ENCOUNTERS WITH VIOLENCE IN LATIN AMERICA

Latin America is both the most urbanized and the most violent developing region, where the links between social exclusion, inequality, fear and insecurity are clearly visible. The banal, ubiquitous nature of drug crime, robbery, gang and intra-family violence destablizes countries' economies and harms their people and social structures.

Encounters with Violence in Latin America explores the meaning of violence and insecurity in nine towns and cities in Colombia and Guatemala to create a framework of how and why daily violence takes place at the community level. It uses pioneering new methods of participatory urban appraisal to ask local people about their own perceptions of violence as mediated by family, gender, ethnicity, and age. It develops a typology which distinguishes between the political, social, and economic violence that afflicts communities, and which assesses the costs and consequences of violence in terms of community cohesion and social capital. This gives voice to those whose daily lives are dominated by widespread aggression, and provides important new insights for researchers and policy-makers.

Caroline O.N. Moser is a social anthropologist and social policy specialist. She is currently Senior Research Associate at the Overseas Development Institute and Adjunct Professor at the New School University, New York. Her publications include *Gender Planning and Development* (1993) and *Victims, Perpetrators or Actors?* (with Fiona Clark, 2001).

Cathy McIlwaine is Senior Lecturer in the Department of Geography, Queen Mary, University of London. She has co-authored and co-edited *Women of a Lesser Cost* (with Sylvia Chant, 1995) and *Challenges and Changes in Middle America* (with Katie Willis, 2002).

ENCOUNTERS WITH VIOLENCE IN LATIN AMERICA

Urban poor perceptions from Colombia and Guatemala

Caroline O.N. Moser and Cathy McIlwaine

Routledge
Taylor & Francis Group

NEW YORK AND LONDON

First published 2004
by Routledge
29 West 35th Street, New York, NY 10001

Simultaneously published in the UK
by Routledge
11 New Fetter Lane, London EC4P 4EE

Routledge is an imprint of the Taylor & Francis Group

© 2004 Caroline O.N. Moser and Cathy McIlwaine

Typeset in Times by Wearset Ltd, Boldon, Tyne and Wear
Printed and bound in Great Britain by MPG Books Ltd,
Bodmin, Cornwall

Library of Congress Cataloging in Publication Data
A catalog record for this book has been requested

British Library Cataloguing in Publication Data
A catalogue record for this book is available from the British Library

ISBN 0–415–25864–2 (hbk)
ISBN 0–415–25865–0 (pbk)

TO THE NEXT GENERATION OF PEACEFUL
YOUNG MEN, TAGE, MAX AND SAVVA

CONTENTS

CONTENTS

FIGURES

TABLES

ACKNOWLEDGMENTS

This book has crossed the divide of time and place, from its inception as part of an 'Urban Peace Program' in Washington, DC in 1998, through the research fieldwork undertaken in both Colombia and Guatemala during 1999, and the associated descriptive studies completed in 2000, to this final book written electronically interconnected between Washington and London. A large number of people have supported us along the way. To each we would like to express our profound thanks.

The research utilized a participatory urban appraisal methodology and the four research teams in each country with whom we undertook the fieldwork were the essential backbone of the study. In Colombia these comprised:

Julián Arturo	Isabel Ortiz
Haidí Hernández Córdoba	Christiane Lelièvre
Lya Yeneth Fuentes Carlos	Carlos Arnulfo Mendoza
María Eugenia Vásquez	José Luis Muñoz
Santiago Parra Román	Ana Daza
Claudia Zulima Jiménez	Angélica Acosta
Margarita Molina	Juan Pablo Fayad
Rafael Román	Francisco Hurtado
Titus Moser	William Rodríguez

In Guatemala these comprised:

Juan Carlos Martínez Aniorte	Doris Irene García Posadas
María Carina Baquero	Vilma Ovalle
José Antonio Gómez	Zoila Calderón
Francisco Reyna Lemus	Tomasa Cortez Guanas
Alberto Fuentes	Carmelina Ixay León
Sulma Natalia Gálvez de Maldonado	Carlos Mendoza
Fernando A. Solares	Lucrecia Rodríguez Illescas
Brenda Liliana Xulú Guitzol	Servio Vanegas

The original research was undertaken as part of an 'Urban Peace Program' directed by Caroline Moser, when she was Lead Specialist in Social Development in the World Bank's Environmentally and Socially Sustainable Development Department in the Latin America and Caribbean Region. The Swedish International Development Cooperation Agency (Sida) funded the project. Eivor Halkjaer showed profound vision in supporting this new initiative, while Goren Holmqvist maintained commitment throughout the project.

Daniel Selener of the Instituto Internacional de Reconstrución Rural (IIRR) in Quito participated as the PUA trainer in both Colombia and Guatemala. In Colombia, Donny Meertens, as research advisor, assisted in identifying research teams, while Felipe Saez, Jairo Arboleda and Maria Teresa de Henao provided invaluable support. In Guatemala, Patricia Ardon, Alfredo Stein and David Holiday helped identifying research groups, Carlos Mendoza managed research logistics and José Roberto Lopez-Calix provided support.

The World Bank granted permission to reprint the following: Tables 1.2, 2.2, 4.2, Figures 2.2, 2.4, 2.5, 2.6, 3.1, 3.4, 4.1, 4.2, 4.3, 4.4, 4.5, 5.1, 5.2, 5.3, Boxes 3.1, 3.3, 4.1, and 4.4.

Fiona Clark, Carolina Ladino and Roddy Brett, as members of the Urban Peace Program Team, and then Annalise Moser made important contributions to the organization, data analysis and drafting of this study. At Routledge, Julene Knox commissioned the book, while Christopher Cudmore brought it to publication. Finally, Ailsa Winton provided invaluable and extensive editorial assistance in the final stages of the book – without her it would not have been completed. To all these people and many others who have given help in one way or another we would like to express our deep gratitude.

In addition, Cathy McIlwaine would like to thank the Department of Geography, Queen Mary, University of London, for granting her a year's leave of absence to pursue this research, as well as Ed Oliver from the Department who prepared the maps.

Caroline Moser would like to acknowledge the support of the following people: Howard Glennister for inviting her to be a Visitor at the Suntory and Toyota Centres for Economic and Related Disciplines (STICERD) at the London School of Economics during the early stages of writing up in 2000; Robert Chambers and Andy Norton for their support over the quantification of PUA; Andres Solimano, Santiago Parra, Angélica Acosta, María Eugenia Vásquez, Sally Yudelman and Titus Moser for their sustained commitment to the importance of the research during this extremely difficult period in Colombia's history.

Above all, we are deeply indebted to the many people who participated in the research in the communities where we worked both in Colombia and in Guatemala. They welcomed us into their lives, shared their time and perceptions, and in some cases took risks in order to contribute to the research. For safety reasons, they must remain anonymous.

Finally, we would like to thank Peter Sollis and Lee Drabwell for their stoic support, solidarity and sufferance over the past years as first the research and then the book slowly reached fruition.

Washington, DC and London
May 2003

1

URBAN VIOLENCE AS A CONTESTED DOMAIN

Background to the book

How do local women, men and children, living in the slums of Latin American cities, cope with the daily violence that pervades their lives? What do they think about it? Does their attitude vary in terms of their age, gender or ethnic group? What is their response? Are the causes of violence grounded in the local reality or is it the wider structural context – be it at country or city level – that is the critical determinant? Above all, why are such questions of current significance?

It is the growing scale and enormity of violence that provide the basis for its importance. While violence increasingly dominates the daily lives of citizens in cities globally, it is particularly problematic in Latin America. The region is usually categorized as the most violent in the world, with rates of crime and violence increasing every year, especially in its towns and cities (Kruijt and Koonings 1999). Consequently, violence is now recognized as a complex, multidimensional phenomenon. Not only does it permeate the very core of many Latin American societies, it is also interlinked with an extremely high incidence of insecurity and fear.

This book provides a comparative analysis of daily violence in eighteen urban communities in two Latin American countries, which reflect different political, economic and social contexts. While Colombia is in the middle of civil conflict, Guatemala is currently experiencing a post-conflict 'transition' to democratic governance. The book's objective, first and foremost, is to contribute empirically to this increasingly important work on violence, by documenting the multiple complexities and positioning of so-called 'everyday' violence, fear and insecurity. Members of poor communities, whether victims or perpetrators, experience violence in different ways. This depends on socially constructed identities that are cross-cut by a series of axes that include gender, ethnicity and generation. In turn, a comparative study such as this also provides the opportunity to examine the influence of differences in context and place on experiences of violence.

Linked to the growing recognition of the importance of violence has been a dramatic increase in research on the phenomenon. Although such investigation is by no means new, it is the range of academic disciplines and associated methodological approaches that focus on different aspects of violence, fear and (in)security that have grown exponentially in the past decade. These vary from quantitative approaches such as those of economists and political scientists, to the more qualitative perspectives presented by sociologists and anthropologists. However, among different research disciplines there is a tendency to compartmentalize knowledge, with an associated lack of consensus about the way in which violence is constructed, negotiated, shaped and resolved. Violence, in general, and urban violence, in particular, remains a highly contested domain with diverse definitions, measurements and categorizations. Equally contested are interpretations of the causes, costs and consequences of the phenomenon. A second objective of the book, therefore, is to contribute to these conceptual debates from a specific methodological perspective, that of participatory appraisal. This gives agency and identity to local people's perceptions of the violence they experience in their daily lives. Do their interpretations of reality concur or differ from those of political scientists, economists or sociologists? Can this research methodology, whose contribution to the study of poverty is already formally established (Brock and McGee 2002), also contribute to the study of violence?

The research on which this book is based was conceived within a development policy environment, with the intention of influencing violence reduction policy initiatives. For many development policymakers this is an entirely new agenda. Until very recently violence was regarded largely as an issue of criminal pathology. Increasingly, however, it is recognized as a fundamental development problem in itself, particularly in urban areas (Ayres 1998). As with research disciplines, the focus of policymakers also varies. Here the tendency towards sector-specific approaches means that there are few integrative frameworks providing 'holistic' integrated policy solutions. Those concerned with economic development, for example, most commonly focus on crime and violence as economic problems because of the ways they can weaken business confidence and affect private sector security expenditure. In contrast, practitioners preoccupied with 'societal violence' such as gangs, youth, or gender-based abuse have sought to prevent, punish or alleviate violence through sector-specific interventions ranging from criminal justice, citizen security, public health, social welfare or community development approaches.

Finally, there are important differences in interpretations of violence between academic researchers, who often seek to show the complexity of the phenomenon, and policymakers, who simplify reality in order to provide concrete 'hands-on' solutions. As they struggle to make sense of the world from a policy or project-oriented perspective, pragmatic practitioners often classify and categorize complicated realities in ways that researchers reject as unacceptably simplistic. Can participatory research contribute to bridging the divide between academics and policymakers? The third, and final, objective of the book is to address this issue. While participatory methodologies foreground the realities of the poor them-selves, allowing people's individual experiences to be heard, they can easily be dismissed as anecdotal evidence or 'apt' illustration (Moser 2001). Quantifying and categorizing this information simplifies it so as to make it accessible to more policymakers not only within the research countries but also in a broader context. Does this make the findings less academically relevant? Ultimately this is the challenge the book addresses. In so doing, it highlights the contribution that participatory methodologies can make to the development of a holistic conceptual approach, or frame-work, that seeks to identify the categories, causal factors, costs and con-sequences of violence within poor urban communities.

The rest of this chapter and Chapter 2 elaborate in further detail the substantive issues summarized in this brief introductory section. While this chapter provides a discussion of urban violence in Latin America, Chapter 2 focuses on the policy debates and the contribution of participatory methodologies. Together, these two chapters provide the background introduction for the research findings discussed in the subsequent chapters.

Violence in urban Latin America

The multiple complexities of everyday violence

In poor urban communities in Latin America everyday violence is neither simple nor straightforward. In this 'seamless fabric' of lived experience (Latour 1993: 7), different manifestations of violence contrast, overlap and interlink with each other to form a highly complex layering of multiple, and at times contradictory practices. The overall totality is a context of endemic fear and insecurity. The fact that it permeates the daily realities of living in cities, especially for the poor, is reflected in such terms as 'everyday' (Scheper-Hughes 1995), 'common' or 'endemic' violence (Koonings 1999; Poppovic and Pinheiro 1995) or even 'unbound violence' (Romanucci-Ross 1973).

In Latin American countries this so-called 'ubiquity of violence' (Torres-Rivas 1999: 287) or 'peace-time crimes' (Scheper-Hughes 1997) often interrelates with, or follows on from, national-level political conflicts. For countries still experiencing such turmoil, it is often difficult for the political aspects of everyday violence to be separated from other types. In Colombia, for instance, Pecaut (1999: 142) identifies the interconnections between different types of violence. These include armed confrontation between guerrillas and state troops, or between paramilitary and drug

traffickers, protection rackets by urban militia, 'social cleansing' operations,[1] political assassinations, organized and petty crime, as well as youth
inter-gang warfare, brawls and vendettas. To these should be added social
violence within households and between individuals, primarily sexual
abuse both inside and outside the home. Another example of the interrelationship between different types of violence comes from Peru. González-
Cueva (2000: 100) discusses how soldiers, and especially those conscripted
forcibly to fight against *Sendero Luminoso* (Shining Path) guerrillas, end
up committing different types of violence in the name of legitimate political aims, such as sexual violence against women, racist violence against
indigenous groups and class violence against the poor.

Countries emerging from political conflict, such as Guatemala, often
experience similar processes, with increasingly diverse expressions of
everyday violence flourishing (Koonings 2001). This often manifests itself
in a proliferation of street gangs made up of former guerrilla or military
members, a growing drugs industry with networks established during times
of conflict, as well as an increase in domestic violence (Kincaid 2000;
Pearce 1998). In this way the boundaries between political and non-
political violence are becoming more porous and permeable, particularly
in urban areas where endemic violence is more visible (Guerrero Barón
2001; Meertens 2001).

Not only are there multiple forms of violence, but as the types proliferate, violence becomes 'routinized' or 'normalized' as an essential part of
the functioning of society (Bourgois 2001; Foucault 1977; Pecaut 1999).
For certain sectors of society, violence may be seen as the most logical way
of dealing with conflicts or pursuing interests, the only option in order to
survive, or the only way certain groups feel they can get their voices heard
(Tedesco 2000). While in the past, civil society or social movements provided avenues for representation, today, violence may be viewed as more
expedient (Call 2000). As Pinheiro (1993: 3) has commented in the case of
Brazil: '[r]ebellion against injustice now often takes the form of endemic
violence, rather than of an organized movement to demand civil rights.' In
turn, Pecaut (1999: 142) argues that the very 'banality and ordinariness' of
violence begin to hide the terror associated with it. Indeed, generalized
violence often serves to make the 'unreal' real, thus allowing people to
survive. While it is difficult to disentangle the motives for everyday violence, part of this process of banalization or normalization is a shift
towards identity-based rather than ideologically based forms of violence
(Colletta and Nezam 1999).

The associated fear and insecurity

Inextricably interlinked with the uncertainty generated by everyday violence is fear and insecurity. Defined as 'the institutional, cultural and psy-

4

chological repercussion of violence' (Kruijt and Koonings 1999: 15), fear has also been identified as an outcome of destabilization, exclusion and uncertainty (ibid.; see also Garretón 1992). The notion of a 'culture of fear' or 'terror' in Latin America has its origins in such brutal violence as that noted by Taussig on the frontier lands in the twentieth century (Taussig 1984, 1987, on rubber extraction in Colombia).[2] Nevertheless, in many countries, the contemporary construction of fear is more closely linked to state-sponsored political violence, such as that associated with the military and civil-military dictatorships of the 1970s and 1980s in Brazil, Chile, Argentina and Uruguay. Such violence manifested itself in repression, torture, 'disappearances' or deaths and numerous other abuses of freedoms of civilian populations usually perpetrated by the military, state or organizations linked with them (Corradi *et al.* 1992; Kruijt 2001). This generated fear of both the 'known' and the 'unknown.' While the former included actual physical repression, death threats and propaganda, the latter resulted from omission through disinformation, the absence of places for people to meet and the arbitrariness of violent state actions (Garretón 1992: 23). Although different 'phases of fear' were associated with evolving military regimes (ibid.),[3] overall, the reproduction of fear was aimed at securing order (Lechner 1992), leaving societies more disorganized, with a lack of confidence permeating to the interpersonal level (Torres-Rivas 1999).

Since the dismantling of military and state violence has not always accompanied democratization processes, the legacies of fear remain firmly rooted in contemporary Latin America (Rotker 2002). In many countries security forces continue to perpetrate considerable violence despite attempts to reform the police and military. Equally, once victimized by past state-sponsored violence many people remain traumatized and in a state of constant fear. Commenting on Guatemala, Lira (1998: 56) notes: '[f]ear becomes a chronic response to a situation that is constantly threat-ening and where there seem to be no boundaries. Arbitrariness is "normal," even in a context that is supposedly democratic.' Often, silence remains the only way that people can survive, forming a veil of protection (Torres-Rivas 1999). Past suffering from politically motivated atrocities can also undermine any attempts to reconstruct society after the brutality has officially ended.[4] In countries such as Guatemala and El Salvador, truth commissions have been established in order to build collective memories to facilitate healing and reconciliation (Chirwa 1998).[5] The Recovery of Historical Memory Project (*Recuperación de la Memoria Histórica*, REHMI) in Guatemala is one such example. Its aim was to recognize the lives of those who were murdered as well as give voice to the victims and perpetrators who lived through testimonies. In some places, exhumation of mass graves was conducted to allow relatives to bury the victims with respect (ODHAG 1999).

While political violence continues to engender fear in local populations, the upsurge in endemic 'banal' everyday urban violence compounds this. Fear of such violence produces a sense of 'insecurity' and vulnerability (Arriagada and Godoy 2000). Although perceptions of insecurity are not always borne out by statistical evidence, they are often more important than the incidence of violence itself and fundamentally affect well-being (Kaplinsky 2001). In the current context this refers not only to personal security but also another important legacy of armed conflict in the form of economic fear and insecurity (Kaldor and Luckham 2001; Kaplinsky 2001). Indeed, 'livelihood security,' denoting the ability to access resources to ensure survival, is closely interrelated with a series of structural factors underpinning urban violence (McIlwaine and Moser 2003).

Frequently, citizen insecurity is also associated with the failure of public security on the part of the state.[6] As this increases, efforts to maintain public security systems, such as the police force, become more fragmented. Kincaid (2000) notes that this leads to the emergence of three key actions: (1) militarization, signifying the use of the military to maintain order in addition to the police; (2) informalization of public security involving the emergence of neighborhood vigilance committees or the use of criminal gangs to protect neighborhoods, death squads or paramilitary activity, or lynching suspected criminals; and finally (3) the privatization of public security and the growth of private security firms, armed guards and house protection systems. Informalization and privatization vary according to socio-economic status, with the poor usually opting for the former, while higher-income groups pay for private security services (Arriagada and Godoy 2000; UNCHS 2001). Both processes of informalization and priva-tization assist in continuing the perpetration of violence. In totality, the memory of previous, politically motivated violence, coupled with contemporary everyday violence, means that fear continues to permeate urban societies. While in the past, it was the police or military that was most feared, now it is local criminal organizations, neighborhood gangs, and drug dealers.

The dramatic growth in multiple forms of violence

Violence is by no means a new phenomenon, with coercion and force his-torically as much a part of everyday life as are markets and economic exchange (Bates 2001). Nevertheless, in Latin America the current com-plexity is closely linked to the fundamental growth of multiple forms of violence in general and urban violence in particular. As mentioned above, Latin America is now the most violent region in the world. Regional and country statistics tell a grim story. In the late 1980s and early 1990s regional level murder rates stood at around 20 per 100,000 (Ayres 1998: 3), but by 1995 they had risen to an estimated 30 per 100,000 (Arriagada and

Godoy 2000: 116). The rate of intentional murders had increased by 50 percent from the early 1980s to the mid-1990s (Fajnzylber *et al.* 2000: 220). Between the 1980s and mid-1990s the highest murder rates were in the Andean region, while the lowest were in the Southern Cone countries. Overall, murder rates increased in nine out of twelve countries in the region, with three increasing by a factor of between four and six (in Panama, Peru and Colombia) (ibid.; see also Ayres 1998). Other forms of crime and violence have also increased in the region, particularly kidnapping (in Colombia, Guatemala, El Salvador and Honduras) and violent crimes against property (Arriagada and Godoy 2000). Finally, riots and violent social protest have also increased, especially in Central America (Call 2000).

At the city level, UNICRI data for eighteen cities in developing countries shows that Latin America and Africa share first place for all types of crime (UNICRI 1998).[7] When the 'contact crime' rate (denoting robbery, assault with force and sexual assault) is analyzed separately, Latin American cities outstrip African and Asian cities. Using murder rates as a proxy indicator of levels of violence, Latin American cities such as Medellín in Colombia, Diadema in Brazil and Guatemala City, have especially high rates (248 per 100,000, 146.1 and 101.5 respectively) (Moser and Grant 2000: 14).

Within Latin America, cities rather than rural areas have experienced dramatic increases in violence, especially in Brazil, Colombia and Mexico and more recently in Argentina (Vanderschueren 1996). For instance, in Buenos Aires the urban crime rate increased by 65 percent between 1995 and 2000 (Tedesco 2000: 536). In Mexico, urban violence increased as a whole, but most significantly in Mexico City with violent crime peaking during some of the worst economic recession years in 1992 and 1994 (Mexican Health Foundation 1999; Pansters 1999). In Rio de Janeiro, increased urban violence is largely associated with the growth of organized crime and arbitrary police violence (Koonings 1999), with children and youth often being the main targets as well as perpetrators (Scheper-Hughes 1996). Within countries, some cities are more violent than others. In Jamaica, in 1994, more than half of all violent crimes occurred in Kingston and St. Andrew, with almost three-quarters of murders and more than 80 percent of shootings taking place in Kingston, St. Andrew or Spanish Town (Moser and Holland 1997: 1).

Urban violence has particular characteristics in that it tends to be linked to crime against property, theft, burglary and mugging (Vanderschueren 1996; see Tedesco 2000).[8] In addition, it is frequently associated with alcohol and drug misuse, illicit drug dealing, and prostitution (Ross 2001). Gang violence, particularly among young men predominates, possibly because a critical mass of youth is necessary for a gang to emerge (Rodgers 1999). These gangs often draw their inspiration or experience from gangs in the United States (see Márquez 1999, on Caracas; Moser and Winton 2002, on Central America). Other organized crime linked with drugs or political activities, for example, also tends to proliferate in cities. A critical mass can precipitate violence as resistance through riots. In the 1990s the most common form was the so-called 'austerity protests' or 'IMF riots' against public expenditure cutbacks or the rising costs of basis commodities associated with Structural Adjustment Programs (Green 1995: 165–174).

Other types of violence such as murder, assaults and rape, many of which are gender-based, while not exclusive to urban areas, are often more common there. Gender-based distinctions often differentiate between violence in private arenas (violence in the home, *violencia en la casa*) from violence in public arenas (violence in the street, *violencia en la calle*) (Jimeno and Roldán 1996, on Colombia). Women in urban areas may be more at risk from domestic violence than those residing in rural areas. In Nicaragua, a study on domestic violence found that rural women had a significantly lower level of risk of violence than those residing in cities (Ellsberg *et al.* 1999, 2000).

Within cities themselves, violence levels vary according to socio-economic group and across space. Violence is often geographically concentrated in poor, marginal, informal settlements, located on the peripheries of cities in areas lacking the resources to control it (Soares *et al.* 1998). In contrast, upper-income areas tend to be well maintained, often in walled compounds with comprehensive security measures. Violence-risk maps undertaken in four Brazilian cities identified high and low risk areas across the cities. In São Paulo, levels of intra-urban violence closely reflect socio-economic differentials with violence concentrated in the poorest areas (CEDEC 1996; see also Barata *et al.* 1998; Landmann *et al.* 1999).

Contested definitions, measurements and categories of violence

Definitions of violence

Despite this extensive description of urban violence in Latin America, we are left with a fundamental question. What do we mean by violence? Given its complexity, multiplicity and chaotic nature, as Michael Taussig (1987) has commented, violence is slippery and escapes easy definition. Violence is also highly contested, with no agreement as to what actually constitutes the phenomenon. As Robben and Nordstrom (1995: 5) point out: '[V]ested interests, personal history, ideological loyalties, propaganda and a dearth of first hand information ensure that many "definitions" of violence are powerful fictions and negotiated half-truths.' Nevertheless, the starting point for most generic definitions, including the definition used in this book, denotes violence as the use of physical force, which causes hurt to others in order to impose one's wishes (Keane 1996). Expanded, this refers to the 'unwanted physical interference by groups and/or individuals with the bodies of others' (ibid.: 67). While such a narrow physical conceptualization underlies many definitions (Riches 1991), others have been broadened to refer to psychological hurt, material deprivation and symbolic disadvantage (Bourdieu 1998; Galtung 1985, 1991, 1996; Schröder and Schmidt 2001).

Underlying such definitions, however, is the recognition that violence and power are inextricably interrelated. Violence involves the exercise of power that is invariably used to legitimate the use of force for specific gains. Indeed, violence is often viewed as legitimate when exercised by the powerful, and illegitimate when performed by the powerless. Yet it is not simply about power. Robben and Nordstrom (1995) contest the notion of affixing violence to a single domain or one locus of power since it results in a victim/perpetrator dichotomy, reducing populations exposed to violence as helpless undifferentiated masses while stereotyping perpetrators as brutal 'power mongers.' In their own words (1995: 8): '[I]n reality violence is constructed, negotiated reshaped and resolved as perpetrators and victims try to define and control the world they find themselves in.'

Definitions of violence also often overlap with those of conflict and crime as reflected in widely used terms such as 'violent crime,' 'criminal conflict,' 'conflictual violence' and 'violent conflict.'[9] For instance, in their review of violence, the U.S. National Academy of Science distinguishes between individual behavior involving violence and the collective violence that underpins wars, state violence, riots and organized crime (Reiss and Roth 1993). As such, there are important distinctions between violence and conflict. While both are concerned with power, conflict-based power struggles over scarce resources do not necessarily inflict physical or mental harm on others, while violence by its very nature does (Soley 1996). Conflict therefore can be peacefully resolved through negotiation without recourse to force but becomes violent/armed conflict when it includes fighting and killing. Alternatively, crime by definition is an act (usually a grave offense) punishable by law – the breach of a legal prohibition. In turn, violent crime has been defined as any act that causes physical or psychological damage and which is against the law (Vanderschueren 1996).

Perceptions of which crimes are violent, or which types of violence are unlawful, differ widely, determined less by objective indicators of degree of damage or injury than by local cultural values and power relations that determine who constructs such definitions. What counts as a tolerable level of violence in one society may be condemned in another society as excessive (Robben and Nordstrom 1995). In Brazil, for instance, the term violence and crime are often used synonymously due to the violent nature of much contemporary crime (Pinheiro 1993). In this book, the use of perception data illustrates the diversity of people's perspectives as to what violence means to them, influenced not only by context and location but also by such factors as age and gender.

The measurement of violence

Equally contested is the measurement of violence, with associated methodologies also fraught with difficulties.[10] The most common constraints result from the use of mortality statistics as proxies for levels of violence. Such statistics are notoriously unreliable due to under-reporting, difficulties in interpretation and lack of reliability of data (Short 1997).[11] In addition, national and regional differences in data collection methods, recall periods, and cultural definitions of crime and violence make valid cross-country comparisons hard to achieve. Consequently, these are only possible through specific global data sets such as the International Crime Victimization Survey (UNICRI 1995, 1998) and the United Nations World Crime Surveys (Fajnzylber *et al.* 1998; Newman 1998). Along with victimization surveys, other commonly used data sources include official crime statistics (usually obtained from police figures), murder or intentional injury statistics from hospitals and morticians including death certificates, and judicial records such as offender rates and surveys (Glaeser 1999). Diverse sources within the same city or country often record markedly different rates of murder, even though this indicator remains more reliable than others. Data problems are exacerbated by the fact that no Latin American country carries out systematic public opinion surveys on levels or perceptions of violence and security (Arriagada and Godoy 2000). Finally, such quantitative methodologies fail to capture how people actually experience the multiplicity of different forms of violence on a daily basis.

Complementing quantitative research has been an extensive range of sociological and anthropological studies using combined methods, but frequently more reliant on qualitative approaches. Of particular note is work on poverty and violence (Scheper-Hughes 1992), terror and healing (Taussig 1987), male violence and gangs (Gutmann 1996; Lancaster 1992) and gender-based violence (Ellsberg *et al.* 2000). Participatory appraisal techniques, that form the core of the study on which this book is based, constitute a relatively new methodology that gives voice to people's perceptions of violence (Moser and McIlwaine 1999). This also pioneers the quantification of community perceptions of different types of violence, and in so doing it challenges the orthodoxy about the separation of qualitative and quantitative methodologies (see Chapter 2).

The categorization of violence

Finally, the categorization of violence is contested around its boundaries or axes (Gasper 1999; McIlwaine 1999). Violence can be classified descriptively according to whether it is physical, psychological or sexual in nature. Equally, it can be classified in terms of victimization, for instance, violence against women or children. Motivation, such as political or racist, provides another axis, as do the agents of violence, such as gangs, drug dealers, and youth. The relationships between the victim and the perpetrator such as relatives, friends, or strangers has been used more commonly as the basis for categorization than the place of occurrence, in terms of domestic, street or workplace violence (Arriagada and Godoy 2000; Buvinić *et al.* 1999).

Further categorizations are analytical in nature. Of particular relevance to the Latin American context are Salmi's (1993) human rights distinction between 'direct,' 'indirect,' 'repressive' and 'alienating violence,' Pecaut's (1997, 1999) differentiation between 'organized violence' (politically motivated, organized in groups) and 'disorganized violence' (individual crime, delinquency, vandalism) and Pinheiro's (1993) account of 'institutional violence' as perpetrated by police and other state institutions. Policy-oriented classifications include the Inter-American Development Bank's distinction between 'criminal' and 'social violence' (Buvinić *et al.* 1999), with the latter closely associated with 'gender-based violence' (Pickup *et al.* 2001; see also below). Galtung (1996), in a categorization that encompasses many such facets, distinguishes between 'personal or direct violence' (relating to a subject or person inflicting physical or psychological hurt), 'structural violence' (referring to the uneven distribution of economic or political power and resources in society), and 'cultural violence' (denoting the symbolic and ideological sphere of existence that can be used to justify personal or structural violence).[12]

Chapter 3 explores the multiple complexity of everyday violence for the urban poor in Colombia and Guatemala. In so doing it illustrates the way micro-studies of this sort can contribute to important debates identified above. It first outlines the complexity of perceptions of violence, fear and insecurity, and then builds on the categorizations of Latin American violence experts to categorize and quantify these perceptions in terms of three broad encompassing categories of social, economic and political violence.

Theorizing the causes of violence

The wide range of approaches that seek to understand the causal factors that underpin or determine violence are equally diverse, complex and widely contested. Theorizing violence has a long history (Arendt 1969), with widespread disciplinary fragmentation. Historically, within development theory, analyses of violence, especially urban violence, have evolved along with dominant paradigm shifts. Thus in the 1960s, criminologists writing from a modernization perspective focused on how young unemployed male migrants, psychologically unable to cope with urban anomie, turned to violent criminal behavior (Sichor 1990). Oscar Lewis, in his seminal work on the 'culture of poverty,' identified the psychological inability of some individuals to cope as the root cause of violent crime, which in turn, was closely linked with poverty (Lewis 1961). In contrast, dependency approaches in the 1970s focused on structural causes, with levels of crime and violence perceived as an outcome of unequal power relations both between and within countries, as well as the product of colonial criminal law systems (Sumner 1982). Here, crime and violence were viewed as a form of resistance by economically and socially disadvantaged individuals (Arthur and Marenin 1995).

Just as development theory itself has recently reached somewhat of an impasse (Schuurman 2000), so too are theories of violence in relation to development yet to be integrated into the mainstream of development theory, tending still to be compartmentalized into specific academic and professional disciplines. Thus, biomedical and psychological violence theories focus on the physiological, genetic or psychological tendency that some individuals have towards violent behavior, with considerable emphasis placed on socialization processes through childhood, where violent behavior becomes a 'learned' activity taught through social processes. In contrast, epidemiological public health approaches liken the spread and prevention of violence to disease, and identify 'risk factors' that make some people more likely to commit crimes and violence than others (Concha-Eastman 2002; Guererro 1998; Turpin and Kurtz 1997).

Political scientists have long prioritized structural and institutional issues such as the state and criminal justice systems in influencing the propensity for violence (Keane 1996), while a more recent focus highlights the violence associated with 'fragile' or 'crisis' states and stateless societies (Crisis States Programme 2001; Nef 1995). Political economy approaches focusing on wars and complex political emergencies suggest that violence is rational and functional from the perspective of social actors. Drawing on Foucault's (1977) notions of the utility of violence, it is often proposed that political leaders and entrepreneurs, as well as ordinary civilians or low-ranking soldiers can benefit from violence and may often have vested interests in its maintenance (Berdal and Keen 1997). Depending on the social actors involved, there are political and non-political (economic, security and psychological) advantages of violence (ibid.; see Richani 1997 on Colombia).

Echoing political scientists' preoccupation with the correlates of violence, economic research on violence tends to focus on quantitative modeling of statistical relationships between violence and other variables (Arthur and Marenin 1995). These may include economic variables such as inequality, unemployment and income distribution, as well as other non-economic variables such as deterrence factors (police, laws, judiciary), demographic and cultural issues, prevalence of illegal activities such as drug trafficking, and political factors (Fajnzylber *et al.* 1998, 2000). Following Becker (1993), much of the economic analysis of the causes of crime and violence uses cost-benefit analysis of individual involvement in illegal or violent activities.

In contrast, anthropologists and sociologists tend to consider the relationships between culture and social structures to explain violence, distinguishing between theories of individual socialization and those of structural rupture or anomie. Within this vein, Galtung's (1996) 'positive peace approach' identifies fulfilling basic needs, fighting oppression and inequalities and promoting a culture where peace rather than violence is legitimated as the way to promote real peace. In summarizing anthropological approaches, Schröder and Schmidt (2001) identify three overlapping theoretical approaches. First, is the 'operational approach' based on the 'etics of antagonism' that links human nature and rationality with measurable material and political causes of violence. Second, is the 'cognitive approach' that deals with the 'emics of the cultural construction of war,' with violence culturally constructed in historical context. Third, is the 'experiential approach' that focuses on individual subjectivity, whereby each individual develops a fragmented view of violence depending on particular circumstances and situations. Although each approach tends to place greater emphasis on certain causes over others, most recognize that several factors interrelate, which in turn, is influenced by both culture and context. As discussed in Chapter 4, this book builds on such an approach in identifying underlying causal factors in terms of the interrelationship between structure, identity and agency.

The causes of urban violence in Latin America

Explanations of the causal factors underlying violence in urban Latin America vary widely depending on the types of violence and the discipline within which they are interpreted. Although no single cause predominates, probably the most important debate concerns the extent to which crime and violence are causally rooted in poverty or inequality (Arriagada and Godoy 2000; Rosenburg 1999). While poverty has long been considered the predominant determinant of violence, more recently this linear relationship has been challenged as simplistic and indeed, harmful. Interpretations based on statistical modeling, for instance, have demonstrated that inequality is more influential than poverty in relation to national murder rates (Fajnzylber *et al.* 1998, 2000). At the same time, the daily living conditions of the urban poor heighten the potential for the emergence of conflict, crime or violence (Concha-Eastman 2002; Vanderschueren 1996). In reality, poverty and inequality frequently overlap to generate conditions in which some people resort to crime and violence. A case study from São

Paulo, Brazil, for example, shows that the highest violence rates are spatially concentrated in areas with the lowest indices of socio-economic status (Barata *et al.* 1998).

Increased levels of violence have also been identified as closely associated with the two interrelated processes of globalization and neoliberalism (Willett 2001). Thus, it is argued that not everyone has benefited from increasing global interconnectedness and greater global volumes of trade and capital mobility, with many losers now identified (UNDP 1999). As Castells (1998: 144) argues, the ongoing processes of polarization and differentiation between those who are 'connected,' and those who are not, increasingly overlap with the spatial segregation and economic differentiation of disadvantaged groups, neighborhoods or even cities. Those excluded from 'connectivity' to the dynamic new sectors (through lack of education or infrastructure) are more likely to turn to crime, violence and a drugs culture.

As mentioned above, one pervasive aspect of the current phase of globalization is the spread of economic neoliberalism, particularly as enshrined in Structural Adjustment Programmes (SAPs) that since the 1980s have been closely associated with an upsurge in inequality throughout most of Latin America (Killick 1999; Moser 1998; Willett 2001). Although evidence as to whether SAPs have directly increased poverty remains inconclusive, in many countries they have exacerbated social cleavages and exclusion among the poor, and created a class of 'new poor' (Pansters 1999, on Mexico; Tedesco 2000, on Argentina).

Globalization has also facilitated the spread of global criminal networks, critical for the functioning of local endemic urban violence in Latin America as elsewhere. These include the Mexican and Colombian cartels, and the Jamaican Posses or Yardies, all of which are major players in what Castells (1998: 166) refers to as the 'global criminal economy.' Such mafia-style groups and drug cartels have a tendency to tap into other illegal economic activities such as prostitution and extortion rackets. In turn, as drug syndicates become more aggressive, so too do levels of violence, augmented by the free trade in firearms (Muggah 2001). Neoliberal imperatives have also resulted in a paring down of the state such that in some contexts it has been unable to provide legal and legitimate means to resolve social conflicts, either through the use of its security forces or judicial system. Despite efforts to reform security forces, especially in Central America, the use of state-sponsored arbitrary violence is widespread, further bolstered by corruption (Call 2000). The upshot is extensive impunity, which allows crime and violence to flourish (Chevigny 1996, on Mexico City and Kingston, Jamaica).

At the same time, during the past decade, democratization processes have swept across many Latin American countries, with shifts from authoritarian regimes of the past, especially in the Southern Cone, to post-conflict transitions, particularly in Central America. Kruijt and Koonings (1999: 11) argue that along with such processes, the phenomenon of violence itself is democratized, as it has ceased to be primarily a resource for the traditionally powerful or the 'grim uninformed guardians of the nation.' In many countries, democratization is confined to elections, with other democratic procedures such as rule of law, separation of powers, freedom of association and expression often absent (Kaldor and Luckham 2001). In contrast to this, violence and crime serve important economic functions particularly in 'uncivil democracies' and 'collapsing states' where 'greed' as well as 'grievance' may underpin the phenomenon (Collier and Hoeffler 2000). Often, the engine of violence is the battle over resources, as in the case of Colombia where drugs and oil are primary motivating factors (see Kaldor and Luckham 2001).

Are broad and macro-level analyses of the causal factors influencing violence, such as those described above, relevant at the local micro-level? Among the range of issues identified, which are prioritized by poor people themselves? Chapter 4 explores the causal factors underlying violence in poor urban communities in Colombia and Guatemala from the perspectives of the social actors themselves. Since identities vary geographically, it examines these in relation to experiences of violence both within and between Colombia and Guatemala. Not only do the structural contexts differ, so too do other dominant axes of differentiation in terms of gender, age and above all ethnicity. For instance, while Colombia has relatively small indigenous and Afro-Colombian populations (Wade 1993), in contrast, almost half the population of Guatemala is of indigenous origin (PNUD 1998). Finally, the use of participatory methodologies strengthens local people's agency and voice. This is well illustrated by the multiple interpretations of causal factors which focus groups in the different communities identify. These in turn can be analyzed in terms of broader contextual concerns. Thus, in an iterative manner, structure, identity and agency provide a framework for the analysis of community perceptions of causal factors influencing violence.

The costs and consequences of violence

Closely related to the causal factors underlying violence are the costs and consequences of violent action. If there is less of a contested debate about this aspect of violence than others, this can be attributed to current limitations in measurement methodologies. To date, most Latin American research is based on the economic measurement of monetary costs, which provides a common, interpretable metric for understanding the impact of crime on both individuals and society. This allows for a comparison with the costs of other social ills, and as such is a useful comparative tool for cost-benefit assessments of different policy options – such as preventative as against curative interventions (Macmillan 2000).

The costs of violence are generally categorized in direct and indirect terms, with an associated distinction between the gross costs borne by the victim and the net macroeconomic costs.[13] Regional Inter-American Development Bank-funded research distinguishes between the direct costs to the health system, police, justice system, housing and social services, and indirect costs, such as higher morbidity and mortality due to homicides and suicides, abuse of alcohol and drugs, depressive disorders. In addition, economic multiplier effects, defined as macroeconomic impacts, influence the labor market and inter-generational productivity, as well as social multiplier effects which include the effect on inter-personal relations and the quality of life (Arriagada and Godoy 2000).

Probably the greatest advances have been made with measurements of the direct economic costs of violence, the associated losses due to deaths and disabilities, and 'transferrals' resulting from property crimes, calculated as percentages of GNP or GDP (although this does not necessarily imply that GDP would have increased by that percentage had these losses not occurred). Londoño (1996) argues that the net accumulation of human capital in Latin America and the Caribbean over the past 15 years has been cut in half due to the increase in crime and violence over this period. Loss of human capital due to violence has been estimated to amount to 1.9 percent of GDP in Latin America, which is equivalent to the total spending on primary education (CIEN n.d.). Colombian data on the economic costs of violence show that from 1991 to 1996, net costs associated with urban violence and armed conflict were assessed as totaling 18.5 percent GDP, representing a yearly average of 3.1 percent of GDP (Trujillo and Badel 1998: 25). Similarly, the total costs associated with guerrilla conflict, including private and public expenditures and human capital costs, averaged over 4 percent of GDP from 1990 to 1994 (Granada and Rojas 1995). Nevertheless, despite decades of research, the costs of violence in Colombia, as elsewhere, remain difficult to measure. Constraints include not only methodological issues but also, in many contexts, lack of access to information on violence-related expenditure assessments by the police, the judiciary, the penal system and even the armed forces, that can result in wide discrepancies in research results.[14]

Violence, livelihoods and capital assets

At the same time, many of the components of indirect costs and consequences for individual victims as much as for society as a whole, are intangible and in this case no reliable quantitative data exist – indeed it may be futile to attempt to quantify something so complex and subjective. Yet it is clear that both the levels and types of endemic daily violence in poor urban communities, impact dramatically on people's well-being in terms of their livelihood security, and the functioning of local social institutions. This book, therefore, focuses on the linkages between violence and capital assets and capabilities associated with livelihood security – with the intention of contributing to a more robust qualitative approach to understanding the consequences of daily violence at the local level.[15]

Concepts such as capital assets, capabilities and livelihood security, heavily influenced by Amartya Sen's (1981) path-breaking work on famines and entitlements, are now widely used to better understand the risks and vulnerabilities experienced by the poor. These identify how, for instance, the poor withstand short-term shocks and longer-term trends by mobilizing entitlements, assets or capabilities such as income from wage labor, income from the sale of assets, and resources from their own production such as food, and social security claims.

To date, however, the close relationship between asset ownership, vulnerability, violence and insecurity has not been widely acknowledged. Yet they are closely linked. The more assets people have, the less vulnerable and more secure they are, and the greater the erosion of people's assets, the greater their insecurity (Moser 1998). Consequently, such concepts also provide a useful framework for assessing the consequences of violence. To achieve positive livelihood outcomes a range of assets is required, with no single category of assets sufficient on its own (DFID 2000). This is particularly true for poor people with limited access to any single category of assets and who therefore have to manage a complex asset portfolio. From the extensive debate on capabilities, assets and livelihoods, there is a widespread consensus that the five most important capital assets of the poor can be usefully categorized as physical, financial, human, social and natural capital assets (Carney 1998; Chambers and Conway 1992; Moser 1998; Moser and Norton 2001). The consequences of violence can be analyzed in terms of their direct and indirect effects on various capital assets.

For instance, physical and financial capital comprises the stock of plant, equipment, infrastructure and other productive resources owned by individuals, the business sector or the country itself, as well as the financial resources available to people (savings, supplies of credit). Costs of violence include the drain on savings and losses in earnings and other capital stock in terms of the resources allocated to reduce or control the phenomenon. The inability to control rising violent crime often results in households and businesses relying on private security to control or prevent violence (Arriagada and Godoy 2000).

Human capital assets include individual investments in education and health and nutrition. Labor is a critical linked asset; health status determines people's capacity to work, and skill and education determine the returns from their labor. One of the direct consequences of violence is increased private and public spending on health. Gender-based domestic violence, for instance, has serious associated consequences for human capital assets. These include the impacts of serious injuries experienced by victims particularly if pregnant, injuries to children, unwanted and early pregnancy (due to rape or lack of control over contraception) and sexually transmitted diseases (STDs) (including HIV), as well as the psychological consequences such as suicide, mental health problems, and effects on children (World Bank 1993, cited in Heise *et al.* 1994). But domestic violence can also impact on women's economic productivity in terms of their earnings and participation in the labor force. Children living in a violent household are affected in terms of their health, and also their own use of violence within relationships. In addition, living in an environment of abuse can lead to a long-term loss of human capital through reduced educational performance.

Social capital is defined as the 'rules, norms, obligations, reciprocity, and trust embedded in social relations, social structures, and societies' institutional arrangements, that enable its members to achieve their individual and community objectives' (Narayan 1997: 50; also Moser 1996). Social capital is thus embedded in social institutions at the micro-institutional level – communities and households – as well as referring to the rules and regulations governing formalized institutions in the marketplace, the political system, and civil society.[16] Of particular relevance to the book is the debate as to whether violence erodes social capital when it reduces trust and co-operation within communities, or whether it reconstitutes social capital in different forms (Colletta and Cullen 2000; Moser 1998; Moser and Holland 1997). The policy implications of this revolve around the extent to which high levels of social capital may reduce violent crimes (Lederman *et al.* 1999). Two key analytical distinctions of particular relevance to the relationship between violence and social capital, and examined in greater detail in Chapter 8, are cognitive and structural social capital (Uphoff 2000), and productive and perverse social capital (Rubio 1997a; also McIlwaine and Moser 2001).

It is important to emphasize that local people in the research communities in Colombia and Guatemala did not articulate the costs of violence specifically in terms of capital assets. Nor do participatory methodologies lend themselves to numerical calculations of the costs of violence. Therefore, these concepts are used more as guiding principles underlying the description of the consequences of different manifestations of violence as prioritized by members of local communities. Thus Chapter 5, which explores perceptions of intra-household violence, highlights the health impacts of domestic violence or abuse in terms of their implications for human capital assets. Chapter 6 turns to the particular impact of drug- and alcohol abuse-related violence on local households and communities. Again, both have important implications for well-being in terms of human capital assets.

Two further chapters focus on the consequences of the sustained multiplicity of everyday violence on community members in terms of the extent to which it fundamentally impacts on levels of well-being. Chapter 7 specifically focuses on the nature of organized violence in communities, illustrating both the huge diversity of different organizations involved in violence, as well as their dominant hold over communities. In turn, it explores how these groups formed for reasons such as making a living, extending their power in the face of widespread exclusion, or as a major pole of socialization in the case of young people and especially young men who join gangs.

Chapter 8 focuses more analytically on social capital using this concept to explore the effects and consequences of violence on the social cohesion of communities. Violence often erodes the governance capacity of formal institutions with particular implications for human rights violations and impunity rates (Turshen 2001). When judicial, educational, health, media and security institutions are unable to function appropriately and transparently, this can reduce even further the existing unequal access to such institutions on the basis of gender, ethnicity or age. In addition, the capacity for informal community-level organizations to function depends not only on levels of cohesion but also on the ability to meet locally – which hinges on levels of insecurity and personal safety. High levels of conflict and violence reduce mobility. Since women, in their role as community managers, are most active in a voluntary capacity in local level community organizations, fear of leaving the home affects the functioning of such groups (Moser 1993). However, in some contexts of extreme armed conflict, female-dominated organizations can be perceived as the most trusted institutions during conflict, and can play a critical role in rebuilding social capital during peace processes (Coral 2001). In quantifying perceptions of trust in social institutions in communities in both Colombia and Guatemala, this chapter highlights the importance of both productive and perverse social institutions. In providing voice to the perceptions of different social actors in diverse communities, what emerges is a highly complex picture in which violence both erodes and reconstitutes social capital in a range of different ways, depending on the context. Leading on from this, Chapter 9 addresses the strategies and solutions identified by people in communities, as well as how these fit within existing types of interventions to reduce violence.

As mentioned in the introductory section of this chapter, this research was conceived within a development policy environment. Therefore, before turning to the research contexts of Colombia and Guatemala, Chapter 2 outlines the policy debates and the contribution of participatory methodologies to the study of violence, fear and insecurity.

2

TOWARD A POLICY-RELEVANT POSITIONING OF VIOLENCE

The role of participatory research methodologies

This chapter turns to a second important area of contestation. This concerns the ongoing debate between theory and practice as it relates to the issue of urban violence. In seeking to bridge the divide between the different worlds of academic research and policy action, it outlines the potential contribution of recently developed participatory methodologies. Finally, by way of background, it provides a brief description of the research communities. Associated with this are the particular methodological constraints in implementing participatory appraisals in areas with such high levels of gratuitous daily violence that communities live in 'cultures of fear' or 'silence.'

Contradictions between theory and practice

The disjuncture between the complexity of daily violence and simplification of violence-reduction policy interventions

Not only do diverse academic disciplines differ in their analysis of violence and the causal factors underlying the phenomenon, they also vary in their attitude toward policy interventions. As government and civil society policymakers have increasingly come to recognize that violence is not only a political, social and economic problem, but also a constraint on development itself, this gap between theory and practice becomes increasingly significant (Trivedy 2001). This is illustrated, among other things, by the fact that a high incidence of crime, robbery and gang violence increases private sector security expenditure while weakening investment confidence, both of which affect a country's economic growth and productivity (Fajnzylber *et al.* 2002). In urban areas, policymakers now acknowledge that there is a relationship between inequality, exclusion and violence (Lederman *et al.* 2002). Because of its impact on human rights, governance and democratic political procedures, this is now a global concern (see Chapter 1).

The nature of policy approaches to violence varies according to academic discipline. This is clearly illustrated by the fact that well-established violence-focused professional disciplines such as criminology and epidemiology, whose research methods have traditionally been based on formal 'etic' quantitative methodologies, have well-developed solutions associated with their particular approaches to the problem. In contrast, other disciplines, particularly those based on 'emic' methodologies, are more reluctant to translate research results into practical solutions, in this sense disputing 'whose narrative and vision of the world can be considered more persuasive or "valid" ' (Arce and Long 2000: 3).[1] As Nordstrom (1995: 138) admonishes: 'rather than recognizing that violence is experiential and real, we have a legacy of thinking about violence as a concept, a phenomenon, a "thing." We reify it, we "thing-ify" it as Taussig [1987] cautions.'

Such criticism is strongest in its resistance to the categorization of quantitative knowledge to provide packaged solutions. This is usefully illustrated by Halbmayer (2001) in his anthropological study of war among the Yukpa of north-western Venezuela. He clearly states that it is not his intention to give a final or monocausal explanation as to why war or violent behavior occurs: '[n]or is my aim to provide statistical data ordered by "etic" western categories on the frequency of different forms of violent behaviour' (ibid.: 49). Because of the complexity and interconnectedness of everyday violence, many anthropologists also strongly resist attributing specific causality, or identifying the functionality of violence, preferring to see it largely as socially and culturally constructed. Causality itself is played out in terms of identities. In their analysis of violence as a dimension of living, Robben and Nordstrom (1995: 6–7) argue that: 'our search is not for cause or function but for understanding and reflexivity.' Attempts to apply equations of rationality are seen to be based on misguided assumptions that violence should be understood in terms of its function or objective.

What emerges is a dualistic divide and associated lack of collaboration between academic interpretations that emphasize the complexity of violence, and a policy-focused analysis that seeks to categorize types of violence, measure its costs and delineate its consequences based on murder records and victimization surveys. Can we reconcile the 'emic' multiple layering of different forms of violence in the everyday reality of poor urban populations and the 'etic' needs of policymakers to systematize and categorize complex realities in order to advocate appropriate interventions? While recognizing the need to be inclusive of such complexity, we need to go beyond the issue of contestation and explore the middle ground between the 'purity' of research and the 'impure' domain of operational policy solutions.

Participatory appraisal methodologies bridging the research policy divide

The empirical evidence on which this book is based uses participatory urban appraisal (PUA) methodologies. As mentioned in Chapter 1, one of the objectives here is to explore the contribution of this methodological approach to understanding the complexity of everyday violence in poor communities in Latin America. In so doing it seeks to play a catalytic role in bridging the divide between academic researchers and pragmatic policy-makers. This is similar to the role played by participatory methodologies in the recent debates on the reconceptualization of poverty that has involved a shift from static, quantitative, poverty line approaches toward dynamic, qualitative and participatory approaches (Moser 1998).[2] The latter have sought to bring the 'voices of the poor' to the attention of poli-cymakers.[3] This 'co-production with poor people of information about poverty which reflects their perspectives' has resulted in a convergence between participation, poverty and policy (Brock 2002: 1). Most recently the methodology has received the double-edged legitimacy of being main-streamed into the World Bank's annual *World Development Report* on Poverty through the 'Voices of the Poor' research project (World Bank 2000; also Narayan *et al.* 2000, 2000a).[4]

It is important to stress that methodologies that pertain to 'give voice' are not new. Indeed, one of the most vehement unresolved debates within the social sciences concerns the ability, or right, of researchers to speak for others (see Jackson 2002). Spivak (1988), for instance, challenges Western anthropologists when they 'speak' for those among whom they work, on the basis that research and representation and political power are completely intertwined. By contrast, Taussig (1987) and Scheper-Hughes (1996), both of whom are research pioneers on Latin American violence and fear, challenge anthropologists to speak out against the injustices they encounter. In a similar vein, Robben and Nordstrom (1995: 11) argue that in a world not governed by 'the positivists' dream of rational coherency,' it is not an option but a duty to write against repression and injustice. Unable to resolve such dilemmas, anthropological fieldwork seeks to reduce the degrees of distortion by ensuring the direct gathering of local knowledge through such methodological techniques as participant obser-vation and the collection of testimony.

Policy-focused researchers using participatory methodologies have grappled with similar dilemmas as they have developed analytical tools that provide greater voice, agency and representation to people them-selves (Cornwall and Jewkes 1995). In so doing they have sought to go beyond ethnographic notebooks and people's testimonies. Participatory methodologies are rooted in Paulo Freire's advocacy of popular education as empowerment (1950–60), as well as in a range of anthropological and

22

agro-systems research tools. However, the current trend in participatory urban and rural approaches dates back to the 1980s, prompted by grass-roots organizations reacting against externally imposed development agendas (see Chambers 1994a, 1994b, 1994c, for comprehensive, detailed reviews of this approach). Such has been its popularity that by the 1990s, interest in participatory methodologies reached: 'frenzied levels of global interest ... [as] the new synonym for "good" or "sustainable" develop-ment' (Guijt and Shah 1998: 4). Participatory methodologies differ from other research methods in terms of the 'location of power in the various stages of the research process' (Cornwall and Jewkes 1995: 1667–8), rather than merely in the tools used. Key elements of participatory rural appraisal (PRA) or participatory urban appraisal (PUA), as the methodol-ogy has become known, therefore relate to the way in which local people carry out research. This means, in theory at least, a transfer of power to local people, rather than researchers, with local knowledge valued over other 'external' sources.

With their roots firmly in the policy arena, participatory approaches continue to have much to offer policymakers. McGee (2002) identifies four different channels through which participatory research can ideally influence policy. First is the informational channel in which new informa-tion collected not only fills gaps, but also challenges the descriptive cat-egories and concepts previously used, demonstrating poor people's capacity to analyze and problematize their own experience. A second important channel is the stimulation of local level action. In this case poor people involved in participatory research are stimulated by their experience to undertake advocacy and action to address their needs. A third channel concerns the broadening of the 'epistemic' community. This refers to the impact that participatory poverty research can have on the relationship between actors involved in poverty reduction issues, and the formation of new relationships such that the policy dialog is opened to a larger group of stakeholders with more diverse perspectives and priorities. A final channel concerns the experiential learning of policymakers whose first-hand contact with poor communities can engender empathy and a process of reflexive critical learning.

Not all channels are necessarily applicable to each research project. Policy-focused participatory studies that seek to reach national-level government officials, for instance, are essentially more extractive in objec-tive than grassroots-based studies. Consequently, they are less concerned with the direct empowerment of people within communities, although this may be an outcome of the research process, at least in part. For instance, researchers often return to research communities after the completion of the study to share the final analysis, with the information providing the necessary basis for the development of a community plan which can then be used to lobby for funding (Moser and Holland 1998).

The limitations of participatory methodologies

In seeking to bridge the divide between the 'emic' multiple layering of reality and the 'etic' needs of policymakers to systematize and categorize complex realities, PUA has its limitations. For instance, if 'participation' itself is not problematized, there is a tendency to ignore the fact that it may mean different things to different people (Cornwall and Jewkes 1995; Lewis and Gardner 1996). While some may view participation merely as consultation with local people, others may assume it refers to genuine empowerment involving self-determination and action. Indeed, some go as far as to suggest that the opposite may occur, effectively leading to the disempowerment of communities (Cooke and Kothari 2001; Mohan 1999).

Another limitation relates to the concept of 'community' as the primary unit of participatory research. Here it is essential to recognize that this does not imply a homogenous entity with defined boundaries (Guijt and Shah 1998). Assumptions such as this deny agency to individuals within communities and ignore internal power struggles and conflicts that are an inevitable part of community life. Communities not only have porous boundaries, but also are made up of a diverse range of people with different perceptions. Certain identities are particularly important in recognizing potential lines of conflict. The lack of a consistent gender perspective within the participatory paradigm has been particularly problematic, with women often sidelined in discussions, especially among community leaders (Cornwall 2000a; Guijt and Shah 1998; Jackson 2002; Lennie 1999). Ethnicity and age are also important axes of diversity. Such constraints are not insurmountable and can be overcome when researchers ensure that groups who may traditionally lack voice are included in the research process (Cornwall and Jewkes 1995: 1667).

There are also constraints associated with the analysis of PUA data. As Norton *et al.* (2001: 16) have commented, such analyses are: 'mediated representations of the realities, experiences, priorities and perceptions of poor people.' These are the result of interactions and relationships generated during the research process. As such, they do not differ from other forms of inductive research where the reliability and validity of results depend on a professional approach which emphasizes prolonged engagement, persistent observation, triangulation and cross-checking as methodological tools for ensuring credibility (ibid.; Pretty 1995). Caution therefore needs to be exercised to ensure against the 'filtering' of policy messages such that 'certain messages disappear from view' (Norton *et al.* 2001: 16–17).

Above all, there are dangers associated with the power of researchers. Chambers (2002) has commented that, in development practice, many of those undertaking participatory research find themselves being intermediaries between people and data, on the one hand, and those with power, on the other. In reflecting on the exercise of power in the construction and use of knowledge, he comments:

> Power forms and frames knowledge and interpersonal power dis-
> torts what is learnt and expressed. Each of us has to take respons-
> ibility for our part in the methodological, epistemological and
> ethical struggle to achieve representations of realities which opti-
> mize a multitude of trade-offs.
>
> (ibid.: 159)

As such, there should be explicit acknowledgment that researchers as well as participants play an important role in the summary and interpretation of results, with researchers invariably holding disproportionate levels of power (Pain and Francis 2003).

The research methodology

Turning to the research project, it is important to describe the research contexts as well as to mention the participatory tools found to be particularly important for studying violence. Finally, a mention is made of the way in which qualitative PUA data were quantified.

The research locations and communities

Since participatory urban appraisals are qualitative in nature, they rely on in-depth investigation of a small number of communities and use purposive rather than random sampling. This means selecting communities that are considered broadly representative of the issue under investigation and conducting a PUA with sufficient groups to be representative of each community. In both Colombia and Guatemala, fieldwork was undertaken in nine highly diverse, yet predominantly low-income urban settlements in a range of cities and towns. While the PUA methodology in no way claims a level of representativeness of national level household surveys, nevertheless its coverage and selection criteria make it representative of the nine communities studied and, as such, more widely significant than simply providing anecdotal evidence (Moser 2001b).

Communities in both Colombia and Guatemala were selected to be broadly representative of different geographical areas as well as the range of urban characteristics. In addition, they sought to reflect different types of violence as well as diverse types of armed conflict associated with particular regions, both past and present. In both countries, pseudonyms rather than the actual names of communities and participants were used to ensure safety. Thus, names were changed in field notes and analysis to protect both individuals and communities from possible retribution. In many cases, it was the community leaders themselves who chose settlement pseudonyms.

In Guatemala, communities were also selected to include a range of different ethnic groups. However, the fact that ethnicity was not the primary research focus, and that this was an urban study, meant that the proportions of indigenous groups included in the study was lower than the national average. Nonetheless, two communities were predominantly indigenous (Santa Cruz del Quiché and Chinautla), and many indigenous people participated in the other research communities. The study used a number of indicators to identify predominantly urban poor communities: lack of legal land tenure, limited access to basic urban services, as well as the detailed local knowledge of the community among researchers. In each country, research communities can be usefully categorized into four main urban area types (see Tables 2.1 and 2.2).

Colombia

In Colombia, research was undertaken in nine communities with locations including three major cities, an oil-rich area associated with intense armed conflict, and a region with a large displaced population of rural dwellers fleeing violence for refuge in the cities (summarized in Appendix 1; see Figure 2.1). The first category, 'large metropolitan area/capital city' refers to the capital city of Bogotá, with fieldwork undertaken in the three communities. While Embudo is located in the central area of Santa Fe, which was originally part of the colonial settlement, the other two communities of Jericó and 14 de Febrero were both established on the southern urban periphery in the 1970s and 1980s.

The second category, 'large metropolitan areas with drug cartel history,' refers to Medellín and Cali, the country's second and third largest cities, in which the two communities of Pórtico and El Arca are located. Despite government efforts to dismantle the cartels, both are internationally renowned as centers of the drug trade.[5] They are dominated by drug cartel-related violence, together with political violence on the part of guerrillas and paramilitary groups, as well as the proliferation of gangs, militias and the *sicarios* (paid assassins) dating back to the 1970s (Ceballos Melguizo 2001; Salazar 1994). Both research communities were founded through land invasion in the 1970s and 1980s and were thus relatively well consolidated.

The third urban category is 'intermediate cities and small towns with high levels of displaced populations.' This refers to Bucaramanga, a major secondary city and the departmental capital of Santander, as well as to Girón, a small historical town close to Bucaramanga where the research communities of Amanecer and Rosario respectively are located. Although all research locations have displaced populations, metropolitan Bucara-

Table 2.1 Characteristics of research communities in Colombia

Selection criteria	Community pseudonyms								
	Embudo	14 de Febrero	Jericó	Pórtico	El Arca	Amanecer	Rosario	Cachicamo	Colombia Chiquita
City location	Bogotá	Bogotá	Bogotá	Medellín, Antioquia	Cali, Valle de Cauca	Bucaramanga, Santander	Girón, Santander	Yopal, Casanare	Aguazul, Casanare
City characteristic	Large metropolitan area/capital city	Large metropolitan area/capital city	Large metropolitan area/capital city	Large metropolitan area with drug cartel history	Large metropolitan area with drug cartel history	Intermediate city with displaced populations	Historical small town with displaced populations	Frontier town in natural resource rich area	Frontier town in natural resource rich area
Socio-economic status	Poor	Poor	Poor	Poor	Poor	Poor	Poor	Poor and middle-income	Poor
Intra-city location	Inner-city	Peri-urban	Peri-urban	Peri-urban	Peri-urban	Peri-urban	Peri-urban	Central urban neighborhood	Peri-urban
Date of establishment	1596	1971	1980	1972	1980	1980	1991	1935	1994
Form of establishment	Colonial residential area	Invasion of private land managed by Central Nacional Provivienda– Communist Party	Small-scale invasion of private farm land and purchase of lots	Purchase of lots on private farm land	Invasion of private land managed by group from M-19 guerrilla	Purchase of lots on private farm land	Invasion of disused public land	First settlement registered in municipality	Invasion of private farm land

Table 2.2 Characteristics of research communities in Guatemala

Selection criteria	Community pseudonyms								
	Concepción	Nuevo Horizonte	La Merced	San Jorge	Sacuma	Limoncito	Gucumatz	El Carmen	Villa Real
City location	Guatemala City	Guatemala City	Guatemala City	Chinautla	Huehuetenango	San Pedro Sacatepéquez San Marcos	Santa Cruz del Quiché	Santa Lucía Cotzumalguapa	Esquipulas
Administrative status and spatial location	Capital city in central Guatemala	Capital city in central Guatemala	Capital city in central Guatemala	Small town in central Guatemala	Departmental capital in Western Highlands	Departmental capital in Western Highlands	Departmental capital in Western Highlands	Town in Southern Lowlands	Border town in Eastern Lowlands
Socio-economic status	Poor	Poor	Poor	Poor	Poor	Poor and middle-income	Poor and middle-income	Poor	Poor
Intra-city location	Central urban	Peri-urban	Peri-urban	Peri-urban	Peri-urban	Central urban	Central urban	Peri-urban	Central urban
Date of establishment	1976	1983	1983	Pre-Columbian	1969	1940	Pre-Culumbian	1820	1980
Form of establishment	Land invasion	Land invasion	Land invasion	Historic community	Urban development	Urban development	Historic community	Urban development	Urban development
Ethnic composition	Predominantly ladino	Predominantly ladino	Predominantly ladino	Predominantly indigenous	Predominantly ladino	Predominantly ladino	Predominantly indigenous	Predominantly ladino	Predominantly ladino

Figure 2.1 Colombia: locations of towns and cities where the research was conducted.

manga has been particularly affected due to its proximity to the high-conflict area of the Magdalena Medio region where political violence, especially between the National Liberation Army, or ELN (*Ejército de Liberación Nacional*) and paramilitaries is chronic. In the recently established community of Rosario, located on the outskirts of Girón, displaced people comprise half the population.

The final category is 'frontier towns in natural resource rich areas.' This includes Yopal, the departmental capital, and the smaller town of Aguazul

29

Figure 2.2 Guatemala: locations of towns and cities where the research was conducted.

where the communities of Cachicamo and Colombia Chiquita respectively are located. Set in the plains and grasslands of the *Llanos* in the Department of Casanare, both towns are in the country's oil-producing region. This area is seriously affected by the political violence of the guerrilla and paramilitaries, and is often regarded as one of the most violent regions in the country (Dudley and Murillo 1998). The community of Cachicamo forms part of the central urban area of Yopal, while Colombia Chiquita is a much newer, peri-urban settlement in Aguazul.

Guatemala

The nine research communities in Guatemala can also be categorized into four main urban types. These were located in the Western Highlands, and the Southern and Eastern Lowlands, as well as the capital region. They included localities directly affected by the conflict (Santa Cruz del Quiché, San Pedro Sacatepéquez San Marcos,[6] Huehuetenango), as well as indirectly (Santa Lucía Cotzumalguapa), and a community relatively untouched (Esquipulas) (see Figure 2.2).

The first category, the 'capital city and towns in central Guatemala,' refers to Guatemala City and its surrounding area. Research was undertaken in the communities of Concepción, Nuevo Horizonte, and La Merced all in Guatemala City, as well as in San Jorge, Chinautla. Robberies, delinquency, and gang activity are most pronounced in the capital together with drug-related crimes and a proliferation of small firearms. Indeed, both the homicide and robbery rates are considerably higher than the national average (IEPADES 1998). The communities of Nuevo Horizonte and La Merced are peri-urban while Concepción is more central, with all three resulting from land invasion. In contrast, San Jorge is a settlement in a small town approximately 12 kilometers north of the capital city with a long history as a Pocomam indigenous area (in contrast to the other communities which are mainly *ladino*).[7]

The second urban category, 'departmental capitals in the Western Highlands,' refers to Huehuetenango, San Pedro Sacatepéquez, San Marcos, and Santa Cruz del Quiché, with research undertaken in the communities of Sacuma, Limoncito and Gucumatz respectively. The Western Highlands are populated predominantly by indigenous groups (comprising 75.9 percent of the total population) (PNUD 2000: 58). As one of the areas most affected by the armed conflict, particularly the military's counter-insurgency project, Huehuetenango and El Quiché are two of the most militarized departments. Although political violence has lessened, institutional violence and delinquency increased throughout the 1990s, with lynching a popular form of informal law enforcement. Huehuetenango also has violence problems relating to its border town status. All three communities in this region are centrally located, well-consolidated settlements, with Gucumatz (a predominantly K'iché indigenous settlement) dating back to pre-colonial times.

The third urban category, 'town in the Southern Lowlands,' refers to the town of Santa Lucía Cotzumalguapa located in the department of Escuintla. Fieldwork was undertaken in a peri-urban community called El Carmen. While predominantly a *ladino* settlement, it contains a sizeable indigenous population displaced from the Western Highlands, due to the armed conflict as well as economic hardship. The town itself has strong links with the sugar industry, with much of the population associated in some way with this sector. Violent conflict has increased considerably in the region in the 1990s, with the highest homicide rate in 1996 recorded in nearby Escuintla (PNUD 1998: 149).

The final urban category, 'town in the Eastern Lowlands,' refers to Esquipulas, in the department of Chiquimula where fieldwork was conducted in the mainly *ladino* inner urban community of Villa Real. The town lies close to the borders with both Honduras and El Salvador, with a relatively large transient population from these two countries. This region was relatively immune from the armed conflict, but has traditionally been associated with armed violence and extreme forms of machismo (Palma 1998).

The research teams

In both countries the authors undertook the PUA between January and June 1999 in collaboration with four teams of local researchers. Team selection criteria prioritized researchers and organizations with previous experience working in a low-income urban community. This was essential in ensuring the necessary trust to undertake the research, minimizing entry time, and assisting in negotiations with community 'gatekeepers' to get agreement to enter and work in the community. Above all, to ensure safety for team members, every effort was made to include at least one person in each team with guaranteed trust and access to the community studied. Over and above this critical selection criterion, counterpart organizations comprised a range of different groups, chosen to broadly reflect the different sectors of civil society in each country.

In Colombia, they included a team of academic anthropologists from the *Universidad Nacional*,[8] a non-governmental organization (NGO), CEMILLA (*Centro Microempresarial del Llano*), that worked in local community-based income-generating and education projects, a women's NGO, *Fundación Mujer y Futuro*, that also worked closely with local communities and especially with displaced people. Finally, there was a group of young consultants, some of whom previously had worked with the *Alto Comisionado para la Paz*, as well as with youth organizations in Cali and Medellín. Of a total of nineteen researchers, nine were male and ten were female.

In Guatemala the research was again undertaken with four collaborating teams. These included a research-oriented NGO, AVANCSO (*Asociación para el Avance de las Ciencias Sociales*), a women's NGO, AMVA (*Asociación Mujer Vamos Adelante*) working with community-based women's organizations on educational and human rights issues, a community development NGO, FUNDESCO (*Fundación de Desarrollo y Servicios Comunitarios*), also working in grassroots projects with women and youth groups. Finally, there was a team that combined members from a policy-focused NGO, CIEN (*Centro de Investigaciones Económicas Nacionales*) and an education-oriented NGO, SEPREDI (*Servicios Profesionales Educativos Integrales*). Of the sixteen researchers, nine were female and seven were male. Both the FUNDESCO and AMVA teams included indigenous researchers – with four indigenous women in total.

In both countries, all researchers involved in the research process started with one week's classroom training in PUA techniques. Daniel Selener of the *Instituto Internacional de Reconstrucción Rural* (IIRR) undertook this in collaboration with both the authors.

The PUA methodology in practice

PUA includes a wide range of participatory techniques. Each study began with a transect walk through the community and meetings with local community members for an exchange of ideas about the project. The most important technique was focus group discussions that ranged in size from two to three (such as neighbors or young people on street corners) to twenty people (such as meetings in community centers, crèches, clinics and schools). These were always facilitated by two researchers. In Colombia a total of 1,414 people participated in focus groups in nine communities, while for Guatemala where exactly the same methodology was implemented, 1,860 people participated. To ensure representativeness within each community studied, focus groups were triangulated to reflect age, gender as well as position/status within the community and, where appropriate, ethnicity.

The PUA involved the use of an extensive number of tools. While poverty and livelihood studies commonly prioritize a number of wealth-ranking tools, in studying violence different tools, adapted to the focus of the study, were found to be essential. Among those of greatest importance were listings of violence that provided the basis for the quantitative data analysis. Equally prominent were causal impact diagrams that analyze the causes and effects of different types and categories of violence within communities. Institutional mapping diagrams were highly relevant to identify social institutions perceived as important within communities. Finally, timelines provided a temporal analysis of changing levels of violence within communities (see Appendix 2 for a summary of PUA tools used in this study; also Moser and McIlwaine 1999; Pain and Francis 2003, on the advantages and disadvantages of the tools).

The primary aim of PUA is to allow people to express their own ideas and perceptions of issues of importance to them. Therefore, in all the focus groups community participants were encouraged to write the matrixes or design the diagrams themselves, and in all cases to provide the associated text (which they either wrote themselves or which was noted by facilitators). This process is often referred to as 'handing over the stick' and derives from rural PRA where local community participants in African and Asian contexts wrote on the ground with a stick (Chambers 1994c). In the urban Colombian and Guatemalan context, however, this generally involved pens, pencils and paper that was taped to a nearby wall, door or window, or placed on the ground. This is just one of the transparent ways in which power is transferred from the researcher to the researched in PUAs. It means that people in the communities themselves, using their language, drew all the diagrams reproduced in this book.

As the following chapters reveal, visual representations were very popular with all age groups. Drawings are often important in non-literate communities, or as a useful tool to engage children. In addition, because of the high levels of fear and insecurity in the communities studied, and the associated culture of fear or silence (see below), in both countries focus groups were often far more comfortable drawing visual images to illustrate issues, than to articulate them verbally or in written matrixes. This was particularly the case when identifying the menacing presence of guerrilla and paramilitary groups in Colombian communities through institutional maps. For this reason, this study relies very heavily on the visualization of issues. For publication purposes it has been necessary to transfer the diagrams into computerized form, but reproducing as far as possible the exact words and drawings of the focus group.

Constraints associated with violence-focused PUA

In addition to the general constraints associated with using PUA outlined above, there are some specific limitations associated with conducting PUA in communities experiencing high levels of violence. Not only is violence relatively new as a development issue, as mentioned in Chapter 1, it is also a difficult and sensitive issue to research (Lykes 1997). Despite the recent proliferation of PRA/PUA studies, few have examined issues relating to violence, other than those on natural resource conflicts (see Leach *et al.* 1997). The research on which this book is based was strongly influenced by an earlier PUA of urban violence undertaken by Caroline Moser and Jeremy Holland in urban Jamaica where the methodology was piloted, and safety issues highlighted (Moser and Holland 1997). In this research project, important limitations related both to the safety of researchers and to the understandably high levels of reticence among the population in local communities. Both had an important influence on the PUA process.

The safety of researchers

To ensure the safety of the researchers, the PUA was undertaken primarily during daylight hours. As mentioned above, all the research teams had prior experience of working in low-income urban communities, and at least one researcher was known in the community prior to the project. Nevertheless, in Guatemala in particular, some less experienced researchers felt fearful working in areas with high levels of violence, particularly those who had not previously worked intensively with community members in the informal manner required of PUA. In some cases they were especially anxious when working 'in the streets,' when their previous research experience had been in safer areas such as inside houses, or in community centers working under the 'protection' of local organizations in the area.

This meant that decisions relating to research entry points were critical. In both Colombia and Guatemala, focus group discussions started with the identification of community problems rather than violence issues *per se*. As described in Chapter 3, community members themselves introduced their concerns with violence as part of the broader discussions. Again, this is consistent with PUA's aim that issues emerge from the people themselves rather than being imposed by the researchers. Violence was not *a priori* assumed to be a problem. The first stage of the PUA explored community perceptions regarding the priority given to violence as against other concerns, along with the ranking of the gravity of different types of violence.[9]

Within these parameters of caution, it was also important that the research was conducted as transparently as possible in terms of informing community members of the study aims, and ensuring that key community power-brokers were included in discussions. This assisted in preventing further conflict from developing (Hamilton *et al.* 1998). Indeed, the most expedient way of initiating research in communities was to start with open meetings with community leaders and residents to explain the aims of the research. As mentioned earlier, both communities and participants were all given pseudonyms and their identity remained confidential throughout the research process.

The 'culture' or 'law of silence' in communities

As mentioned in Chapter 1, local populations in both countries have developed important strategies to cope with fear and insecurity, and to protect themselves from outsiders. This not only influenced the research findings, but also the research process itself. Because of their fear, people were often reluctant to discuss certain issues. In some cases, they refused to give information or sometimes gave incomplete information. Kruijt and Koonings (1999: 2) have pointed out: '[o]f all the countries on the continent, Guatemala is one of the most significant examples of a "society of fear,"' and the research project certainly bore this out. Individuals and groups were far more reluctant to discuss topics directly or indirectly relating to violence in local Guatemalan communities, particularly those dominated by indigenous populations, than was the case in Colombia. This was due largely to the different nature of political conflict in the two countries, and specifically whether or not the civilian population was an explicit target, as was the case in Guatemala. In Colombia, this was a problem mainly in communities currently affected by severe political violence, such as Yopal and Aguazul (see Chapter 8).

In Guatemala, the so-called 'culture of silence' (*cultura de silencio*) was a legacy of the armed conflict. This affected all communities, both indigenous and *ladino,* although it was more widespread among the former. As a result of human rights violations and the state's counter-insurgency policy during the civil war, silence was a strategy used by victims of, or witnesses to, violence as a means to avoid violent repercussions (Lykes 1997; see Chapters 3 and 4). Widespread terror perpetrated during the 1980s, in particular, had created a society based on fear – with its effects on the indigenous population documented in the *Recuperación de la Memoria Histórica* (REHMI) project (ODHAG 1999) particularly severe.[10]

Fear was most widespread in the predominantly indigenous community of Gucumatz, Santa Cruz del Quiché, which suffered considerably during the conflict. One man from this community recalled that in the 1980s: 'If someone talked, they were a dead man; for this reason, people kept silent.' This reluctance to speak has continued to the present with another man from the same community noting: 'How do I know you are a good person? . . . You think I'm stupid, that's what they did in the past . . . when you turned round they changed their tune.' In a similar vein, another man highlighted the continuing legacy of the conflict: 'Today no one takes responsibility for anything; only dead men . . . the survivors live in silence.' Many people from Gucumatz pointed out that despite the Peace Accords they were still afraid of repression.[11]

As such, a focus group of four indigenous women working in a tortilla-making shop in Gucumatz abruptly ceased talking about violence when they felt it had become too sensitive. In discussing how violence had changed over time, they said it had been highest in 1978 and then declined in 1982 during the government of Efraín Ríos Montt. They would not carry forward their discussion past 1990, however, choosing instead to simply describe how violence had declined and was now carried out predominantly by thieves. Furthermore, none of the focus groups in Santa Cruz del Quiché were willing to draw diagrams of the causes and impact of violence. One of a group of indigenous people from Quiché, comprising a 40-year-old man and two women aged between 40 and 50, simply stated: 'People are afraid.'

While *ladinos* did express such views, indigenous people in focus groups were most likely to comment on the implications of political conflict. Although people still feared the return of political violence, in many cases this was now manifested in fear of delinquency, robbery, and gangs (*maras*) resulting from insufficient state security force protection. Women in particular feared rape which affected their mobility; this was further exacerbated by the gossip about the types of crimes committed in the *colonia* (see Chapter 8). People also complained of the stigma associated with their *colonias*. In Concepción, Guatemala City, for instance, residents explained that people from outside refused to come into their *colonia* because they were afraid of violence, and that shops wouldn't give them credit when they heard where they lived (see Chapter 4).

In both Guatemala and Colombia, despite an evident reluctance to share experiences in many communities, a number of strategies were employed to address this issue. In Guatemala, this included speaking to children and youth who were too young to have direct experiences of the atrocities of the 1980s, and who tended to be more affected by other types of violence currently affecting communities, such as *maras* and drug-related violence. As noted above, in Colombia, the 'law of silence' (*ley de silencio*) was an especially important issue in the communities affected by political violence. Consequently, it was most evident in one community in Aguazul where guerrilla and paramilitary groups were active, regularly entering the community and threatening, and occasionally killing the inhabitants (see Chapters 4 and 8). One of the strategies developed to deal with the fear of talking about violence here involved making appointments with community members to return to talk with them at 'safe times' when there was no danger of the guerrillas and paramilitaries arriving. In addition, focus groups were often conducted in back rooms of houses out of sight of the rest of the community, rather than in the street.

In both countries there was also a widespread reluctance by some community members to openly discuss intra-family violence. Here, however, there were important age and gender-based differences. For instance, young people were more willing to discuss violence within the home than were older community members. In addition, women were much more likely to raise the issue than men, mainly because men were the primary perpetrators. It was often only possible to explore intra-family violence from the perspective of alcohol abuse. When alcohol arose as a topic in focus group discussions, it was often a conduit to talk about violence in the home, given that it was cited as a major cause of domestic abuse (see Chapter 5).

The analysis of the data: quantifying the PUA results

Finally, by way of background it is important to briefly mention some of the challenges encountered in the analysis of the results from the extensive field notes as well as summary reports that were the outcome of the project. The fieldwork on which this book is based was undertaken as part of a larger project – the Urban Peace Program – directed by Caroline

Moser, when Lead Specialist for Social Development in the World Bank's Latin America and Caribbean Region. This included two country-specific descriptive reports (see Moser and McIlwaine 2000, 2001a).

Particularly in Colombia, the contextual background to the research project influenced both the research methodology adopted as well the approach taken in the original analysis of the data. In the late 1990s, the Colombian government, together with the World Bank, had undertaken a participatory country assistance strategy (CAS) process. This identified violence as Colombia's most important development problem with significant implications for levels of vulnerability and poverty. The subsequent Sector Study undertaken by the World Bank in collaboration with local researchers revealed two further issues of importance (Moser et al. 2000). First, was the overriding preoccupation of politicians and researchers with the country's political violence, and, second, was a serious lack of information of the poor's perceptions of the issue of violence and its relationship to poverty. The Colombia PUA was a direct outcome of this lack of information.

Since it was conceived within a development framework, in analyzing the research results it is important to recognize the inherent tension that exists between the necessity to remain true to the participant's perceptions and the need to synthesize results in a form accessible for policymakers (Jackson 2002; Moser and Holland 1998). To ensure that the descriptive findings from the research project are relevant for policymakers, as much as for researchers, it has been important to 'push the analytical envelope' in terms of the quantification of qualitative, participatory research (see Moser and McIlwaine 2000, 2001a). Here again, the issue of power is pertinent since planning the methodology itself entails the exercise of power to set boundaries on what will and will not be found (Chambers 2002). As mentioned above, both the choice of research communities and the purposive sampling of focus groups within communities have been designed to ensure that the results provide broadly representative rather than anecdotal information. Similarly, the quantification of the research results has been essential to provide robust data rather than 'apt' illustration (Gluckman 1958; Mitchell 1956).[12]

The research analysis has included quantification of the extensive numbers of focus group listings of community perceptions of different types of violence. As Chapter 3 shows, this has resulted in somewhat counter-intuitive results, demonstrating that the perceptions of violence of local low-income communities are not always the same as those of the country's politicians, policymakers and journalists. Also of considerable importance is the quantification of institutional maps. These provide a graphic visual tool for local people to illustrate their perceptions of local institutions, and as such are important in understanding the complexities of levels of trust and mistrust, and associated social capital. Again, the quantification of data provides important policy relevant results.

The contestation between theory and practice, and associated with this the debate concerning the advantages and limitations of quantifying PUA data, are themes that run throughout the book. This chapter, therefore, is intended to provide the background for the following chapters that explore in greater detail, through a discussion of the empirical findings, the contribution of participatory methodologies to our understanding of urban violence.

3

THE MULTIPLE COMPLEXITY OF DAILY VIOLENCE IN URBAN COLOMBIAN AND GUATEMALAN COMMUNITIES

Although 'banal' or 'ubiquitous' violence is now endemic in many Latin American cities, little is known about how this affects the daily lives of the urban poor. The PUA methodology gave voice to local members of eighteen research communities in Colombia and Guatemala to describe how they themselves perceived the multiple complexity of daily violence. The methodological tools also visually illustrate how associated perceptions of fear and insecurity were spatially manifested.

By way of background, the chapter begins with a brief review of the historical origins and the current nature of violence at the national level in the two countries. Turning to community-level data, the types of violence are then identified through focus group listings and rankings, showing both the multiplicity of types of violence, as well as the way people deal simultaneously with interrelated types. It highlights the importance of violence relative to other livelihood problems facing the urban poor and, given population diversity, explores how violence is experienced in a wide range of ways depending on gender, ethnicity and age.

Finally, in seeking to reconcile the disjuncture between the complexity of daily violence and the level of simplification required by policymakers, it categorizes the multiple types of violence within the community in terms of three categories of social, economic and political violence. While this reduces multiple realities to non-complex classifications, it nevertheless provides the opportunity to challenge existing stereotypes as to the relative importance of different types of violence in the lives of poor people themselves.

National level historical and contemporary perspectives on violence

The focus on Colombia and Guatemala as the countries in which the research was conducted provides interesting comparative experiences of violence at the national level. Aside from their location in Latin America, there would appear to be as many contrasts as similarities between them.

These relate not only to the geographical and socio-economic character-istics of the two countries, but also to the historical roots of violence, embedded as they are in very different socio-political contexts. Colombia is a middle-income country currently experiencing severe recession along with an expanding civil war. Guatemala, by contrast, is one of the poorest nations in the region, but with a relatively steady economic growth rate.[1] It is in a 'post-conflict' transition phase in which decades of civil war have left an indelible imprint on society. However, regardless of such differ-ences in political histories and economic resource bases, in both countries daily violence dominates the lives of ordinary people.

Colombia

With one of the highest homicide rates in the world, three times the rate in Brazil and Mexico, and 50 times a typical European country, Colombia has the dubious reputation of being characterized as one of the world's most violent nations (Gaviria 2000: 2). This may seem surprising given its reputa-tion as one of South America's oldest and most enduring democracies, its middle-income status and its richness in natural and human resources. However, even in the late 1970s and early 1980s its homicide rates were high by international comparisons, standing at 20.5 per 100,000 of the population (compared with Brazil with a rate of 11.5 which was the next highest in the region). In the late 1980s and early 1990s, the rate increased to an alarming 89.5 (compared with 19.7 in Brazil) (Ayres 1998: 3). This dramatic increase was most marked in the three largest cities of Bogotá, Cali and Medellín, where around 40 percent of all violent deaths in the country occurred (Rubio 2001: 55). Peaking in 1993, homicide rates have since declined nationally, although conflict has intensified in other ways.

Such a situation is not new, however. With eight general civil wars and fourteen local civil wars occurring during the nineteenth century, the roots of violence in Colombia extend back over a century or more. These con-frontations were both political and economic in nature, contested between the Liberal and Conservative Parties, the two principal parties that consti-tuted the central power of Colombia's aristocratic state. In competing for political power, both parties were closely tied to the interests of large coffee and cattle barons. While the Conservative Party historically represented the social structures consolidated in the colonial era, the Liberal Party, in break-ing away from the power bases of the Catholic Church and traditional politi-cians, became associated with emerging social structures linked to the diversification of the economy and territorial expansion of the power base (Chernick 1997; Deas 1998; Reyes Posada 1998).

Contemporary political violence is closely identified with '*El Bogotázo*' that erupted in 1948 as a violent response to the assassination of the Liberal politician Jorge Ulcer Gaitán. His widespread popularity related to his identification as the first popular figure to protest against a social and political system that sustained an oligarchy and allowed them to enjoy arbitrary privileges and wealth. Gaining power in 1946, the Conservative Party had already begun a wave of violence aimed at Liberal rural peasants and farmers in order to consolidate its power base by force. With the outbreak of the 1948 insurrection, however, systematic violence let loose a flood of pent-up rage and hostility, resulting in an undeclared civil war known as *La Violencia* that cost the lives of some 200,000 Colombians between 1948 and 1958. Beneath the Liberal–Conservative conflict there emerged a host of regional and local issues that fueled the violence in the absence of any state authority or mediating mechanism, including land conflicts, social conflict, family and inter-personal feuds (Ocquist 1978).

The impact of *La Violencia* was deep, lasting and extensive. Over two million rural peasants and farmers were displaced and forced from their lands. Slums and shantytowns sprang up in almost all the major cities, and a new wave of pioneers, displaced by the violence, migrated to marginal lands along the country's borders. Social and institutional networks were destroyed, and widespread trauma frequently converted itself into violent waves of revenge killings and murder. Political party membership became an important measure of identity, as much as a means of differentiating allies from enemies, a situation that has clearly affected any sense of citizenship and weakened respect for the legal rights normally indicative of belonging to a state. During the past five decades, as the numbers of social actors and the intricacy of their interdependent relationships have multiplied, so the spatial density of conflict has worsened. As the complexity of these relationships has increased, so too have the constraints associated with successfully resolving the conflict been compounded (see Appendix 3 for a summary of the main social actors involved in political conflict in Colombia, 1948–98).

One major trend has been the numerical and territorial expansion of armed groups. In 1997, there were 132 guerrilla groups, divided principally into the Revolutionary Armed Forces of Colombia, known as the FARC (*Fuerzas Armadas Revolucionarias de Colombia*) and the National Liberation Army, or ELN (*Ejército de Liberación Nacional*).[2] In addition to the guerrilla forces, there were some 100 paramilitary organizations operating in around 300 municipalities, with the United Self-Defense Forces of Colombia (*Autodefensas Unidas de Colombia*, AUC) the best known among them (Ferreyra and Segura 2000). Throughout the 1990s, total membership of insurgent groups rose by 60 percent and the number of municipalities with a guerrilla presence increased fivefold (Rubio 2001).

It is essential to recognize that insurgent groups are highly diverse, constantly changing and difficult to classify. Ceballos Melguizo (2001: 111), for instance, divides them into three main groups: (1) the 'counterstate powers' such as the guerrilla groups and some urban militias; (2) the 'parastate powers' such as the paramilitary and self-defense groups; and (3) 'organized crime' groups such as the drug cartels, arms traffickers and money-laundering organizations. All such groups are involved in complex negotiations over drugs, territory and associated power. Combined with the growth in their number and size has been an expansion of the violence associated with them. This includes massacres, terrorist acts and kidnappings, as well as petty crime, car theft and bank robberies (Gaviria 2000). For instance, in 1999, the highest number of massacres for the decade was reported, with more than one occurring every day (Rubio 2001: 59). In particular, Colombia has become synonymous with kidnapping. The rate is 50 times higher than the average for the ten countries where 90 percent of all global kidnapping occurs (ibid.: 60). Most significant of all, however, has been the manner in which politically motivated conflict has increasingly merged with other types of crime and violence (Pecaut 1999). While officially, it is still maintained that over 95 percent of homicides are not linked directly with the state–guerrilla confrontation, in practice it is often not possible to distinguish between political and economic motivations for murder (Gaviria 2000: 6).

The situation has been exacerbated by additional political and economic factors. Along with economic liberalization and Colombia's first economic recession for sixty-two years, increased oil exploration has intensified armed conflict (Watson 2000). Opposition to privatization of the oil industry has come from legitimate and illegitimate groups alike. Both the ELN and the FARC have opposed increased multinational interests in the oil industry, blowing up pipelines and attacking and kidnapping oil officials (especially foreign workers), with the paramilitaries and private security armies also involved in the fight against the guerrilla forces (Dudley and Murillo 1998; Dureau and Florez 2000). To add to this, most recently, U.S. intervention through Plan Colombia, drawn up between Colombia and the U.S.A. and implemented in September 1999, is also reported to have intensified the armed conflict. Aimed primarily at curbing the supply of drugs to the U.S.A., most of Plan Colombia comprises military aid, with minor components allocated for alternative cultivation schemes for coca farmers and human rights and judicial programs.[3]

While the actors involved in violence have multiplied, so the people affected by it have also increased. Until the 1990s, armed conflict mainly affected those involved in the conflict itself as well as marginal populations in remote rural areas, with urban violence primarily impacting on low-income *barrio* (community) dwellers. Daily violence now affects the lives of all Colombians. Not only has this prompted frequent public demonstrations against armed groups, but also widespread emigration of more wealthy Colombians; several surveys have reported that over 50 percent of those interviewed wanted to settle abroad (Rubio 2001: 55).

This multiplicity of violence has been allowed to flourish in a context of widespread impunity. In 1996, it was reported that between 97 and 98 percent of all crimes went unpunished, with 74 percent of crimes unreported (Giraldo 1999: 31). Such extreme levels of impunity have demonstrated the failure of the state to enforce its sovereignty and the rule of law, and in turn, bred widespread fear and insecurity. With both armed actors and the civil population questioning the legitimacy of the state, a plethora of different armed actors have developed their own alternative forms of governance and protection, including a range of private security firms and informal militias and gangs. Thus, in Colombia, violence, fear and insecurity have developed a self-sustaining momentum with interrelated causes, manifestations and consequences.

Guatemala

In contrast to Colombia, Guatemala is one of the poorest nations in the region with far fewer natural resources. In turn, it is generally considered the most violent country in Central America, with the highest regional homicide rate (CIEN 1998) (although it often vies with El Salvador). Violent deaths per annum increased from 2,699 in 1992 to 3,657 in 1995, with the number of crimes doubling from 11,711 in 1992 to 22,742 in 1995 (PNUD 1998: 148). By 1998, violent deaths per 100,000 had reached 76.99 compared with 63.7 in 1991, with the total number of crimes increasing by 50 percent between 1996 and 1998 (Call 2000: 9). Also important has been a reported increase in gendered violence, especially within the home. Of some 800 women interviewed in 1997, 38.7 percent cited domestic violence as their principal family problem (PNUD 1998: 151–152). Rape is also common, with one reported every two to three days (ibid.).

As in Colombia, violence is not a new phenomenon. Political conflict has characterized the nation's history since its sixteenth-century conquest at the hands of Conquistador, Pedro Alvarado, to the last century of domination of Mayan indigenous groups, and the concentration of power in the hands of the *ladino* elite. Here, unlike Colombia, inequality has developed largely along racial and ethnic lines, with the indigenous populations experiencing widespread oppression.[4] This group represents just under half of the nation's population (41.7 percent) and comprises 23 ethno-linguistic groups, 21 of which are Mayan (PNUD 1998: 219). After independence from Spain in 1821, for instance, liberal and conservative regimes contributed to a state-building process that excluded the majority indigenous population and poor *ladinos*. In the first half of the twentieth century, a major factor underpinning levels of violence was the forced labor of indigenous groups. Imposed after the Liberal Revolution of 1871 and in response to the coffee boom, indigenous groups were forced to work on plantations or risk imprisonment, with a series of authoritarian military dictatorships designed to enforce this.[5]

Despite a brief period of democracy in the 1940s, the last five decades have been characterized by widespread conflict, repression and violence. The exceptions were the administrations of José Arévalo (1944–52) and

Jacobo Arbenz (1952–4), which oversaw liberal policies that widened participation and the political franchise, and implemented socio-economic reforms. In particular, the Arbenz administration instituted programs of nationalization and land reform, expropriating land from, among others, the U.S.-owned United Fruit Company and redistributing this to peasant farmers in the highland and coastal regions. These changes were overturned with the CIA-orchestrated coup of 1954.

The internal armed conflict, which began in 1960 with the first military-led insurgency, grew out of divisions within the military institution following the CIA-orchestrated coup.[6] Between 1960 and 1996, four guerrilla groups (*Partido Guatemalteco de Trabajo*, PGT; *Las Fuerzas Armadas Rebeldes*, FAR; *La Organización del Pueblo en Armas*, OPRA; and *El Ejército Guerrillero de los Pobres*, EGP) operated across the country, combining in 1982 under the umbrella organization the URNG (*La Unidad Revolucionaria Nacional Guatemalteca*). During this period, between 150,000 and 200,000 civilians were assassinated, kidnapped, tortured or disappeared in the state-led counter-insurgency, the majority of whom were indigenous people (ODHAG 1999; Wilson, R.A. 1997). This was defined by the Commission for Historical Clarification (*Comisión de Esclarecimiento Histórico*, CEH) as genocidal (CEH 1999).

The early 1980s were the bloodiest period of the country's history with a series of brutal atrocities and massacres concentrated in rural areas (CEH 1999; ODHAG 1999). A principal element of rural militarization was the establishment of the civil self-defense patrols (*Patrullas de Autodefensa Civil*, PACs), initiated under the regime of General Lucas García (1978–82) and institutionalized under General Efraín Rios Montt (1982–3) through the counter-insurgency campaign known as 'beans and bullets.'[7] Political violence continued throughout the democratic transition, initiated with the return to civilian rule in 1985, although it began to decrease toward the mid-1990s. With the signing of the Oslo Agreement in 1996, Guatemala completed the peace process and became a 'post-conflict' nation–state (Palencia Prado 1996; Wilson, R.A. 1997).

However, this did not signal the eradication of violence. In fact, much contemporary crime and violence affects urban areas that were previously relatively immune from the worst of the civil war. Thus, it has shifted from the North Western (Huehuetenango, El Quiché) and North Central (Alta Verapaz, Baja Verapaz) regions of the country, to the South Western (San Marcos, Sololá, Totonicapán, Quetzaltenango, Suchitepéquez, Retalhuleu) and North Eastern departments (Izabal, El Progreso, Zacapa, Chiquimula) (Palma 1998; PNUD 1998). Compounded by intense media attention, widespread insecurity and fear now exist across the country.[8] Indeed, it is often reported that there is more violence now than during the armed conflict (de León *et al.* 1999).

Along with the increased murder rates, mentioned above, kidnapping, car theft and bank robberies increased throughout the 1990s. Kidnappings, concentrated in Guatemala City, increased from 162 in 1995, to 182 in 1996, and were estimated to generate approximately Q300 million (U.S.$48.8 million) (PNUD 1998: 148).[9] While only seven bank robberies were reported in 1996, this increased to forty-nine in 1997 (with sixteen outside the capital region) (ibid.). Similarly, robberies of vehicles has also become a major issue, with a reported eighteen armed gangs involved in between 4,000 and 7,000 robberies per year (ibid.). Gang violence has also increased dramatically, especially since 1986. Known locally as '*maras*' or less frequently by their generic name of '*pandillas*,' gangs usually comprise young, unemployed men with a minority of women. They are most prolific in the capital, where estimates on the number of gangs range from 60 (PNUD 1998) to 330 (PRODEN 1996). Membership in each gang ranges from tens up to hundreds (AVANCSO 1996). Gangs are involved in robberies, attacks, rapes and street fighting (usually over territory), and generally copy the gang culture found in the United States. Although some have suggested that the *maras* are a direct outcome of the dissolution of the URNG, others maintain that they are linked with frustration and exclusion experienced by youth (ibid.).

As in Colombia, impunity is widespread throughout Guatemala. This is related to the weakness of the judicial system and the lack of trust in the state security forces, especially the police force. In an effort to reduce institutional violence, the Peace Accords called for the creation of a new police force, the *Policia Nacional Civil* (PNC), as well as the reform of the judicial system. However, this process is still in its infancy and impunity remains a widespread problem (Molina 1999a). This has contributed to an increase in lynching as an illegal and informal way of dealing with accused criminals (Rodríguez 1996). In this case, local populations take the law into their own hands, injuring or killing someone accused of committing a crime, usually involving dousing the target with petrol and setting them alight. While not unheard of in the past, lynching is on the increase, mainly in rural areas (MINUGUA 1998). While official concern is growing, lynching is met with widespread public approval. For example, a public opinion survey undertaken in 1996 showed that 75 percent were in favor of taking justice into their own hands (Ferrigno 1998).

This brief account of violence, as both an historical and contemporary phenomenon, provides a backdrop for the situation within the eighteen urban poor communities in both countries.

Community perceptions of daily violence

The scale of violence

Research results from the PUA broadly correspond with the national level picture above in showing that the lives of local community members in both Colombia and Guatemala were dominated by violence. First, and most revealing, was the scale of the phenomenon as manifest in the diversity of types of violence experienced. In Colombia, people identified a total average of twenty-five different types across all nine *barrios*, with one community (Embudo, Bogotá) distinguishing sixty different types of violence. Even more alarming, in Guatemala, there was a total average of forty-one types of violence, with one community (Sacuma, Huehuetenango) distinguishing between an acutely high seventy different types.

In both countries most focus groups used the generic term 'violence' (*violencia*) in their listings. Nevertheless, fear and insecurity associated with the 'culture of silence' (discussed in Chapter 2), meant that in some cases other words were used as synonyms. In Guatemala, for instance, a more locally acceptable term was 'danger' (*peligro*). *Peligro* referred to all types of violence and insecurity, in contrast to *violencia*, which was often perceived as political violence and conflict associated with the civil war. For others, danger denoted the threat of force, whereas violence denoted the act itself. Figure 3.1, for instance, provides an example of the way in which a group of young men in Villa Real, Esquipulas, listed and distinguished types of violence and danger, ranging from gang and drug violence to violence within the home.

Sphere of influence	Types of danger	Types of violence
Individual	People who kill Drunk people	Parents who hit their children Children in prostitution Adults who abuse children
Group	Gangs Arms Inhalants	Drugged people who can kill
Community	People from other places who come over with negative attitudes	Drunk people who push people People who mistreat others physically and verbally
City	Some people that carry arms Adolescents carrying arms Gangs Going out at night	Child abuse Gangs that abuse people Assaults

Figure 3.1 Types of violence and danger in Villa Real, Esquipulas, Guatemala (identified by three young men aged 14–17).

Sphere of influence	Violence	Insecurity
Individual	Physical and verbal aggression	Fear
Household	Fights between husbands and wives Fights between grown-ups	Bad neighbors Drug addicts Leaving children alone in the house Deficient housing construction
Interpersonal	Disharmony Armed fights among friends	Hypocrisy Lack of confidence or knowledge to talk to friends
Neighbor	Armed robbery Killing wife and burying her in the yard Lack of conscience	Lack of telephone to call Bringing strangers to the *barrio* Dangerous friends Lack of unity
Community	Guerilla confrontations with civilian victims Army accusations of civilians being guerilla members	Naming people from outside the *barrio* as representatives Unknown neighbors Politicians
City	Youth gangs Satanic sects	Policies of Pastrana Government coup

Figure 3.2 Listing of violence and insecurity in El Arca, Cali, Colombia (identified by three women and three men aged 24–40).

In Colombian communities, the majority of focus group listings again referred to types of violence. However, in some cases a more locally acceptable term was 'insecurity' (*inseguridad*). This catch-all term included phenomena such as robbery, fights, drug abuse and general delinquency. As in Guatemala, some focus groups deconstructed the term, listing its constituent parts, while others used it collectively. Figure 3.2 illustrates how a mixed group of adults in Cali distinguished between insecurity and violence.

Violence was also seen as multidimensional. Figure 3.3 for instance, reveals the types of perceived violence faced by people in La Merced, Guatemala City, according to a young woman. As with other listings, it is

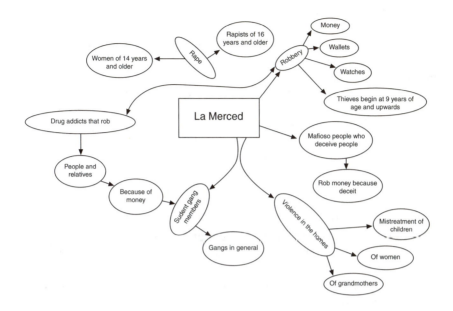

Figure 3.3 Causal flow diagram of types of violence in La Merced, Guatemala City (prepared by a 16-year-old young woman).

the multiplicity of types of violence that was striking, and also in this case how different types of violence were interrelated.

Daily violence and identities: perceptions of violence by different population groups

Not everyone in poor communities experienced violence in the same way, with perceptions varying according to gender and age. Once again, the two countries highlight both similarities and differences. As noted in Chapter 2, in both Colombia and Guatemala, adult women were more likely to discuss sexual violence than men, who in turn were more preoccupied with political conflict and drug-related violence and delinquency associated with young people (see below). More specifically, in Colombia, elderly women and men were most concerned about insecurity and drugs. Elderly men discussed how young women were involved in violence and drug use, something that represented a new phenomenon for them (and whom they referred to as '*muchachas vagas*' or 'wild girls'). In Guatemala, the elderly and adults of both sexes were more reluctant to talk about violence in general. When discussed, elderly and middle-aged women tended to focus on intra-family and sexual violence, often in relation to alcohol abuse.

Men, on the other hand, concentrated their discussions on robbery, delinquency and *maras*.

Young people in both countries were especially concerned with drug-
related problems. However, while young men also mentioned gang and
militia violence in Colombia, young women were more concerned with
sexual violence, especially rape outside the home. In Guatemala, the
maras were most frequently discussed among children. Here, perceptions
were elicited from drawings. In response to the question 'What are you
afraid of?' almost half of the drawings dealt with violence, with two-thirds
of them associating fear with guns. In 80 percent of these, men were
depicted as perpetrators of violence. Of a total of 244 children's drawings
from the Colombian communities, almost half (115) dealt with themes of
violence. As in Guatemala, this was usually in response to the question
'What are you afraid of?' (see Figure 3.4). The most striking issue to
emerge was the association between fear and guns (drawn in two-thirds of
the drawings). Men were depicted as the main perpetrators of violence (in
80 percent of cases), with most violence in the streets (in 82 percent of
cases). In both countries, children often found it more difficult to draw
intra-family violence. These invariably showed victims with tears, usually
adult women or children (see Chapter 5). Drawings of drugs usually
depicted men inhaling cocaine or *bazuco* (crack), or smoking marijuana
on street corners in the evenings (see Chapter 6). Finally, specifically in
Guatemala, indigenous groups were more likely to identify political violence in relation to human rights and police abuses than *ladino* people.
However, both indigenous and *ladinos* equally identified social and economic violence as important problems.

In both countries, focus groups also ranked, or prioritized, the most
serious types of violence. In Guatemala, *mara* or gang issues were prioritized as important in five of the nine communities. These included Nuevo
Horizonte and La Merced, Guatemala City; San Jorge, Chinautla;
Limoncito, San Marcos; and El Carmen, Santa Lucía Cotzumalguapa. In
the other communities, robbery, assaults, and delinquency were considered particularly important. Intra-family violence in particular and
sexual violence in general also emerged as especially significant. In Colombia, in the seven communities where the PUAs prioritized violence, drug-
related violence was the main priority in three: Embudo and 14 de
Febrero in Bogotá, and Rosario, Girón. In Jericó, Bogotá, intra-family
violence was considered the most significant, while in Pórtico, Medellín,
murder was viewed as the most serious. In El Arca, Cali, mistreatment of
children, and robbery were jointly prioritized as particularly severe.

Within community-level rankings, there were interesting variations that
reflected perspectives of different groups, highlighting important limitations in quantitative data. This is well illustrated by two very different
examples. In Jericó, Bogotá, for instance, a group of four 11-year-old girls

Figure 3.4 Drawing of 'what are you afraid of?' in El Arca, Cali, Colombia (drawn by a 13-year-old girl).

Note
Peleas, fights; *Violaciones*, rapes; *borrachos*, drunks; *maltrato*, mistreatment; *pandillas*, gangs.

listed and prioritized the main types of violence affecting their community. Allocating a score of 4 for the most important type, 3 for the next most serious, and 2 for the third, they unanimously identified drug-related violence as the most serious problem (with marijuana, *bazuco*, cocaine, and 'Boxer,' a type of glue, the most common drugs). Three of the four girls had experienced pressure to take drugs from their friends, with one girl noting that a female friend said sniffing Boxer 'was like being on the moon.' Trying drugs was a sign of bravery, and refusal meant being called '*pollo*' (chicken) or '*bobo*' (fool). The girls also felt the pressure of rape, ranking it in second place, and commenting that it was men they already knew (friends, boyfriends, and male relatives) who threatened them most. Robbery, fights among gangs and verbal aggression were ranked of least importance. In a similar exercise undertaken by a mixed group of four teachers in a local primary school in Concepción, Guatemala City, both child abuse and child abandonment were ranked as the most important problem followed by child sexual abuse and family disintegration. This reflected the particular preoccupations of primary school teachers and as such differed from the more prevalent community preoccupations with *maras* and drugs.

The importance of violence relative to other community problems

It would be facile to think that violence was the only problem local populations faced. Indeed, as noted in Chapter 2, the PUA did not assume *a priori* that violence would necessarily be an important issue in people's daily lives, although it emerged as paramount, with problem listings in both countries revealing two similar trends. Problems relating to violence, crime and physical security were not only their greatest concern, but also had tremendous impact on other livelihood-related problems (see Table 3.1).

Consequently, while quantification of problem listings revealed slightly higher figures for Guatemala (47 percent) than Colombia (42 percent), in both cases violence represented almost half of all problems. At the same time, there were variations within the category of violence-related problems. In Colombia, drug-related problems – linked mainly with consumption rather than sale or trafficking – coupled with insecurity, constituted just under half of all violence-related problems (see Appendix 4; also Chapter 6). In Guatemala, by contrast, theft and robbery (both property and mugging), as well as gang-related violence were the two most important preoccupations (see Appendix 5; also Chapter 7). A ubiquitous problem in both countries was intra-family violence that was often perceived to underpin other types of violence and related problems (see Chapter 5).

Violence-related problems were identified as the most serious in seven of the nine communities in Colombia, and in all the Guatemalan communities (see Appendices 4 and 5). But local variations were revealing. Interestingly, in Colombia these problems were not perceived as the

Table 3.1 Frequency listings of types of problems identified in nine communities in both Colombia and Guatemala (%)

Type of problem	Percentage of total problems cited	
	Colombia	*Guatemala*
Violence-related	42	47
Lack of physical capital assets	23	21
Lack of social capital assets	14	10
Lack of human capital assets	12	9
Lack of natural capital assets	3	8
Lack of financial capital assets	5	4
Total ≈	100	100

Source: 159 listings in Colombia, 199 listings in Guatemala. Adapted from Moser and McIlwaine (2000, 2001a).

most serious issue in Pórtico, Medellín. This can be attributed to a local peace process between warring territorially-based gangs and illustrates the time-bound nature of people's perceptions of problems. Between 1994–6, an extensive Peace and Conciliation Process had been initiated in the Metropolitan Area of Aburrá in which the community was located. This resulted in a perception of relative calm compared to previously high levels of violent conflict. By contrast, in Colombia Chiquita, Aguazul, the lack of violence-related problems was more a reflection of the 'law of silence.' With fourteen assassinations in the *barrio* between 1998 and 1999, community members were extremely reluctant to discuss violence due to fear of reprisals from both the guerrillas and paramilitaries. Similarly, in Guatemala, violence-related problems were identified more frequently in some communities than others. In Sacuma, Huehuetenango, with the highest proportion (60 percent of all problems), community members blamed these on the city's proximity to the Mexican border and its attraction for other Central Americans. In contrast, in San Jorge, Chinautla, violence represented only one-third of the problems identified. Such problems were perceived to have gradually spread geographically from Guatemala City itself to this mainly indigenous small town.

When community members ranked problem listings, again, it was violence that predominated. Drawings, such as the so-called 'onion diagram,' provided a visual tool for focus groups to decide the relative importance of different types of violence as well as in terms of other problems. Figure 3.5, drawn by four children aged 10–13 in Sacuma, Huehuetenango, Guatemala graphically illustrates this. Violence related problems were positioned at the onion's epicenter, with the two non-violence specific problems on the periphery.

Listings of other problems across communities in both countries (summarized in Table 3.1) revealed a comparable picture. These only require a brief mention here, with their violence-related implications spelt out in subsequent chapters. Regardless of differences in the economic or infrastructure investment context, inadequate public services and lack of employment opportunities, loosely categorized as a lack of physical capital assets comprised between a quarter (23 percent) and a fifth (21 percent) of problems in Colombia and Guatemala respectively. Within this category, however, public services deficiencies were more frequently mentioned in Guatemala than Colombia. This referred to sanitation facilities, especially the lack of adequate drainage systems that plagued many of the communities in Guatemala City, as well as Villa Real in Esquipulas, and lack of, or irregularity of drinking water supply, which was a major problem in four Guatemalan communities (see Appendix 5). In contrast, unemployment problems were mentioned more frequently in Colombia, totaling 9 percent of all problems cited (see Appendix 4). Aggravated by the recent decline in national economic performance, lack of employment

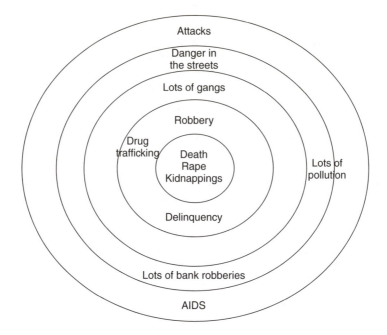

Figure 3.5 Onion diagram of problems in Sacuma, Huehuetenango, Guatemala
(drawn by four young people aged 10–13).

opportunities was severely undermining the productive capacity of many communities (see Chapter 4).

Communities also identified lack of trust, unity, community networks and low level of social organization, loosely categorized as social capital assets and closely linked to livelihood security. This was perceived as a significant problem in both countries, constituting 14 percent in the Colombian communities and 10 percent in Guatemala (Table 3.1). Community members themselves widely used such terms as 'social fabric' (*tejido social*), 'social unity' (*unidad social*), and 'union' (*unión*) to describe such social relationships. For instance, an adult woman from 14 de Febrero, Bogotá, noted that her community had a 'heavy atmosphere' (*ambiente pesado*) characterized by an unwillingness to help others. Another woman, from Jericó, also in Bogotá, commented that 'the community is becoming more isolated, and now there is not much communication within the community.'

Elderly women in particular, recalled with nostalgia earlier days when everyone knew one another and worked together for the good of the community. In Guatemala, elderly indigenous women focused on the loss of traditions and the lack of respect among youth in contemporary society, especially among the indigenous community. In Colombia, elderly men often blamed young people of the community for violence problems, describing young men as 'full of vices' (*viciosos*) and young women as 'street girls' (*niñas callajeras*). In Guatemala, the elderly tended to blame most community ills on the gangs, as well as on 'foreigners' (most commonly in the border towns of Huehuetenango and Esquipulas where the Hondurans and El Salvadorans were often scapegoated). In Colombia, the 'Community Mothers' (*Madres Comunitarias* – community childcare providers)[10] often listed problems such as mistreatment of children, lack of adequate recreation for youth, and lack of community unity.

Lack of education was the most frequent human capital concern (see Appendices 4 and 5). In Colombia, this was often associated with insufficient primary school places. The economic crisis meant fewer people could afford to send their children to private school, while lack of money meant that even state school matriculation fees had become a problem for the poorest. Young men, for instance, bemoaned the lack of educational opportunities and recreational facilities, and linked this to police harassment and drugs. They complained of not being taken seriously, as one young man from Bucaramanga pointed out: 'no-one takes us into account.' In Guatemala, education problems related to the lack of services provided within primary schools, the poor quality of teaching provided, and the scarcity of secondary-level educational establishments. Here, boys also identified school-related violence, especially physical abuse on the part of teachers. In one school in San Marcos, Guatemala, for example, one boy complained that the teachers hit them when they were disobedient and forgot their books.

Lack of, or inadequate, health care services was also widespread in the majority of communities which was further compounded by increasing costs for private health care. This particularly affected older people. In Guatemala, in particular, environmental problems, associated with natural capital assets, were also a problem. While this accounted for 8 percent of all problems, it rose to 21 percent in Esquipulas and 18 percent in Chinautla. Both communities were located adjacent to a flood-prone river, endangering both the lives and livelihoods of community members. The same concern was voiced in two Colombian communities in Girón and Aguazul, which were also severely affected by flooding.

Finally, although all the communities included in the study were broadly defined as 'low-income,' the issue of financial capital and particularly income poverty was not always explicitly articulated. Overall, poverty was perceived as a minority problem (5 percent of the total in Colombia and 4 percent in Guatemala). What was more common was for people to prefix discussions with, 'we're very poor,' yet to discuss other factors that affected their lives more severely. In Guatemala, indigenous groups in all the communities were most likely to identify poverty as a serious problem, as well as discrimination and dismay at the loss of their traditions. In turn, these groups were the only ones to identify human rights abuses as serious concerns in their communities. In a minority of cases, socio-economic status emerged as a source of differentiation. Within essentially low-income communities were pockets of higher socio-economic groups, especially in the well-consolidated urban settlements, such as Yopal in Colombia. These people were more likely to emphasize such issues as corruption, payment of bribes, and the national macro-economic situation. In Colombia, such groups were preoccupied with the impact of political conflict on their businesses. In a discussion with professional people in Yopal, for example, the issue of corruption and having to pay bribes to the guerrillas and paramilitaries was prioritized (see McIlwaine and Moser 2003, for further discussion of poverty and livelihoods).

The spatial dimensions of urban violence

The fear and insecurity associated with violence were undoubtedly most visible when drawn in terms of their spatial manifestations. Community maps helped different groups in both countries to highlight the manner in which various types of violence were spatially concentrated. This also allowed for temporal distinctions to be made between day and night, and here gender and age-based differences were particularly important.

In Colombia, it was possible to identify spatial variations in the incidence of violence at national, urban and community levels. At the national level, spatial variations were captured by the range of the research communities in different areas of the country. Table 3.2 highlights the main types of violence by category and by particular sub-categories. While drug-related violence, insecurity and robbery were important in all the urban areas, intra-family violence was especially important in Bogotá. In the large metropolitan areas with a history of drug cartels, gang violence was especially marked. The effects of political violence in the countryside were experienced in the intermediate towns and cities through the arrival of displaced populations, especially in Bucaramanga and Girón, where the issue of *vagancia* (street loitering) among youth was also perceived to be important. Finally, in frontier towns rich in natural resources, various types of political violence including war, paramilitary violence and assassinations were the most marked.

In addition, within Colombian urban areas, violence was perceived to be spatially concentrated in peri-urban communities located on the outskirts of the city. Here people often felt ostracized from the city itself due to 'area stigma' associated with perceptions of high concentrations of violence. In Bucaramanga, for instance, the city center is located on a plateau (*meseta*), while the community of Amanecer is situated in a large low-income lowland area around the city. A 19-year-old woman, who had lived in the *meseta,* noted that Amanecer was primarily associated with insecurity and

Table 3.2 National variations in predominant types of violence in Colombia

Urban category	Predominant types of violence
Large metropolitan capital city	
Embudo, Bogotá	Drug-related violence
14 de Febrero, Bogotá	Insecurity and robbery
Jericó, Bogotá	Intra-family violence
Large metropolitan area with drug cartel history	Drug-related violence
El Arca, Cali	Insecurity and robbery
Pórtico, Medellín	Gang violence
Intermediate cities and small towns with high levels of displaced populations	Drug-related violence
Amanecer, Bucaramanga	Insecurity and robbery
Rosario, Girón	Street loitering (*vagancia*)
Frontier towns in natural resource rich areas	
Cachicamo, Yopal	Insecurity and robbery
Colombia Chiquita, Aguazul	War
	Paramilitary violence
	Assassinations

Source: Adapted from Moser and McIlwaine (2000).

'people who make you afraid,' and as a result, residents were discriminated against.

At the community level, community maps highlighted concentrations of violence, with many dangerous locations linked with drugs and gangs. Most commonly mentioned were street corners, basketball courts, parks and river banks, all places where drug addicts, sellers or gangs congregated. Girls and women particularly feared river banks due to the additional danger of rape in these secluded locations (see Chapter 6). Figure 3.6, a community map of El Arca, Cali, identified the high proportion of the *barrio* which was perceived as insecure. While some areas were dangerous only at night, many were also dangerous during the day. Basketball courts were dangerous for men and women, although places where drugs were sold and gangs met were reported to be more insecure for women. Ironically, the police station was perceived as a place feared by all people both by day and by night, reflecting negative attitudes toward the police.

Within urban areas in Guatemala, dangerous areas were commonly identified as the *zonas rojas* (red zones), and linked with gangs, drugs and prostitution, which included the markets, bus terminals and sometimes entire communities. In Villa Real, Esquipulas, for example, a group of community leaders noted how the mayor, the municipality, and the rest of the population of the town had until recently labeled their *colonia* as *rojo* (red) and *peligroso* (dangerous). Many places identified as dangerous were linked with

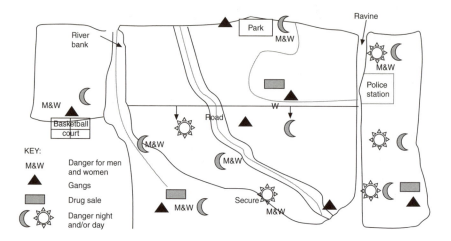

Figure 3.6 Map of dangerous places in El Arca, Cali, Colombia (drawn by two young men and two young women).

gangs and, in Guatemala City in particular, with drug consumption. Most commonly mentioned were places where gangs congregated, such as football pitches, basketball courts, parks and river banks. Figure 3.7, a community map of La Merced, Guatemala City, shows how different gangs were linked with particular spaces and territories, which in turn, were co-opted and became associated with violence and danger. Since many of the areas identified as dangerous were those intended to be safe recreational areas, such as football pitches, such maps have implications for policymakers in challenging the assumedly positive impact of such facilities.

In addition to drug consumption, there was also a strong association between danger and drunks (the latter sometimes referred to as *bolos*). This was a common pattern in many communities where the *cantinas* (bars) and brothels were usually identified as dangerous. However, women rather than men tended to fear drunks and the *cantinas*, with the latter out of bounds for women of all ages.

Policy perspectives on the multiplicity of violence

(Re)categorizing violence

Bridging the divide between theory and practice, as discussed in Chapter 2, requires some measure of 'negotiated compromise' between the multiple complexity of daily violence in the lives of poor urban communities, and policy requirements for some level of systematization and categoriza-

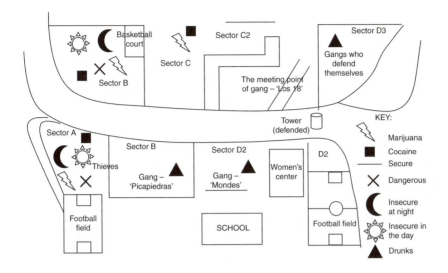

Figure 3.7 Map of dangerous areas in La Merced, Guatemala City (drawn by a group of young male gang members aged 12–22).

tion. To develop conceptual congruency requires a holistic, integrated framework that seeks to (re)position violence in terms of the manifold interrelationships between different categories, causal factors, consequences and impacts. This is elaborated through the course of the different chapters of the book. It draws on a number of texts that include Latin American academic research on violence by anthropologists, sociologists and political scientists, mentioned in Chapter 1, as well as the policy-focused debates of criminologists and epidemiologists. Above all, it is informed by the empirical evidence from the PUA as articulated by the men and women, girls and boys whose daily lives are determined by the banality of everyday violence, insecurity and fear.

Following the description of multiple forms of violence, this chapter introduces the systematization of categories of violence. While this needs to be bounded in order to be manageable (Dower 1999), it is important not to oversimplify, if accusations that these are no more than the impositions of alien Western and inappropriate ideas are to be avoided (Long 2000). Thus, the diversity of types of violence identified by local people in the two countries needs to be systematized in terms of an overarching, or 'umbrella' typology. This is based on the primary motivation behind the exercise of the violence identified, within which it is also possible to place a variety of other types of violence as they are also experienced, whether by nature, victim or perpetrator. The typology identifies political, economic and social violence as the primary motives of violence. As described in Table 3.3, each type of violence is identified in terms of the physical act that consciously or unconsciously is used to gain or maintain power.

Table 3.3 also summarizes some of the common types of violence for each category, in terms that are deliberately broad. Thus, social violence (mainly interpersonal) is motivated by the will to get or keep social power and control. Much social violence is gender-based, both inside and outside the home, including domestic violence and child abuse, often linked with constructions of masculinities (Greig 2000). It can also refer to ethnic violence, arguments among peers or territorial or identity-based violence associated with gangs. Economic violence, motivated by material gain, refers to street crime such as mugging, robbery, drug-related violence and kidnapping. Finally, political violence, such as guerrilla or paramilitary conflict or political assassination, is inspired by the will to win or hold political power. While often associated with wars, political violence is also committed during peacetime.

Since any categorization by its very nature is static, this threefold typology is conceptualized as a continuum with important reinforcing linkages between different types of violence. Social, economic and political violence are overlapping and interrelated. Individuals, households and communities experience different types of violence simultaneously. Equally, from the perspective of the social actors themselves, these are not mutually exclusive categories in terms of violent acts committed. The same act can be committed for different reasons based on diverse, multiple identities.

Table 3.3 Categories of violence

Category	Definition	Manifestation
Political	The commission of violent acts motivated by a desire, conscious or unconscious, to obtain or maintain political power.	Guerrilla conflict; paramilitary conflict; political assassinations; armed conflict between political parties; rape and sexual abuse as a political act.
Economic	The commission of violent acts motivated by a desire, conscious or unconscious, for economic gain or to obtain or maintain economic power.	Street crime; carjacking; robbery/theft; drug trafficking; kidnapping; assaults including killing and rape made during economic crimes.
Social	The commission of violent acts motivated by a desire, conscious or unconscious, for social gain or to obtain or maintain social power.	Interpersonal violence such as spouse and child abuse; sexual assault of women and children; arguments that get out of control.

Source: Moser (1999).

A categorization that distinguishes political, economic and social violence serves a number of purposes. First, in recognizing the interconnections among different violence types such a continuum assists policymakers to move from individual reduction interventions toward more integrated strategies. Second, it highlights the policy implications of multiple identities, and associated motivations, of perpetrators. For instance, ending political violence in countries dominated by guerrilla campaigns may require both a negotiated peace that addresses guerrilla political motives, as well as job creation for demobilized combatants. Only in this way can the economic motives behind much guerrilla group membership also be tackled. Since the reinsertion of male and female ex-combatants into society may be shaped by perceptions of their gender roles and identities, this may require different resources to assist them in this process.

Gender-based 'domestic' violence provides another example of the importance of identifying different identities. Economic independence through job creation may aid some battered women to leave their husbands (see, for example, Sen 1999). However, while this intervention removes women from their dependence on spouses, it does not address the root causes of violence, which are based on gender power relations (O'Toole and Schiffman 1997). Finally, such a categorization facilitates explanations as to why interventions to reduce one type of violence may not result in similar reductions in other types. Indeed, reductions in one sphere can be accompanied by increases in another. On a broad scale, for example, many post-conflict settings – including Guatemala – have experienced an upsurge in social and economic violence in conjunction with a reduction in political violence (Kincaid 2000; Pearce 1998).

Categorizing violence in Colombia and Guatemala

As shown in Table 3.4, listings of violence from both countries were quantified and grouped together using the threefold categorization of political, economic and social violence (see Appendices 6 and 7 for a detailed country-specific breakdown). Within the category of social violence, a further distinction was made between violence within the home, violence outside the home and violence in either sphere, to categorize rape when it was not clearly specified where it occurred. The types of violence represent a continuum where none of the categories are mutually exclusive, but instead intersect. For example, drugs are categorized as economic violence, because in the eyes of the community, drug consumers were mainly perceived as a problem linked with robbery to feed their habit. However, from the point of view of the consumers themselves, taking drugs was primarily linked with seeking an identity, conforming to youth culture and peer pressure (of which violent acts were a part), therefore making it more a social violence issue.

Table 3.4 Types of violence identified in communities in Colombia and in Guatemala (%)

Types of violence	Identified in Colombia (%)	Identified in Guatemala (%)
Economic	**54**	**46**
Drugs[a]	15	10
Insecurity	13	1
Robbery	15	12
Gangs[b]	5	11
Other[c]	6	12
Social	**32**	**50**
Inside the home	10	14
Outside the home	18	28
Outside or inside	4	8
Political	**14**	**3**
Police abuses	4	1
War	3	–
Paramilitaries/guerrilla	3	–
Assassinations	2	1
Other	2	1
Total	**100**	**100**

Source: 104 listings in Colombia, 154 listings in Guatemala. Adapted from Moser and McIlwaine (2000, 2001a).

Notes
a Drugs were classified as economic violence due to their close link to theft and mugging.
b Gangs were classified as economic violence due to their close links to theft.
c The four largest categories of economic violence were individually identified, with all remaining categories identified as 'other.'

For policymakers, probably the most significant implication of this violence categorization was that in both countries economic and social types of violence were mentioned far more frequently than political violence. While this might be expected in Guatemala as indicative of a post-conflict context, in the case of Colombia this result was essentially counter-intuitive. Although the low prioritization of political violence – particularly in Colombia – is in part a reflection of the 'culture of silence' that still surrounds such violence, it is nonetheless highly significant that other types of violence were so overwhelmingly dominant. At the same time, there were slight differences in prioritizations between countries. In Colombia, economic violence dominated, representing over half of all types of violence (with drug-related violence the single most important category), social violence accounted for a third, with political violence constituting 14 percent. In contrast, in Guatemala, social violence was slightly more dominant, representing exactly half of all types of violence (50 percent), and economic violence making up just under a half at 46 percent nationally, while political violence constituted only 3 percent.

A threefold violence categorization also assists in differentiating between perceptions of violence based on diverse identities. Most profound of all are gender-based differences in the ranking of different types of violence with important similarities across countries. Men were more preoccupied with political violence, while women, in contrast, were much more concerned with social violence, particularly in Guatemala (see Moser and McIlwaine 2001b).

As noted earlier, there were also intra-country differences, reflecting context-specific local realities. Although drug and armed conflict were of particular importance in Colombia, they did not necessarily determine community priorities. In Embudo, Bogotá, almost 60 percent of violence was identified as social rather than economic, despite the fact that drugs dominated the community. Intra-family violence was highest in Jericó, while in the Santander communities economic violence represented between 70 and 80 percent. In communities with a history of drug cartels, economic violence predominated, although political violence was also important. In both Cali and Medellín, levels of violence have escalated as guerrilla groups, militias and informal protection forces and gangs have fought one another within communities. In Casanare, political violence represented between a third and a half of violence listed. This related to a widespread guerrilla and paramilitary presence associated with the oil boom. While these organizations initially competed for territory and power, with the collapse of the labor demand generated by the oil sector, they turned to economic extortion and corruption – terrorizing the local population.

There was similar diversity in Guatemala, with the frequency of violence again reflecting context-specific complexities. In Limoncito, San Marcos, economic rather than social violence was the most prevalent (59 percent), with one of the higher levels of robbery, assaults, and delinquency of the nine communities. However, levels of robbery and assaults were highest in El Carmen, Santa Lucía Cotzumalguapa, because of the instability of the local plantation economy. In contrast, in San Jorge, Chinautla, social violence represented three-quarters of all types of violence, with the highest incidence of intra-family violence nationally (29 percent). Political violence was identified in seven of the nine Guatemalan communities. It was most frequently cited in Gucumatz, Santa Cruz del Quiché (8 percent) and in Sacuma, Huehuetenango (7 percent) – both areas in the indigenous highland region that was particularly affected by the civil conflict and where the majority of massacres took place during the war (ODHAG 1999).

The interrelationships between different types of violence

While such categorizations of violence provide important guidelines for policymakers seeking to prioritize appropriate interventions, these are essentially static categories that simplify the situation. In the context of daily realities, local people do not necessarily think in single categories, and thus often may be more aware of the complex interrelationships among different type of violence. Consequently, their qualitative perceptions are essential for policymakers in complementing the quantitative measurements of the phenomenon.

This is well illustrated by Figure 3.8 from Bucaramanga, Colombia. This shows how three young men perceived the interrelationships between different types of violence in their daily lives. Intra-family (social) violence was seen as the basis of other types of violence, leading some young men to leave home and join gangs (as alternative support structures), or turn to drugs, which were connected with insecurity, together with the economic violence of crime, robbery and delinquency. The outcome was not only increased fear, but also the erosion of unity, trust and social institutions, that have come to be analyzed by policymakers and academics alike in terms of social capital.

In this way, Figure 3.8 sets the scene for subsequent chapters of this book. It illustrates the tensions inherent in making sense of specific types of violence in a world where ultimately it is their inter-connectedness that creates the fabric of fear and insecurity that pervades local communities. The focus of this chapter has been largely descriptive, outlining in detail the perceptions of multiple types of violence by local communities, as well as their subsequent classification into categories potentially useful for policymakers. The following chapters turn to the causal factors underlying political, economic and social violence examining in turn their roots and consequences in the daily lives of men, women and children in Colombia and Guatemala.

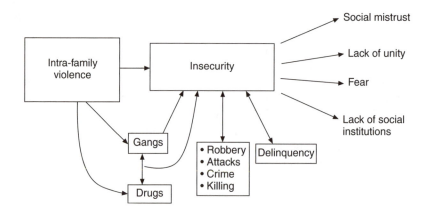

Figure 3.8 Causal flow diagram of intra-family violence and insecurity in Amanecer, Bucaramanga, Colombia (drawn by three young men from a youth center).

4

COMMUNITY PERCEPTIONS OF THE STRUCTURAL FACTORS UNDERLYING POLITICAL AND ECONOMIC VIOLENCE

The highly complex structural factors underlying violence in both Colombia and Guatemala have been widely analyzed, and debated by generations of academics including the so-called Colombian 'violentologists,' together with those working within well-established disciplines of political science, economics, criminology and social science.[1] Given the complicated nature of the phenomenon, no clear consensus exists as to the causes or roots of violence, with different interpretations widely contested.[2] Chapter 1 illustrated this at the regional level with a brief summary of debates concerning the theorizing of violence, as well as a description of some of the most important interpretations of the causes of current violence in Latin America. In addition, Chapter 3 provided a more specific focus, at the national level in Colombia and Guatemala.

This chapter focuses specifically on the contribution that members of poor communities offer to this debate, discussing their interpretations of causal factors underlying the daily violence they experience. While this is the comparative advantage of this study, it also has limitations which are necessary to re-emphasize. Since such information is based on people's perceptions, it is often partial and subjective in comparison with academic interpretations. Yet this is their reality, and despite such tools as triangulation, it is important not to exaggerate or complicate 'mediated representations of realities' (Norton *et al.* 2001: 16; see Chapter 2). To ensure such representation, this chapter foregrounds community perceptions of structural factors underlying political and economic violence in particular, drawing on the wider academic literature only as appropriate to provide further elaboration or understanding of the factors identified.

Understanding the causes of violence

The most salient characteristic of everyday violence in urban communities in Colombia and Guatemala, as highlighted in Chapter 3, is the complex, overlapping layering of different types. Consequently, an understanding of causal factors requires a holistic approach, rather than one that focuses on a specific level, or type of violence. It needs to take into account the fact that no single factor explains why some individuals behave violently toward others or why some communities are more violent than others. Circumstances relating to the individual, the family, the community and the broader national context all combine to play a role in violence perpetration or victimization (Moser 2001a).

Of the different approaches grappling with the interrelated nature of violence, to date, one of the best known is the 'ecological model' originally used by Bronfenbrenner (1977) to explain human development. This has been adapted by violence researchers, particularly those working on public health issues in the U.S.A., to reveal the roots of different types of violent behavior.[3] It identifies violence at structural, institutional, interpersonal and individual levels, explores the relationship between individual and contextual factors, and considers violence as the product of multiple levels of influence on behavior (Moser *et al.* 2000; WHO 2002).

Another interpretation based on the distinction between different levels is Turpin and Kurtz's (1997) differentiation of the causes of violence at interpersonal, collective, national and global levels. In addition, in the case of Central America, Arriagada and Godoy (1999) suggest a multi-causal epidemiological approach that identifies three types of contributory factors. First is social and familial position and situation, in terms of gender, age, education, socialization, and alcohol and drug consumption. Second are social, economic and cultural factors such as unemployment, poverty, overcrowding, social inequality (which threatens social integration and leads to exclusion), violence in the media and the culture of violence. Third are institutional and contextual factors such as war, drug trafficking, corruption and availability of firearms.

The interrelationship between structure, identity and agency

Recent anthropological and sociological discourses have emphasized the need, in terms of both methodology and representation, to give space to different voices in order to combine structure and agency in understanding sociological phenomenon (Arce and Long 2000; Giddens 1991; Simon 1998; see Chapter 2). Rethinking these concepts in relation to perceptions of urban violence in poor communities allows for recognition of the need to locate the specific nature of people's experience of violence within a broader structural context. To embrace this, in this book a holistic framework is adopted that identifies the factors underlying violence, fear and insecurity in terms of the interrelated concepts of structure, identity and agency. Figure 4.1 shows diagrammatically how these associated concepts may be represented, as well as illustrating the outcomes of violence in

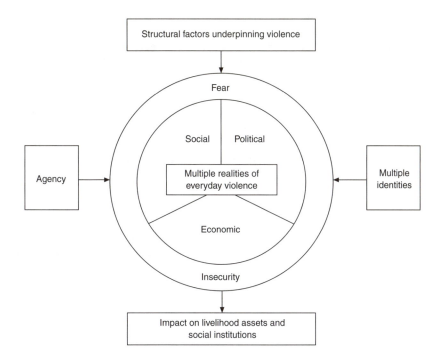

Figure 4.1 Framework for analyzing everyday urban violence.

terms of impacts on livelihood assets and social institutions. A brief description of each concept from the perspective of violence further clarifies their use in this framework.

Recognition of the context-specific nature of people's experience does not preclude an analysis of the structural inequalities of power that underlie these variations. Since issues of power and powerlessness are fundamental to understanding the causal factors that underpin violence, at the outset it is critical to analyze the wider political and socio-economic power structure within which local and individual realities are manifest. As Foucault's definitive study *Discipline and Punish* (1977) illustrates, at its most extreme, violence can be embedded in social and material structures that are taken for granted by Western society as normal, natural, just, humane and even enlightened. Similarly, Gramsci (1971, cited in Robben and Nordstrom 1995: 7), in his notion of hegemony, points to the way in which violence, force and power are embedded in social institutions.

As described in Chapter 1, violence is deeply embedded in the historical evolution of Latin American societies and their institutions (Kruijt and Koonings 1999). Among many structural factors mentioned in the current context, probably the most important are severe inequalities in the distribution of economic, political and social resources in countries across the region, which are also closely linked to poverty. In the past decade, macroeconomic processes of globalization and structural adjustment, as well as political democratization occurring in many countries, have exacerbated both poverty and inequality.

It is also important to recognize that people experience violence in different ways not only because of a diversity of underlying structures of power, control and domination, but also because of differences in their identity positioning. Indeed, violence itself can shape people's perceptions as to who they are, forging as well as affecting their identities (Feldman 1991). Basic elements in individual identity formation and primary signifiers of relationships of power include gender, age, ethnicity and race. Identity formation is not only dynamic, but also geographically and historically context-specific. Castells, for instance, states: 'by identity as it refers to social actors, I understand the process of construction of meaning on the basis of a cultural attribute' (1998: 6).[4] He notes that for any given individual there may be a plurality of identities, which is a source of stress and contradiction in both self-representation and social action. This is significant in the context of violence. For instance, a guerrilla involved in political violence and armed conflict in a struggle against oppression may at the same time be physically abusing his wife (see González-Cueva 2000, on Peru). Finally, identities can be collective or individual. As noted in Chapter 1, new forms of violence and conflict are increasingly based on individual identity, rather than on more traditional ideological issues.

Identity formation is a process. While gender identity, for instance, may be initially constructed around whether a person is born male or female, socialization processes in turn also play a part. Predominant notions of what is deemed as appropriate ways for men and women to behave (referred to as 'hegemonic masculinities' and 'hegemonic femininities', Laurie et al. 1999) are of particular importance in relation to violence, since the construction of masculinities is considered to be closely linked with the exercise of male power over women, and manifest in violence against them (Greig 2000). In this sense, discourses relating to 'women as victims, and men as perpetrators' are usually based on the assumption that the concept of masculinity is immutable rather than diverse and contradictory (Cornwall 2000b; Jackson 1999). Of equal significance are identities of masculinities and femininities in relation to political violence or armed conflict (Jacobs et al. 2000; Large 1997; Moser and Clark 2001).

Since gender is relational, gender identities are also constructed in relation to other axes of social diversity with race, ethnicity, generation and sexuality now all acknowledged as equally important (Cornwall 1998; Marchand and Parpart 1995; Mohanty 1991, 1997; WGSG 1997). So too is the notion that individuals and social groups have 'multiple' identities

(Pearson and Jackson 1998). These most frequently cut across race and ethnicity, especially in the case of Latin America. Not only are ethnic and religious violence often more overtly manifested within cities, but racial minorities usually experience heightened levels of crime and violence (Pinheiro 1996, on Brazil). In turn, ethnicities are not constant, but reflect high levels of diversity. In the case of Latin American countries, they may include indigenous, Afro-Caribbean or Amerindian identities. In certain countries ethnic minority groups commonly are blamed for rising levels of crime and violence (McIlwaine 1997). Generation and age also interact with both gender and ethnic identities, with implications in terms of violence (Chant and McIlwaine 1998). Life course or life cycle experiences vary according to age (Clark and Laurie 2000; Varley and Blasco 2000). Consequently, the elderly and the young are particularly vulnerable to violence in ways that differ from the adult population in general. Violence against children, for instance, focuses not only on child soldiers, street children and child labor, but also their exposure to violence within families and local communities (McIlwaine 2002b; Schlemmer 2000).

Just as violence is experienced in multiple ways depending on people's identities, so too are perceptions of insecurity that vary according to socio-economic status. In urban poor areas, fear is most closely associated with personal attack, while in higher-income areas it is linked mainly to fear of property theft. Although higher-income groups are more at risk from kidnapping and being involved in bank robberies, levels of insecurity are most marked in the poorest communities (see Gaviria and Pagés 1999). In turn, it is women who are most likely to express feelings of insecurity (Kaplinsky 2001; Pain 1991).

Since each participant or witness to violence brings his or her own perspective, identity is closely interrelated with individual 'human agency.' This relates to recognition of individuals as social actors who face alternative ways of formulating their objectives. As such, any stereotypical essentializing of groups or individuals by gender, age, ethnicity or nationality into universal simplified categories denies individual agency. The importance of human agency lies at the heart of a paradigm that recognizes the role of social actors. As Long (1992: 23) clarifies: 'the notion of agency attributes to the individual actor the capacity to process social experience and to devise ways of coping with life, even under the most extreme forms of coercion.' At the same time, social life is not built on a single discourse. As social actors, individuals face alternative ways of formulating their objectives, however restricted their resources.

In relation to violence, a host of stereotypes that deny agency abound in both research and popular belief. Individuals and groups are often disproportionately associated with perpetrating or experiencing violence, such as the poor being more likely to commit crimes which, in turn, often dangerously suggest that all poor people are violent. Such a positioning, in treating the poor as 'objects,' denies each their agency and associated role as 'actors' in the processes. Again, a constant universal interpretation of agency across cultures cannot be assumed. 'Multiple realities' and the importance of place and location in the construction of identities and difference determine how identity and agency are differently constituted (Momsen and Kinnaird 1993; Parpart and Marchand 1995). This in turn, affects how actors attempt to cope with situations they face (Long 1992). Overall, structure, identity and agency combine to influence the causes, consequences and experiences of violence, and therefore provide the basic framework within which local community perceptions of the principal factors undermining violence are identified here.

During the PUA a number of participatory tools identified causal issues. While problem listings, identified in Chapter 3, provided a useful starting point, causal flow diagrams, as well as institutional maps, timelines and drawings, undertaken by focus groups across all the communities, provide much of the information in this chapter. Figure 4.2, a causal impact diagram drawn by a focus group of eight adults in Colombia Chiquita, Aguazul, not only identifies the diversity of factors that they perceive as causing violence but also their proposed solutions (see Chapter 9). Figure 4.2 summarizes some of the most frequently mentioned structural reasons underlying violence cited by community after community, not only in Colombia but also in Guatemala, as well as some which reflect the particular perceptions of this peri-urban community closely linked to rural areas. At the same time, Figure 4.2 illustrates clearly how the reality of daily life is 'messy.' Causal

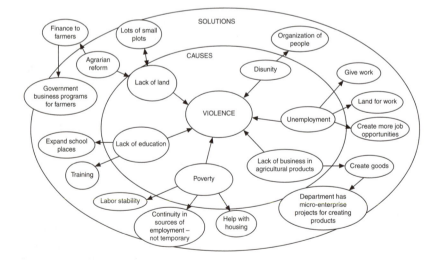

Figure 4.2 Causal flow diagram of violence in Colombia Chiquita, Aguazul, Colombia (drawn by four adult men and four adult women).

factors are never unilinear, but are interrelated in complex overlapping ways; in reality, people do not identify causal factors in isolation.

While acknowledging the interrelations among different types of violence, this chapter starts by examining the roots and effects of political violence as perceived by local communities. It goes on to analyze the role of poverty, unemployment and education in the perpetration of economic violence. Subsequent chapters then focus on social violence in the form of intra-family conflict, as well as substance abuse-related violence and organized violence.

The causes and consequences of political violence

Chapter 3 showed that although at the national level in both Colombia and Guatemala communities perceived political violence as less important than other types of violence, two limitations in this quantitative data need to be recognized. First, these are national level figures. Obviously, political violence was the primary preoccupation only in those communities that experienced it, as against those where it was not such a dominant issue. Second, in both contexts, but particularly in Guatemala, the culture or law of silence meant people were often less willing to discuss this issue (see Chapter 2). For communities located in the midst of conflict, this was undoubtedly the most critical issue. Consequently, this section draws particularly on the research undertaken in communities currently in the midst of paramilitary or guerrilla fighting in Colombia, and those which had been centers of civil conflict in Guatemala. Comparative perceptions from the two countries highlighted the differences between Colombia, that was still in the middle of conflict and therefore directly affected by political violence, and Guatemala, in which fragile Peace Accords had been signed, making the legacy of political conflict a more significant influence than contemporary political violence.

Unequal access to land

Both countries are largely urban in terms of population distribution, particularly in the case of Colombia, where the urban population accounted for 73 percent of the total population in 1999 (UNDP 2001), but also increasingly so for Guatemala with a comparable total of 39 percent in 1999 (ibid.). Nevertheless, the historical roots of political violence in both countries are rural. In turn, they are related to unequal access to both land and natural resources, and also to the political power struggles of successive generations of social actors both inside and outside the state to gain political and associated economic power (Kay 2001). As this section reveals, communities in both countries identified similarities and differences in their perceptions of land as a cause of violence.

In Colombia, unequal access to land was identified as one of the most important factors underlying political violence, as shown in Figure 4.3, a causal impact diagram drawn by a group of adults living in Colombia Chiquita, Aguazul. Their perception was closely related to the community's location in the middle of a highly conflictive area. Aguazul, situated in the Department of Casanare, was not necessarily one of the poorest municipalities. It was the combination of the availability of natural resources (both land and more recently oil) and high levels of inequality that had turned areas such as this into a 'battleground' between different guerrilla and paramilitary groups, all competing for power over land associated not only with cattle ownership but also increasingly with illicit drug cultivation.

At the same time, political violence over land was perceived to be interlinked with social violence, both between neighbors as well as within households. Figure 4.3 clearly identifies this, as well as mentioning a number of impacts or outcomes, some of them also violent in nature. Since in the PUA, women generally were more likely than men to voice their concern about violence in the home, the flow diagram reflected their agency as well as that of the men, on this issue (see Chapter 5). Broadly, Figure 4.3 illustrates two important issues of relevance to the study of violence; first, the interlinked nature of violence and, second, the ways in which violence in itself generated more violence.

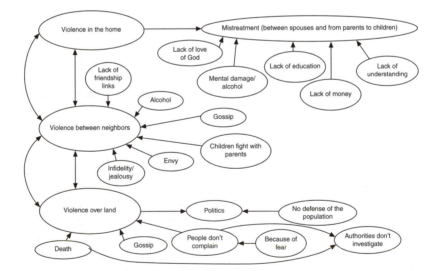

Figure 4.3 Causal flow diagram of the relationship between intra-family violence, violence between neighbors and violence over land in Colombia Chiquita, Aguazul, Colombia (drawn by four men and five women aged 25–60).

This reported connection between access to land and political violence is well documented. Although in the 1960s, the Colombian state did finally try to undertake an effective agrarian reform, ironically this only exacerbated the conflict. Between 1966 and 1970, President Carlos Lleras Restrepo, as part of a reformist trend within the Liberal Party, used the opportunity created by the 1957 National Front (*Frente Nacional*) pact to champion agrarian reform as a means of healing the wounds in the social fabric caused by *La Violencia* (see Chapter 2).[5] In the 1970s, however, cumulative actions by three successive governments curtailed agrarian reform. First, by 1972 the Misael Pastrana government had divided the peasant movement into two wings; second, the Alfonso López Michelsen government in 1974 suspended agrarian reform, replacing it with the Rural Integration Development Program (*Programa de Desarrollo Rural Integrado*, DRI); and finally in 1978, the Julio Cesar Turbay government declared martial law, curtailing the activities of peasant movement leaders under the State Security Act (see Sánchez and Meertens 2001).

Since then, the issue has been exacerbated by the increased cultivation of illicit drugs. Aguazul is located on the edge of one such area in which guerrillas (particularly the FARC) and paramilitary groups are engaged in a deadly conflict for control both of the coca fields and their associated trade routes (see below). These are recognized as essential financial resources for those involved in insurgency as well as in counter-insurgency with both groups taking control of large areas not only in Casanare but also in the Departments of Meta, Guaviare, Caquetá and Putumayo.[6] This had important implications for land ownership, as well as for the associated phenomenon of population displacement. Between 1984 and 1997 small and medium-sized farms in Colombia decreased from two-thirds to one half of the land surface, with the share of large land holdings increasing from one-third to one half of the land surface over the same period (Reyes Posada 1998: 31). Consequently, displaced people and the violence associated with their entry into local communities are another associated outcome of the conflict over land (see below).

In Guatemala, not only unequal access to land but also the lack of land itself has been an historical problem that was exacerbated through the internal armed conflict (see Chapter 2).[7] Historically, the majority of the population excluded from land ownership has been indigenous, a situation that continues to persist despite provision in the 1985 Constitution guaranteeing private property as a human right and recognizing protection of the right to property (Articles 39 and 41).[8] Landlessness played a major role in the guerrilla mobilization during the internal armed conflict, which in turn, had a markedly ethnic dimension with the indigenous population challenging *ladino* control of indigenous land and labor (Kay 2001). Despite the signing of the Peace Accords, problems of landlessness were not adequately addressed. This has had a number of important implications in terms of violence. First, it has continued to plague peasant organizations that are targeted by individual groups opposed to change. Second, the lack of access to land was also a factor that has heightened the population movement from rural to urban areas, which in itself links into the nexus of violence in urban communities through over-population, urban poverty, lack of work and alcohol/substance abuse (see Molina 1999b; also below).

It is interesting, however, that the issue of land was rarely cited by people themselves in Guatemala as a structural cause of violence. Instead, as just noted, it was discussed in relation to poverty and rural–urban migration (see below), and was thus a deep-rooted, yet less direct cause of violence. Since this is an urban study, it is perhaps not surprising that the effects were found to be indirect, and yet no less important given the contemporary ramifications of what was essentially a land-based civil conflict.

The expansion of guerrilla and paramilitary activity in Colombia

> The militias have the same components as the guerrillas. The state views them as guerrillas, the *barrio* views them as militias . . . the militias have more power here than the guerrillas.
> (Community leader from El Arca, Cali, Colombia)

As noted in Chapter 3, a second critically important factor underlying political violence in Colombia was the presence in high conflict areas of a diversity of armed social actors. The civilian population was not only caught in the cross-fire, but far more insidiously was accused by one side of providing support to the other. This was particularly pronounced in natural resource-rich areas such as Colombia Chiquita, Aguazul. Here, the most extreme violence-related organizations, the paramilitaries, or *pájaros* (birds), and guerrilla groups, or *gatos* (cats), dominated the daily lives of the population.[9] In this neighborhood, members described how between 1996 and 1999, two community leaders and twelve other community members were killed, two people had disappeared, and ten families that had been threatened had fled the *barrio*. One community leader noted: 'The people have become accustomed to take away their dead.' By 1999, the main threat was the paramilitaries. Every Friday at 7 p.m. the *carros lujosos* (literally 'luxury cars') arrived and terrorized the population. People suspected of talking to or having links with the guerrillas were threatened and sometimes murdered.

In direct contrast to the peri-urban small town context in resource-rich areas such as Casanare, was the increasing level of political violence associated with large cities such as Bogotá, Medellín and Cali. Guerrilla and paramilitary groups were active in all these cities. Such groups were widely

Figure 4.4 Drawings of guerrillas in El Arca, Cali, Colombia (drawn by a 13-year-old boy).

Note
Text translation: *Ayurdenme* = help me.

known by all members of the community, including children, as Figure 4.4, drawn by a 13-year-old boy illustrates. Another young boy from Cali noted: 'The guerrillas are very bad; the people see them and hide so that they don't kill them.' Organizations committing political violence were often interlinked (see Chapter 7). In El Arca, Cali, for instance, some of the militia groups were closely associated with the ELN.

This expansion of guerrilla and paramilitary activity is widely acknow-ledged (Pecaut 1999). Several commentators also note that their activity has become less politicized over time, as concern for territorial expansion has become paramount. This has also been exacerbated by the drug trade, with drug traffickers funding the FARC, the ELN and paramilitary groups in a range of strategic alliances depending on the geographical area and who holds most power (Pecaut 2001).[10]

The legacy of political conflict and civil war in Guatemala

> Without doubt some political violence is the most serious
> problem that affects Santa Cruz del Quiché, it's a problem
> that is not often verbalized and, what's more, people don't
> want to discuss it.
> (Indigenous woman from Gucumatz, Santa Cruz del Quiché,
> Guatemala)

The Guatemalan context differed significantly from that of Colombia, not
only in terms of the factors underlying violence but also because of the
specific context in which the PUA was undertaken – one in which national
level Peace Accords had been signed. Despite an apparent situation of
peace, the legacy of political violence remained, together with high levels
of inequality. Figure 4.5, a causal impact diagram of the effects of armed
conflict, prepared by an adult man and woman in La Merced, Guatemala
City, for instance, showed how armed conflict was associated with a range
of different types of political violence, and was also linked with delinquency through the migration process (often forced displacement) and

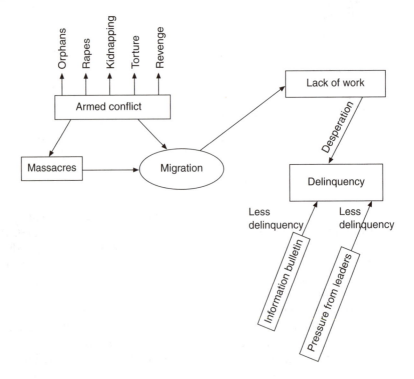

Figure 4.5 Causal flow diagram of the effects of the armed conflict in La Merced,
Guatemala City (prepared by an adult man and woman).

lack of employment opportunities. This in turn linked to forms of economic violence (see below).

As noted in Chapter 3, during the civil war political violence had been concentrated predominantly in the rural highland region rather than in urban localities. This shaped current perceptions and patterns of violence in communities in Santa Cruz del Quiché and Huehuetenango. Political violence also left an indelible imprint on Santa Lucía Cotzumalguapa, as well as some communities in Guatemala City. Although both *ladino* and indigenous populations were affected by the internal armed conflict, the indigenous population suffered most as verified by reports of the complete destruction of 440 indigenous villages during the 1980s (see CEH 1999; ODHAG 1999).

Although political violence was generally not voiced as a major issue in the daily lives of the urban poor, nevertheless, people in seven of the nine communities identified some political violence, especially Gucumatz, Santa Cruz del Quiché, Sacuma, Huehuetenango, and Nuevo Horizonte, Guatemala City. In addition, counter-insurgency institutions active during the conflict and supposedly dissolved were identified as a continuing problem in several communities. For example, the PACs (see Chapter 3), although officially disbanded in 1996, were mentioned in Santa Cruz del Quiché by a group of three *ladino* men who noted how 'the patrols still take people.' The same group of *ladinos* also mentioned that the army still committed human rights violations – although less than in the past. Indeed, human rights violations were mentioned in Guatemala City, Santa Lucía Cotzumalguapa, and Santa Cruz del Quiché. This counter-insurgency violence and its legacy affected both *ladino* and indigenous ethnic groups. In this context, human rights organizations continued to be relevant, and also increasingly broadened their remit. While in the past such organizations mainly represented members of the indigenous population, *ladinos* in one Guatemala City community, for example, were also beginning to use them to resolve intra-family violence.

A particularly sensitive issue in many of the research communities was the alarming preponderance of rape as a form of political violence, which became a fact of life during the civil war. In the post-conflict context this has remained a constant fear, especially for indigenous women. A group of four indigenous women living in El Carmen, Santa Lucía Cotzumalguapa, discussed how in 1980 they had fled Nebaj, Quiché, one of the central arenas of the counter-insurgency, because of the massacres and rapes. One woman described her fear when living in Nebaj: 'We were afraid because the army came into our homes and killed the people; even though they were innocent... many girls and women were raped by the army itself.' Yet the same woman demonstrated resistance to the tactics of the military, stating: 'We wouldn't let the army destroy our people.' Another indigenous woman, who had fled to Guatemala City and lived in La Merced, noted that in general rape was a source of great shame among indigenous people. However, given the scale of rape during the war, parents had to accept daughters who had been raped by the army; often this also included accepting the children born after rape. The same woman noted how raped women rarely married and remained traumatized all their lives. This perception was supported by the REHMI report that documented how rape was used as a tool of war by both the military and the paramilitary groups (ODHAG 1999; see also Moser and Clark 2001).

Ineffective judicial and state security systems

Another critical factor underling the continuation of political violence in both countries was associated with the weakness, or indeed non-existence of important state institutions essential for the maintenance of law and order. Of greatest importance were the judicial and policing systems. For local communities the implications of collapsed or weak state institutions were high levels of impunity, corruption, extortion and the proliferation of arms. All of these had important knock-on effects in terms of economic, as well as political violence. Again, important similarities and differences between the two countries can be noted. The fact that Colombia traditionally had a well-developed judicial system was reflected in community preoccupation with its demise. In contrast, Guatemala had a much less transparent or viable judicial system. Consequently, local communities were less concerned with it *per se*, but prioritized problems with the police system (also an issue in Colombia). In this case they placed more emphasis on violence associated with informal community-level justice solutions such as lynching and social cleansing.

The overall perception in Colombian communities, particularly those in the large cities, was that the power of the government as an effective law enforcement and welfare institution had declined. This was not just the opinion of adults, with even children showing a wide disrespect for such institutions. An 11-year-old boy in Jericó, Bogotá, graphically illustrates this in Figure 4.6 when he identified the government as a 'killer' and 'squeezer,' diminishing since 1950 in its importance and presence to the point of being a mere skeleton. This perception of the historical decline in the legitimacy of the state is all the more interesting given that the boy was not alive at the time, and thus illustrates the intergenerational transfer of institutional perceptions.

Turning to specific state institutions, in Colombia, distrust in the judicial system was widespread. Most people in the *barrios* believed that the police immediately release people after arrest and that even if a case got to court, justice was not served. The case of a new community-based justice initiative, the *Casa de Justicia* (House of Justice) in Bucaramanga, Santander, located near Amanecer, illustrated this. Designed to improve access to conciliation and legal services for low-income people, this was located

Figure 4.6 Depiction of the government, Jericó, Bogotá, Colombia (drawn by a 13-year-old boy).

Note
Text translation: *Lo matto el gobierno* = the government kills; *gobierno exprimidor* = government squeezer.

within the *barrio* itself, yet perceptions as to its effectiveness and useful-ness varied greatly.[11] Figure 4.7, drawn by the institution's director and two of his employees shows their perceptions of the program's function in terms of its institutional links. In contrast, Figure 4.8, drawn by a woman from the same community, revealed a lack of adequate information about the program, associating it with only four roles. In addition, a group of young men in the same community noted: 'No one trusts the House of Justice … It is the same as the police; it plays the same role.' The men maintained that the only justice in the *barrio* was the *ley de defensa* (law of defense), and the use of arms and force.

Indeed, in most communities this concept of justice by force was men-tioned. An inadequate state judicial system, or an absence of faith in such institutions due to high levels of impunity, was a factor underlying the violent resolution of problems. Local community members referred to this as the 'law of the strongest' or the 'law of knives,' and associated it with the use of arms and informal justice systems, particularly social cleansing. In El Arca, Cali, for instance, a previous member of the M-19 guerrilla

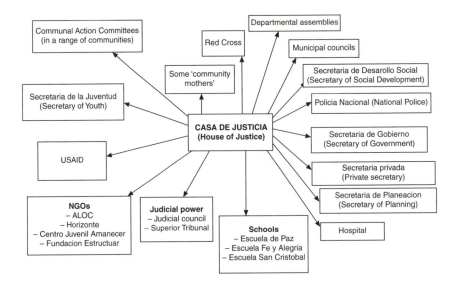

Figure 4.7 Diagram of institutional links of the *Casa de Justicia* (House of Justice) in Amanecer, Bucaramanga, Colombia (prepared by the Director of *Casa de Justicia* and two employees).

group now 'reinserted' into the community described how justice by force had become more violent over time.

Such perceptions are backed up by national level statistical data. As the judicial sector continues to be ineffectual in meting out justice, Colombians have increasingly taken justice into their own hands, with alarming numbers of revenge killings and social cleansing massacres (Klevens 1998). Between 1988 and 1993, social cleansing figures reached 1,926 cases, 77 percent of which took place in urban areas. The highest concentrations of

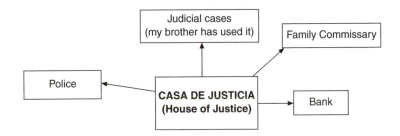

Figure 4.8 Diagram of the function of the *Casa de Justicia* (House of Justice) in Amanecer, Bucaramanga, Colombia (drawn by a mother of two children).

killings were reported in the department of Valle with 585 reported killings (30 percent), followed by Antioquia with 549 killings (28 percent), and Bogotá Central District with 183 (9 percent) (Human Rights Watch/Americas 1994; Rojas 1996).

Likewise in Guatemala, all communities noted the lack of justice and inefficiency of the judicial system, the police and other state actors, including the military. In Gucumatz, Santa Cruz del Quiché, a member of a focus group of three men and one woman complained of the 'slowness of justice – because when a thief is captured he is released immediately.' Even the mayor in Esquipulas identified lack of justice as one of the major problems affecting the town. He reported as the causes the 'lack of application of justice by the judges,' 'lack of police agents,' and 'fear of police agents' (see also below). The outcome had been massacres and fights, especially revenge killings and people taking justice into their own hands. This manifest itself through lynching, which usually involved injuring or killing the accused by dousing them with petrol and setting them alight. All communities identified the presence of lynching, but especially those in Santa Cruz del Quiché, Huehuetenango, Guatemala City and Santa Lucía Cotzumalguapa. In Nuevo Horizonte, Guatemala City, a group of eight young women commented that lynchings in their community were a good way of dealing with robbery and rape. In La Merced, Guatemala City, numerous focus groups recalled the recent lynching of three men who had gang-raped a young girl. Community members had pursued and murdered the men in their frustration with the failure of the police and judicial system to do anything about it. Evidence of perceptions of the inefficiency of the justice system were triangulated by the reports of a group of municipal employees (both men and women) from Santa Cruz del Quiché who identified lynching as a major problem in the town, integrally related to the impotence of the security forces and legal system (see also Ferrigno 1998). They felt pessimistic about the future, stating that lynching would continue until the authorities implemented a fair justice.

National-level data support the significance of lynching in Guatemala. For example, the UN mission in Guatemala (MINUGUA) noted that they were taking place on a weekly basis, mainly in rural areas (MINUGUA 1998).[12] While official concern was growing, lynchings are met with public approval. For example, a public opinion survey undertaken in 1996 showed that 75 percent were in favor of taking justice into their own hands (Ferrigno 1998). The origin of lynching lies in the armed conflict, with evidence suggesting that lynchings are most common in departments where the PACs were strongest and most numerous (de León et al. 1999).

As in Colombia, a more systematic form of informal 'justice' noted in Guatemalan communities was social cleansing. In Villa Real, Esquipulas, for example, this began in 1995 with the arrival of a man called Tito, previously a member of the army, with responsibility in the 1980s for recruiting young men. Tito had received military training courses, including '*kaibil*' that taught extremely violent counter-insurgency strategies. According to those who knew him, such training courses made him insane, turning him into a killer. Together with some companions, he was in charge of killing all the community's 'undesirables' and delinquents. He was ordered to carry out this task by the 'highly corrupt authorities in Esquipulas.' When the bodies began to appear, an atmosphere of terror engulfed the *colonia*. Yet, at the same time, levels of delinquency declined considerably. So, on the one hand, Tito was considered a hero because most people approved of the extra-judicial murders, while on the other, people were afraid of him. Fear increased when he began to kill people who had nothing to do with delinquency, as a paid assassin conducting revenge killings. In addition, he killed former companions who had witnessed his murders. Over time, people hated rather than feared him. On 7 January 1998, some unknown men from outside the *colonia* shot him dead in the back. After his death, many people felt that levels of violence had decreased in the community.

Closely linked to perceptions of the judicial system is trust of the police force, which in both Colombia and Guatemala was lamentably low. The Colombian police force was perceived as a major perpetrator of violence and held in contempt in most communities. As further elaborated in Chapter 8, they were the least trusted institution in local communities. A man in Pórtico, Medellín, thought that the police were untrustworthy and exacerbated bad situations. As a result, he said: 'If I see someone getting killed here and the police arrive and ask questions, I say nothing. Here it's better that way.'

Figure 4.9, drawn by a group of young men in Amanecer, Bucaramanga, described their perception of the relationship between police and local residents, identifying reasons for the antagonism, including harassment – with police constantly asking for papers from people they already knew – and high levels of corruption. The group also noted how children and young people were afraid of the police because they sometimes fired shots to frighten residents. While this reflects the particular experiences of young men – often the group most hostile to law enforcement – their negative perceptions were by no means rare.

People in Embudo, Bogotá, held the most extreme views of the police and perceived them as major perpetrators of drug-related violence, promoting rather than curtailing the sale and consumption of drugs. According to community members, the police ran a well-organized system of extortion from drug dealers, resorting to violence when necessary. Eight-man police patrols worked three shifts a day, with each officer receiving 2,680 pesos (U.S.$1.70) per shift. Drug dealers and consumers usually met the police's demands because of their threat of violence or death through social cleansing (see Chapter 6).

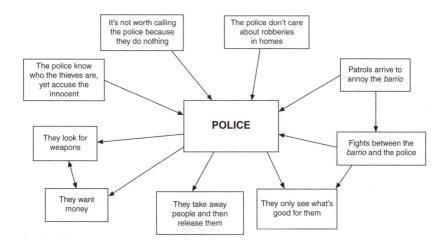

Figure 4.9 Perceptions of the police in Amanecer, Bucaramanga, Colombia (identified by five young men aged 14–23).

Numerous studies have documented the manner in which corruption in one area often leads to corruption in others. Most serious of all has been the manner in which drug-induced corruption has been identified as promoting other types of corruption, which are themselves a common source of violence even when not directly drug-related. Recent analysts have also highlighted the negative effects of guerrilla activity on the workings of the judicial system (Bejarano *et al.* 1997; Rubio 1997b).

In Guatemala, local communities were more preoccupied with the police force than the broader judicial system itself. In this case attitudes varied, depending on whether the community was served by the so-called 'former' force – the National Police (*Policia Nacional*, PN) or by the reformed police force – the National Civil Police (*Policia Nacional Civil*, PNC) – reflecting the importance of police reform changes implemented as part of the 1996 Peace Accords (see Call 2000).[13]

Community members recalled their fairly universal condemnation for the former police, the PN. A 50-year-old woman in Limoncito, San Marcos, commented that they were worse than the delinquents and robbers they were supposed to be catching. They drunkenly traversed the community firing their guns indiscriminately so that people had to hide. She concluded that it was the 'old police force' that destroyed the community. Contempt for the PN had led to violent protest in El Carmen, Santa Lucía Cotzumalguapa. One focus group recalled how the police station was burnt down twice; first, in 1990 because the police did nothing about a North American woman accused of stealing children to take to the

United States; second, in 1991 in protest that the police were not bringing delinquents to justice.

In most communities, the PN had been replaced by the PNC. As a result of police reform involving re-training police officers and appointing new recruits, the new PNC was generally held in higher regard than its predecessor. In communities such as Nuevo Horizonte and La Merced, Guatemala City, and Villa Real, Esquipulas, where the PNC was generally welcomed, many noted that violence had declined when they arrived. For instance, in Villa Real, Esquipulas, people reported that the police made twice-daily 'tours' of the *colonia* and distributed their phone number for emergency needs. An elderly woman noted that they had intervened in domestic disputes, something that the 'old police' would never have done (see Call 2000), while another woman commented that overall: 'we feel more protected now than before.' In a similar vein, in Nuevo Horizonte, Guatemala City, a woman working in a tortilla-making shop spoke of the PNC: 'The police are good now that they're the civil force; they look after the community and when they're called, they come and investigate.' In the same community, numerous people confirmed that they felt much safer now than before. These perceptions were triangulated in a discussion with the Deputy Chief of the Police Station in La Merced, Guatemala City, who observed that the three types of violence he considered as most significant in the community – delinquency, *maras,* and intra-family violence – had all declined since the PNC arrived. He considered that this had been achieved through greater vigilance on their part through patrols, as well as paying more attention to community members' complaints. A reduction in corruption was also noted, with one young man in Concepcíon, Guatemala City, reporting that: 'it was easier to bribe the other police,' although this was not always seen to be the case (see below). In Villa Real, Esquipulas, where community members reported similar patterns, a focus group discussed how violence levels had changed over time (see Figure 4.10). In 1994, the *colonia* was dominated by armed groups, described by some as paramilitaries organized by the military and police force to deal with delinquency, but levels of violence declined markedly after both the death of Tito (see above) and the arrival of the PNC in 1999.

Despite such favorable perceptions of the PNC, many still mistrusted them and reported police corruption everywhere (see also Call 2000). This was most marked in Gucumatz, Santa Cruz del Quiché, especially among Mayan-dominated focus groups. One focus group of young indigenous people maintained: 'The police are really bad because they are not helping the community and they are interested only in causing damage because they don't practise justice.' In El Carmen, Santa Lucía Cotzumalguapa, a Mayan couple noted that the police took bribes of 3,000 *quetzales* (U.S.$429) to release prisoners, and that there was no justice in the town.

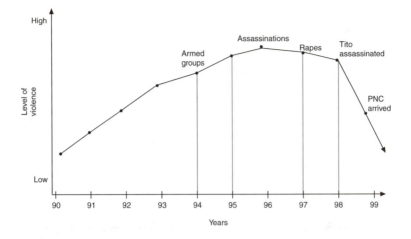

Figure 4.10 Timeline of changes in violence, 1990–9 in Villa Real, Esquipulas, Guatemala (drawn by two young women aged 22 and 23).

As one man in Sacuma, Huehuetenango, commented: 'The police is corrupt and hasn't changed with the new police.' In addition, a *ladino* man in Concepción, Guatemala City, commented that there was no police support in the community because they did nothing to help the population: 'I have never gone to the police because one just becomes another name on the list that is put into the archives,' while a woman in Limoncito, San Marcos, reported that 'now we're abandoned by the police . . . you can call and call, but no-one ever comes.'

Extortion and political violence in Colombia

In contexts of impunity and a lack of justice, extortion was also reported to be a problem in many Colombian communities, and was linked with political violence. One important economic outcome of extortion was the transferral of the costs of war to the local population. In Casanare, for example, guerrillas and paramilitary groups originally arrived with the 'oil boom' in search of territorial control and finance for their activities from the oil companies. With the decline in oil operations, however, they had turned increasingly to the local population as a source of funding. According to the communities of Colombia Chiquita and Cachicamo, in addition to suffering from political violence at the hands of these groups, they also suffered economically through a range of extortion and kidnapping activities. Extortion took a range of forms referred to as *'impuestos'* (taxes), *'vacunas'* (vaccinations) *'boleteos'* and *'subornos'* (extortion).

85

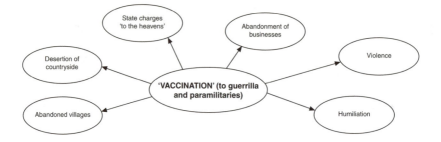

Figure 4.11 Causal flow diagram of extortion in Cachicamo, Yopal, Colombia (prepared by three small-herd ranchers).

The causal flow diagram, Figure 4.11, drawn by three small-herd ranchers, clearly shows how their perceptions related to their identity as a group particularly affected by such extortion. They vividly described the implications of 'vaccinations' not only on their livelihood but also on their sense of well-being. According to them, the paramilitaries were the worst perpetrators of extortion, with the guerrillas targeting large organizations rather than small business people. In addition, they noted that organized crime rings had now joined the guerrillas and paramilitaries in their activities.

Extortion was not only violent and associated with killing, but also had a direct effect on the local economy, with some farmers forced to abandon their land due to the high rate of 'taxes' demanded. Table 4.1, compiled from a diversity of community members showed how 'vaccinations' had to be paid for harvests every six months, annually for certain crops, or in the case of cattle ranching, per head of cattle. Not only was the rural economy collapsing under this pressure, the situation in urban areas was not much better. Both large and small businesses were severely affected. For example, a clothing outfitter in Yopal paid between U.S.$60 and U.S.$125 for every complete set of clothing made, while transport companies had to pay for every trip, whether passenger or cargo. These additional running expenses had led to widespread bankruptcy that affected not only the business owners but also the employees, who lost their jobs.

A lorry driver from Cachicamo, Yopal, exemplified the severe problems associated with extortion and corruption, and complained about having to pay so many 'taxes,' legal and illegal, to so many sources that it had become financially no longer worth his while to continue working. As he put it:

I have a lorry for working and from that I make my living. The man who gives me the cargo takes 10 percent for giving me the

Table 4.1 Cost of extortion activities in Yopal and Aguazul, Colombia

Sector	Unit/measure	Value of payment (pesos)
Rice growers	Hectare/week	15,000 pesos per harvest every 6 months (U.S.$9)
Cattle farmers	Head of cattle	1,500–2,500 pesos (U.S.$1–1.6)
Butchers	3–4 months	100,000 pesos (U.S.$62)
Taxi drivers	Daily	30,000 pesos (U.S.$19)
Salesperson (clothes and shoes)	Complete dressing	100,000–200,000 (U.S.$62–125)
Commercial nursery (plants)	Market produce load (every market trip)	200,000 pesos (U.S.$125)
Transport/haulage	Car/lorry load	50,000 pesos per day (U.S.$31)
Banana farmer	Hectare/year	150,000 pesos (U.S.$94)
Kidnapping for cattle farmers, business people	Per kidnapping	5–10 million pesos (U.S.$3,121–6,242)
Foreigners	Kidnapping/extortion	500–1000 U.S.$

Source: Focus group discussions. Adapted from Moser and McIlwaine (2000).

goods, the company that owns the cargo takes 40 percent, the cargo handlers take 30 percent, the owner of the lorry takes 5 percent, and the driver takes 5 percent. Besides that I have to pay for petrol, oil, tires, or in other words, the maintenance for the lorry. When I'm on the road I have to bribe the authorities when I'm stopped because I don't have all the transportation papers. Sometimes I'm attacked and stopped by the guerrillas to whom I have to give more contributions – more expenses. As a result, I'm working at a loss. I can't pay the taxes for the lorry and I'm charged a fine of 35,000 pesos per month. I therefore don't have enough money to maintain the lorry, and much less to maintain my family.

This final example reiterates the interconnected nature of different types of violence, in this case with political violence intricately linked with economic violence in the form of extortion. The role of extortion in funding paramilitary and guerrilla activity has been widely discussed at the national level, often in conjunction with the notion of 'narco-guerrillas' in the case of the FARC and ELN (see earlier). Indeed, it is now accepted that the guerrillas depend on so-called 'revolutionary taxes' to fund their operations, and in turn, many of these taxes relate to coca production. As well as drugs, as shown in Aguazul, 'taxes' are also imposed on a wide range of legal and illegal transactions, from imported chemical precursor agents, to the refining of cocaine as well as on cattle ranchers, cotton farmers, rice growers and most other commercial agricultural producers (Chernick 1998; Vargas Meza 1998). The paramilitaries were similarly engaged in extortion activities as noted below, although they also receive funding from large landowners and business people (Dudley and Murillo 1998).

The roots of economic violence

The research in Colombia and Guatemala showed that the roots of economic violence, especially robbery, lay in the interrelations between poverty, unemployment and lack of education. Yet between the two countries there were also important structural differences reflecting not only the political context but also the level of economic development. Thus, while in Colombia unemployment rather than poverty *per se* was prioritized by community members, in Guatemala, poverty as much as unemployment was identified as underlying economic violence.[14]

Unemployment, poverty and economic violence in Colombia

> If they don't let us work, we are pushed into robbing. You can't let yourself die from hunger, and less so your children.
> (Unemployed man from Jericó, Bogotá, Colombia)

Among the complexity of causal factors influencing economic violence in Colombia, unemployment and its associated poverty emerged as especially important. These in turn, were interrelated with inequality, especially over natural resources, internal population displacement and area stigma, all of which affected people's livelihood security in both economic and physical terms.

In all the communities, the national economic recession was seen as generating violence and insecurity. From the perspective of community members, *la crísis del país* (the crisis in the country) was a primary cause of unemployment, in turn generating violence and insecurity. An 18-year-old unemployed man from Rosario, Girón, previously a construction laborer, summed up the situation in the following terms: because of the economic crisis, there were no sources of work that meant there was no money. With no money, there was little food, especially in urban areas. In addition, people, and especially young people had nothing to do and so got involved with bad company which in turn, led to drugs or '*vicios*' (vices), insecurity and robbery.

These sentiments, repeated throughout the communities, reflected national-level figures on Colombia's economic recession. Between 1998 and 1999, Colombia had a negative growth rate of 1.9 percent of total GNP, and a decline in growth of 3.6 percent per capita GNP during the same period (World Bank 2000: 274). Moreover, annual growth in GDP has declined from 3.6 percent (1980–90) to 3.3 percent (1990–9) (ibid.: 294). The worst affected sectors included manufacturing, construction and retailing, all concentrated in urban areas. This stagnation was reflected in unemployment with levels growing from just under 11 percent in the first quarter of 1991, to over 20 percent in the first quarter of 1999 (DANE 1999: 95). In the seven largest cities unemployment reached 19.5 percent in March 1999 compared with 14.4 percent in the same month in 1998. Unemployment was highest in Medellín, with 22.6 percent of the economically active population without work (ibid.).

Community-level problem listings described in Chapter 3 supported these findings. At the aggregate level, unemployment represented 9 percent of all problems. However, it constituted 13 percent in Pórtico, Medellín, and 11 percent in 14 de Febrero, Bogotá, Yopal and Aguazul (see Appendix 4). At the same time, focus group perceptions of unemployment rates were considerably higher than these figures suggest. For example, in Colombia Chiquita, a group of three adult women and one man estimated that 90 percent of the *barrio*'s population was unemployed, while in Cali, a group of three adult men estimated 80 percent. However, they suggested that the young had greater access to employment than the middle-aged and elderly. There were also variations according to gender, with men reporting greater unemployment compared with women. In general, women found it easier to generate informal sector work and in many communities were the primary income-earners. As one man from Cali commented: 'Today there are more women working and they are maintaining us.'

Unemployment-related violence was perceived as a last resort survival mechanism. In Figure 4.12, seven adults in Medellín identified such causes underlying unemployment as inequality and the current political situation. For them, violent and/or criminal activities were the only strategies available to some people, including prostitution (mainly among women, but also among men), and small-scale drug dealing – a common way of making money rapidly. Another popular strategy was robbery, especially mugging and theft from lorries delivering soft drinks. In turn, drug consumption was frequently cited as a way of dealing with the frustration and desperation of a lack of work (which was again closely linked with robbery through the need to buy drugs), as well as alcohol abuse and intra-family violence (see Chapters 5 and 6).

Local urban economies experienced economic crisis and its interrelated violence in specific ways. For instance, in 14 de Febrero and Jericó in Bogotá, both located close to large industrial zones, people complained about factory closures and retrenchment of workers. The treasurer for a communal action group in 14 de Febrero predicted that the future held only 'further economic crises,' 'war' and 'violence.' In her words: 'a member of the family who has no work and has to respond to their obligations often has to turn to robbery.' In Cali and Medellín, where unemployment was

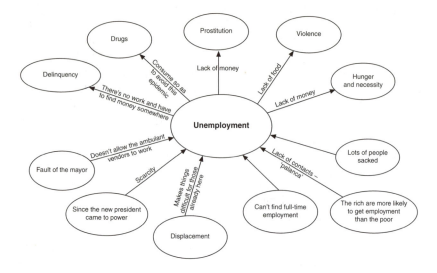

Figure 4.12 Causal flow diagram of unemployment in Pórtico, Medellín, Colombia (drawn by four adult men and three adult women).

associated with the collapse of the construction industry (formerly associated with the drug cartels), effects identified included an increase in insecurity, in armed attack, a greater proliferation of gangs, and a rise in homicides. Also significant in Cali was the link between unemployment and political violence, which was blamed for people, especially young men, joining the guerrillas. An adult woman from El Arca, for instance, said: 'Why do the sons go to the guerrillas? Because in the Valle del Cauca there's no work – they join the guerrillas.' Another woman from the same community similarly pointed out: 'Because there's no work, people join the guerrillas.'[15]

Interrelated with unemployment as a factor underlying violence was poverty. Although less frequently discussed than unemployment, it was still cited as an issue, representing 5 percent of all problems mentioned in the communities (10 percent in one of the Bogotá communities). As one adult man in El Arca, Cali pointed out: 'Poverty is common throughout the *barrio*; it's always present.' Indeed, poverty remains an important issue nationally; although the UNDP estimates that between 1989 and 1998, 11 percent of the population lived on U.S.$1 per day (UNDP 2000: 169), other figures suggest that poverty is much more widespread. Social Watch (2000), for instance, suggests that in 1999, 60.1 percent of all households lived below the poverty line. Regardless of the accuracy of the figures, poverty was identified as an important factor underlying violence in communities, as illustrated in Figure 4.13 from Medellín.

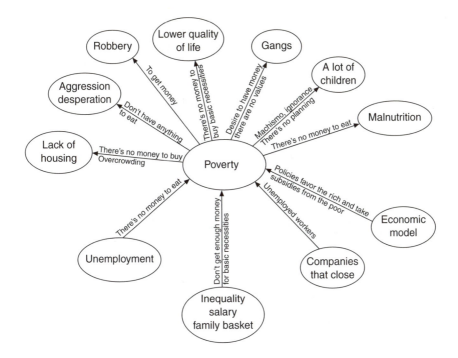

Figure 4.13 Causal flow diagram of poverty in Pórtico, Medellín, Colombia (drawn by a group of seven teachers, six male and one female).

In addition, as also shown in Figure 4.13, inequality was seen as significant and identified in this case in terms of a lack of access to basic necessities, and also in broader terms of economic policies which 'favor the rich and take subsidies from the poor.' Unequal access to the benefits of natural resources in Colombia also emerged as a key violence-related issue, with the most violent areas often those with the greatest wealth of natural resources, especially oil (see above). The potential revenue from oil resources had led to persistent conflict between the various groups seeking to exploit or control the industry (namely the oil companies themselves, together with guerrilla and paramilitary groups involved in extortion), leaving the local population with little besides an unstable labor market and high levels of insecurity and conflict (see Dudley and Murillo 1998).

Internal population displacement

One of the most important impacts of civil war in Colombia has been the dramatic increase in internally displaced people fleeing political violence in rural areas, which has also been aggravated by economically motivated

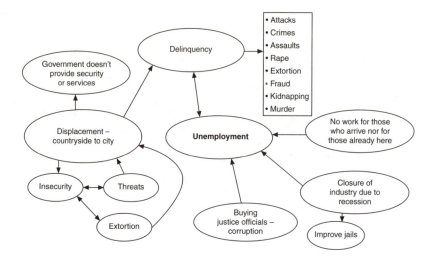

Figure 4.14 Causal flow diagram of unemployment in Cachicamo, Yopal, Colombia (prepared by four men and one woman employed in the *Departamento Administrativo de Seguridad* (Administrative Department for Security, DAS).

migration. Such displacement was seen to exacerbate levels of unemployment and poverty in urban areas, by increasing pressure on already scarce economic resources, thus fueling economic violence. While cities provided refuge (and perhaps opportunities) for the displaced themselves, their presence often generated resentment among the existing population. For example, Figure 4.14 from Cachicamo, Yopal, shows how displacement was perceived as a major factor in unemployment, exacerbating an already difficult economic situation, and leading to further violence.

The reported scale of population displacement was borne out by national-level evidence. This showed that violence-related internal displacement was not a new phenomenon, and that repeated waves of displaced people, fleeing the political violence, had formed the basis of exaggerated urban expansion in cities around the country. It had, however, worsened in recent years. According to one report, over 1.7 million Colombians were displaced between 1985 and 2000, with more than one million of these displaced in the last five years of this period (Social Watch 2000).[16] Women constituted between 51 and 58 percent of displaced persons, and children over 70 percent (DIAL 2001). Furthermore, at least 31 in every 100 displaced households were headed by women, many of whom were widows, or women abandoned during displacement (CODHES 1999; also Meertens 2001).

Area stigma

Another factor linking unemployment and violence was 'area stigma.' Referred to as '*mala fama*' (bad reputation) or '*mala imagen*' (bad image), this related to the manner in which people from all communities felt excluded from the labor market as a result of living in particular *barrios* which were stigmatized as violent and criminal. For instance, a young man from Amanecer, Bucaramanga, who had graduated from high school, said that every time he applied for a job, he was automatically dismissed because he came from the Ciudad Norte (the general area where Amanecer is located). This was because people associated his *barrio* with delinquency, drug consumption and robbery: 'Just because we are from Ciudad Norte no-one will give us work or think that all of us here are thieves.' Similar situations were noted in other communities. In Medellín, people commented about 'discrimination against those from the *comunas*.' This related to recent gang wars and widespread killings after which employers dismissed anyone from these communities, whom they identified as gang members or murderers.

This sense of territorial exclusion was particularly marked in areas affected by political violence. In Colombia Chiquita, Aguazul, many inhabitants complained that they were treated like guerrilla members, as well as thieves, prostitutes and drug addicts. Not only had this made their community a target for paramilitaries, resulting in fourteen assassinations, but it also undermined their ability to secure employment. Figure 4.15 highlights how a focus group identified as a root cause the fact that they had squatted on the land and fought to be recognized by the authorities.

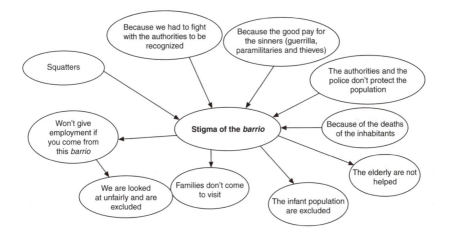

Figure 4.15 Causal flow diagram of area stigma in Colombia Chiquita, Aguazul, Colombia (drawn by one 50-year-old man and three women aged 22–39).

Given the tense political situation, they were soon stigmatized as guerrilla members. Thus, violence (variously social, economic and political) was both a cause of 'area stigma,' as well as a consequence, when the associated lack of work increased levels of economic violence.

Unemployment, poverty, ethnicity and economic violence in Guatemala

> During the conflict, the indigenous people suffered most from the violence, but now we all have similar experiences of suffering.
>
> (*Ladino* man from Gucumatz, Santa Cruz del Quiché, Guatemala)

The underlying causes of economic violence in Guatemala, as in Colombia, were complex and multidimensional, although poor working conditions, poverty and how the manner in which these intersected with ethnicity were the issues most commonly discussed by community members. While these referred to the proximate or immediate causes of economic violence, the post-conflict situation was also viewed as a major longer-term causal factor.

Particularly notable were the clear links identified by community members between a decline in political violence and an associated increase in both economic and social violence. Linked with this shift in the dominant type of violence were changes in its location, with a noted shift from rural- to urban-based violence, including secondary cities and departmental capitals, such as San Marcos and Huehuetenango (see Palma 1998). Thus, while political violence during the civil war predominantly affected the indigenous population, in the post-conflict context, violence increasingly affected all ethnic groups. A group of three indigenous men from Gucumatz, Santa Cruz del Quiché, for instance, said: 'Now the same violence affects all of us in the community, *ladinos* and indigenous.' Comments such as this demonstrated the increasingly equal distribution of violence and insecurity (see de León *et al.* 1999).

Increases in economic violence were attributed particularly to lack of employment and poverty, and the associated increase in gangs known as *maras* (Chapter 7). For example, a group of two men and five women (all *ladinos* except one indigenous woman) in Santa Cruz del Quiché noted that after the Peace Accords, delinquency increased because of the lack of work, and because many refugees had returned to Guatemala from Mexico and Honduras. A group of young indigenous people in the same community noted that since the Peace Accords, some ex-military personnel had joined *maras*.

While unemployment was not as significant as in Colombia, comprising only 2 percent of problems listed, 7 percent mentioned poor and unstable working conditions (see Chapter 3). Thus, many people identified patterns of livelihood insecurity as linked with economic violence, that varied according to fluctuations in labor demand (which produced the need for economic violence) as well as the patterns of pay among those who did have work (who themselves were targets of economic violence). As such, in some areas robbery was closely linked to the annual agricultural cycle. According to a group of four young men in Santa Lucía Cotzumalguapa, scarcity of work when the harvest finished meant that men were so desperate that they robbed. A second mixed group noted that May to November was the period of the highest incidence of robbery because, 'the sugar refineries do not have activities and consequently there is no work for many people.' Figure 4.16 highlights many of these factors, with this man complaining that lack of work, linked with the labor supply instability in the plantations, as well as hunger could lead to war.

The link between employment stability and robbery was further reiterated by several groups who highlighted changes in patterns in robbery levels over both weekly and monthly periods. A group of three women (aged 22–61) from Limoncito, San Marcos, commented that there were more robberies around the 15th and 31st of each month when workers received their pay packets and, according to one, 'were walking around with money.' In a context where many male wage earners worked during the week in Guatemala City (five hours away by bus) returning home only on weekends, robberies were highest on Sunday afternoons and Mondays.

Thus, as in Colombia, the answer to such problems for some was to resort to economic violence. However, older people, in particular, also

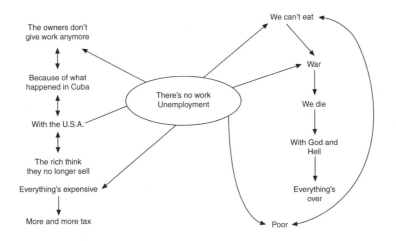

Figure 4.16 Causal flow diagram of problems with employment in El Carmen, Santa Lucía Cotzumalguapa, Guatemala (drawn by one adult man).

cited an unwillingness to work as reason for stealing. A 26-year-old woman shopkeeper in Esquipulas (a single mother whose husband had migrated to the United States) commented: 'There are no sources of work for young people, so they become robbers; however, there are also young people who want an easy life.'

The local importance of unemployment was reflected in national-level data. While the economy in Guatemala is more stable than Colombia, unemployment levels are high. On a national level, only a quarter of the economically active population were employed in the formal sector, within which the Department of Guatemala accounts for over half of all formal sector employment (PNUD 1998: 60–65). Taking high levels of under-employment into account, the national unemployment rate stands at around 40 percent, with the agricultural sector particularly vulnerable to fluctuations in the economy (ibid.: 61–62).

As in Colombia, poverty was also a major issue underlying economic violence in Guatemala. Although it accounted for only 4 percent of the general problem listings, as suggested elsewhere, the lack of specific mention may have related to the fact that everyone was identified as poor in communities and that poverty was effectively taken for granted (McIlwaine and Moser 2003). Nonetheless, several groups did identify poverty as an underlying cause of violence, usually in association with people being desperate for food. An adult man in Nuevo Horizonte, for instance, noted that he knew people who had stolen only to feed themselves and their families, unlike the *maras* who stole for pleasure in his opinion (see Chapter 7).

It was among the indigenous population that the connection between poverty and violence was most commonly made. This was strongly related to racial discrimination, especially in terms of a lack of access to the urban labor market. Linked to this was the strong ethnic dimension of displacement as a result of the civil war. This displacement of largely indigenous rural populations to urban areas (especially the capital region) during the 1980s exerted pressure on local labor markets, and increased overcrowding in low-income marginal areas. In such situations, labor market discrimination against indigenous people was widely reported. Several indigenous groups in Guatemala City, for instance, noted how they stopped using their mother tongue on arrival for fear of discrimination and not being able to get jobs. One woman who spoke Kachikel from La Merced, Guatemala City, discussed how indigenous women in particular were less likely to wear the *traje* (traditional clothing), or would only wear the *corte* (skirt) and not the *huipil* (blouse). Another woman, also from Guatemala City noted that her employer (a private postal company) would not allow her to wear traditional clothing because she was supposed to wear the company uniform. As a result, she had to leave her job.

This local-level economic exclusion of the indigenous population was an extension of broader national poverty trends. While poverty is widespread in Guatemala, with up to 75 percent of the population living in extreme poverty (see McIlwaine 2002a),[17] only 10.5 percent of the indigenous population live above the poverty line, in contrast to 26 percent of the *ladino* population (PNUD 1998).

Education and economic violence

In communities both in Colombia and Guatemala, deficiencies in educational institutions were said to contribute to violence among youth, not least due to the association between a lack of education and low employment opportunities. A group of three young men in Esquipulas, Guatemala, (Figure 4.17) identified a range of issues including the fact that education was associated with employment, well-being (expressed through dressing decently and behaving well) and lack of involvement in drugs and gangs. In contrast, lack of education was linked to unemployment, bad behavior, drugs and gangs and in the case of women, to prostitution and AIDS. A common problem noted in many communities in both countries was that lack of family resources often meant that parents could not afford to send their children to school, further perpetuating economic exclusion. More specifically in the case of Guatemala, low levels of educational attainment among indigenous people exacerbated the problems of finding work.

Nationally, lack of access to education and the quality of education in Guatemala were perceived as major problems affecting young people. As

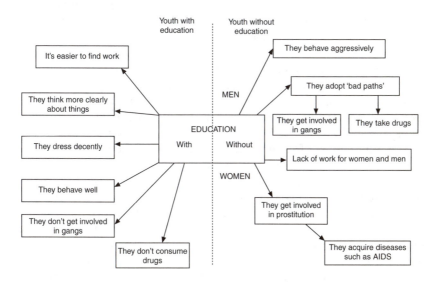

Figure 4.17 Diagram of the influence of education on youth in Villa Real, Esquipulas, Guatemala (prepared by three young men aged 14, 16 and 17).

noted above, several focus groups felt that the lack of education contributed to the greater propensity among some young people to join gangs and engage in robbery as a way of making a better living than that available for those with no qualifications. A group of teachers from Limoncito, San Marcos, for instance, felt that lack of education and especially progression to secondary level, could sometimes lead young people, and especially boys, to 'go off the rails' and get involved in the *maras*. As in other contexts they noted that among young women, lack of education often led to teenage pregnancies rather than involvement in violent activities (see Moser and Holland 1997).

A similar situation prevailed in Colombia where education was valued highly, but access and quality were real problems. For instance, in the majority of communities, people complained about the lack of primary schools places (*cupos*) available as well as the matriculation costs. A displaced woman in Girón, noted that she couldn't afford to send any of her four children (all under 10) to school because of both the lack of places and the costs. She was worried about what would become of them without qualifications, and feared that her two boys might get involved in drugs if they didn't go to school. In Colombia, a group of teachers in Medellín pointed out that violence was a major problem for young people and that an education was one way of trying to stop young people, especially young men from involvement in violence-related activities. However, they were also realistic that even with a high school education, a good job was not guaranteed, especially in the current situation.

Indeed, at the national level in Colombia, it was noted that violent crime was by no means solely the domain of the least educated, in this way demonstrating that improvements in education alone were unlikely to lower violence levels (see Rubio 1997b). While in the rural areas, youth often joined the guerrillas as their sole employment option, in larger urban areas, drug traffickers shrewdly recruited the more successful secondary school students, who realized that area stigma, depressed wages and the precarious investment climate conspired to limit their job opportunities (see also Salazar 1990, 1994). Finally, for others, the school day, with an average three hours of lessons, left a great deal of free time to engage in delinquent, criminal, violent or self-destructive behavior.

This chapter has provided an overview of the main causal factors (and some of the associated consequences) of political and economic violence as identified by the community members in Colombia and Guatemala. Just as it is difficult to discuss different types of violence in isolation from each other, the same is true of the roots of violence. These are inextricably interlinked in nexuses such that the knock-on effect of one factor frequently impacts on another. Consequently, many of the themes introduced in this chapter will be included in greater depth in the subsequent chapters on social violence in the family, substance abuse-related violence, and the nature of organized violence in communities.

5

THE FAMILY AS A VIOLENT INSTITUTION AND THE PRIMARY SITE OF SOCIAL VIOLENCE

> Violence begins in the home, and it is one of the most important factors in the harmony of the community, and this brings about lack of respect in everyone.
> (Young boy from Bogotá, Colombia)

While Chapter 4 outlined the causes of political and economic violence in the communities, the current chapter focuses on intra-family violence as a major manifestation of social violence.[1] Of all the multiple types of violence that poor people in Colombia and Guatemala experienced, intra-family violence[2] was 'routinized' or 'normalized' to such an extent that for many it was not even recognized as a problematic phenomenon. Yet in both countries the PUA showed that the family by its very nature was often perceived as a violent institution, in which acts of violence were perpetrated or experienced by most family members. In exploring intra-family violence, this chapter shows how it was holistically interrelated with other types of violence, both in terms of causal factors underlying it, as well as in relation to its outcomes. Reflecting one of the most frequently made comments by community members in both countries that 'all types of violence begin in the home,' it identifies how other types of violence exacerbated intra-family violence, while intra-family violence in turn also generated other types of violence. The gendered nature of violence in the home also emerged as critically important, linked with constructions of gender identities in the form of masculinities and femininities. Furthermore, the assumedly gendered nature of the perpetrator/victim dichotomy is also challenged by the research findings, highlighting issues of agency. As Greig (2000: 29) has emphasized, it is necessary to 'move beyond the bifurcation of perpetrator and victims into issues of [men's and women's] accountability, complicity and responsibility in relation to the violence of the hierarchies within which they [we] live.' As such, although men were the main perpetrators in both countries, women (albeit a minority) were also involved in the perpetration of violence within the home, usually as mothers.

99

The nature of intra-family violence in local communities

Violence within the home involved the use of coercion and force in the exercise of social power, whether physical, sexual or psychological in nature.[3] This was a daily occurrence in all communities, with focus groups identifying a dramatically large diversity of types. In Colombia, an overall total of twenty different manifestations were identified, while in Guatemala, there were a comparable eighteen types. In terms of average national listings of types of violence identified in the communities, intra-family violence was perceived as slightly more common in Guatemala than in Colombia. In the former, it was the highest single category of violence (14 percent) along with fights outside the home, while in the latter it represented 10 percent of all violence types listed. There were also variations among the communities. In Guatemala, the highest level was identified in San Jorge, Chinautla, (29 percent) and the lowest in Sacuma, Huehuetenango, (6 percent), while in Colombia, it represented only 5 percent in Pórtico, Medellín, compared with 16 percent in Jericó, Bogotá (see Chapter 3).

Types of intra-family violence identified included physical and verbal abuse, as well as sexual and non-sexual violence, and ranged from trauma to incest, sexual abuse, rape and death (see Appendix 8 for detailed listing). In both countries, violence was perpetrated by household members that included men as fathers, step-fathers, husbands and sons-in-law. Importantly, it also involved women as wives, mothers and daughters-in-law, and also boys and girls as sons and daughters as well as brothers and sisters. Finally, extended family members including grandparents as well as non-family members such as renters (men renting rooms in the house) were also involved in carrying out violence within the home. The fact that focus groups identified a range of social actors as perpetrating violence – and that not all men committed violence and not all women were victims – challenged the ways in which hegemonic masculinities and femininities have been constructed in Colombia and Guatemala. This highlighted variations in the experiences of violence within and between gender, ethnic and generational identities. Recognition of individual agency of all community members confronted stereotyped gender identities relating to the 'aggressive male' and 'passive female.' These findings are supported by broader regional level research which challenges assumed homogeneity in terms of the nature of conflict within the home, arguing that the male perpetrator/female victim dichotomy does not always hold, and, indeed, denies agency to women and children in particular (Moser 2001a). Regional level statistics shows that while 75 percent of victims of intra-family violence are women, 2 percent are men and 23 percent of the cases are mutual (Arriagada 1998: 93). It is now recognized that male on male as well as female on female violence occurs in the home (as well as outside the home) (McIlwaine 2002b). This may be among same-sex siblings or other kin members, and critically, is often based on age hierarchies. In terms of child abuse, evidence suggests that both men and women physically or sexually abuse male and female children (Kelly 1991).

The under-reporting of intra-family violence

Overall, however, the levels of intra-family violence identified through listings in both Colombia and Guatemala were low when compared with in-depth discussions in focus groups that reported how widespread intra-family violence was. For instance, in Cachicamo, Yopal, a focus group of five teachers estimated that intra-family violence affected 70 percent of the community, yet in the quantitative listings, only 7 percent of violence was identified as intra-family. Here, as with political violence, the 'law' or 'culture of silence' prevailed with a widespread taboo on discussing intra-family violence despite the extensive nature of the phenomenon (see Chapter 2). In contrast to political violence, strategies of silence with respect to intra-family violence were fairly constant in both countries, although on balance Colombians were slightly more open in discussing the issue.[4] Reticence was linked to the shame and reserve associated with such a sensitive topic, particularly in relation to sexual violence (including incest) on the part of both victims and perpetrators.

Gender, age and ethnic identity also influenced the extent to which people would discuss intra-family violence. Women everywhere were more candid than men, partly because men were more likely to be perpetrators than victims, but also because men were less likely to identify this as a form of violence. In Guatemala, where the culture of silence was even stronger than in Colombia, indigenous women were less likely than *ladinas* to discuss it, and even then often only in relation to alcohol abuse (see also Kulig 1998). Since alcohol was often identified as the cause of domestic male–female violence, this often provided an entry point for discussion. Among men it was boys and adolescents who were more willing to discuss domestic abuse. Overall, young people of both genders were more forthcoming than adults. Although children were influenced by fear and silence in similar ways to adults, focus groups showed how many still retained elements of trust in others that have since been eliminated among the adult population (see Pridmore 1998). Yet, children were not a homogenous category, and girls tended to talk about intra-family violence to a greater extent than boys. This emerged especially through children's drawings where they were asked to draw what they were afraid of. Girls in particular, repeatedly drew violence in the home while boys were more likely to draw violence outside the home (see Figure 5.2 on p. 105). While indigenous children and youth were slightly more reluctant to speak, they had yet to learn the caution of their parents' generation.

The different domains of violence within the family and household

The scale and diversity of violence identified as occurring inside the home in both Colombian and Guatemalan research communities demonstrated the way in which the family itself was perceived as a violent institution and a major source of gender-based violence.[5] Two issues were of particular importance.

First, the fact that intra-family violence was closely interrelated with, and influenced by, the structure and composition of households. It was necessary not to assume that households were universally nuclear in structure.[6] Results from a small quantitative survey conducted in conjunction with the PUA in both Colombia and Guatemala showed a diversity of household structures, and especially the prevalence of non-nuclear forms of households.[7] Male-headed nuclear households represented just under half of all households (41 percent in Colombia, and 45.4 percent in Guatemala). Extended structures were also common, with male-headed extended units making up almost one-third (29 percent in Colombia, and 31.7 percent in Guatemala). Female-headed units comprised around one-fifth in both countries (22 percent in Colombia and 19 percent in Guatemala) the majority of which were extended (22 percent in Guatemala and 14 percent in Colombia) rather than single parent units (7.2 percent in Guatemala and 6 percent in Colombia).[8] The female headship data broadly correspond with United Nations Development Program data that identified 20 percent of Colombian households headed by women and 16.9 percent in Guatemala in 1990 (UNDP 1995: 64).

However, focus group discussions in both countries that complemented this information suggested that these figures underestimated the prevalence of female-headed households. In Colombia, a male community leader estimated the proportion of single mothers as high as 70 percent in Embudo, Bogotá, although a female community leader's estimation in Jericó, Bogotá, was as low as 25 percent. One group in El Arca, Cali, suggested that for every ten young women, four were single mothers. Similarly, in Guatemala a group of three women from La Merced, Guatemala City, estimated that women headed 40 percent of all households in their community while another woman stated that 'there are five single mothers in every block here in the community.' Proportions were even higher in Mayan-dominated communities: in Gucumatz, Santa Cruz del Quiché, the estimation of single motherhood among a group of two indigenous women and one man was 60 percent.

The second issue was the range of actors involved in intra-family violence. Violence between spouses was the most common form of intra-family violence in Colombia and Guatemala. A 25-year-old Colombian woman from Bucaramanga noted: 'Here it is an everyday thing that husbands beat their wives. Some have been wounded with knives and bottles.' Some people feared for their lives because the abuse was so severe, as in the (albeit isolated) case of one man from Medellín, Colombia, who murdered his wife and then buried her in the back yard. Another 35-year-old female market seller from San Marcos, Guatemala, left her drunken husband because of constant beatings. The final straw was when he threatened to kill her with a machete.

Even more common than physical abuse was verbal and psychological violence. There were numerous examples of women being told by husbands that they were worthless. In La Merced, Guatemala City, a single mother who had since left her husband, reported how he came home every night and told her she was 'useless.' Although she eventually left him and regained her self-esteem, she said many other women suffered psychological trauma because they believed and internalized the things their husbands told them. Obviously, this has important ramifications in terms of the constructions of hegemonic masculinities and femininities. Sexual violence was also widespread, although it was discussed less frequently. This was mainly because rape within marriage was widely accepted and condoned, and often seen as part of women's sexual duty to their husbands, regardless of the use of force on the part of men. Nevertheless, a few community members identified rape within marriage as quite widespread and as a source of concern.

Although in many cases men tended to be the perpetrators of violence, some focus groups reported women fighting back at men and beating them either in retaliation, or as their usual way of dealing with their partners. One focus group of adult women in La Merced, Guatemala City, noted that 5 percent of cases of violence among spouses involved women using force against men. In Embudo, Bogotá, with extremely high levels of drug use, a few cases of women physically abusing husbands while under the influence of drugs were noted; according to one community leader, the effects of drugs (usually *bazuco*) gave them the physical strength, and exaggerated psychological bravery to hit their partners in return for their initial blows. Perhaps most common with respect to female perpetrators was verbal abuse on the part of women against men. However, while this was widespread in all communities, it often precipitated further physical violence by men. Indeed, among the men who would discuss intra-family violence, they usually justified it on the grounds of women's 'nagging.'

As mentioned above, although women often admitted being abused themselves, or discussed the situation of their friends or neighbors, it was children who were most likely to identify conjugal violence as a major destabilizing issue in their lives. In a focus group of thirteen girls and one boy in pre-school in Jericó, Bogotá, the main problem affecting them was 'my mother and father fight' followed by 'my mother and father are going to separate.' Indeed, children as young as 5 years old identified physical

Figure 5.1 Drawing of spousal violence in the home in Jericó, Bogotá, Colombia (drawn by a 13-year-old boy).

Note
Madre, mother; *padre*, father; *hijos*, children.

violence between parents as one of the most disruptive aspects of their life. As illustrated by a 13-year-old boy in Figure 5.1, children witnessing violence on a daily basis were often traumatized as a result.

Usually referred to as 'infant mistreatment' (*maltrato infantil*), violence against children took a number of forms, involving physical, verbal and sexual abuse and was alarmingly widespread in both Colombia and Guatemala. For instance, a group of five young girls (aged between 9 and 14) in Santa Cruz del Quiché, Guatemala, noted that 85 percent of children suffered violence in the home. Similarly, in Cali, Colombia, a group of Community Mothers estimated that of every fifteen children in the *barrio*, five were mistreated. Although fathers or father figures, such as stepfathers and uncles, were the most common perpetrators of violence against children, mothers were also sometimes responsible. In a rare incident in Embudo, Bogotá, a woman raped her son while under the influence of *bazuco*. More often, mothers physically beat their children, both boys and girls, for being disobedient, or shouted at them for misbehaving. A young girl from Cali, Colombia, stated: 'My mother loves me a lot but when she hits me, she makes me purple.' Even when they were not responsible, women often colluded in abuse for the sake of trying to maintain family unity and, often more importantly, financial support (see Klevens *et al.* 2000, for similar findings from Bogotá). For example, a 10-year-old boy, Miguel, from 14 de Febrero, Bogotá, described how he was afraid to go home because his father beat him, particularly when he was inebriated. He stated: 'My father hits me with a stick and then follows that with his hands . . . he then calls me a son-of-a-bitch, a homosexual, and a mad person.' While his mother didn't hit him, Miguel felt aggrieved that she did nothing to stop his father's abuse. Thus, boys as well as girls were vulnerable to physical abuse at the hands of parents. In another case from Santa Cruz del Quiché, Guatemala, a teenage woman told how she returned from a party to be confronted by her waiting stepfather, who during an argument cut off her hair with scissors and then stabbed her in the head because he was jealous that she had spoken with other men.

While physical and verbal violence were widespread, sexual abuse of children, and especially incest, were almost reported to be as common, with girls the most likely victims. Girls as young as 7 or 8 years identified rape within the home as one of their major preoccupations, especially in Guatemala (see Figure 5.2). In Santa Lucía Cotzumalguapa, Guatemala, one stepfather was fathering three children simultaneously – one with his wife, and two more with his two stepdaughters whom he had been abusing. Although women were much less likely to be involved in the perpetration of sexual abuse, as with physical abuse, they often colluded with it. In Concepción, Guatemala City, one woman of a group of four teachers noted: 'often the mothers don't believe what their children are saying, because they're afraid of losing their husbands,' referring to the loss of financial support. In Colombia, echoing comments in other communities, one Community Mother in 14 de Febrero, Bogotá, pointed out: 'One hears a lot about the Rights of Children, but there is one rape a day of children.' Again, sexual abuse was most commonly associated with fathers and stepfathers.

Figure 5.2 Drawing of sexual violence against children in the home in El Carmen, Santa Lucía Cotzumalguapa, Guatemala (drawn by a 13-year-old girl).

Note
Text translation: 'I'm afraid that when I'm sleeping I could be raped, that's what I'm afraid of.'

In the Colombian communities, one particularly invisible form of sexual abuse of children within the home was rape by male renters or lodgers. This was especially acute in communities with high levels of renting – either where other families lived in very close proximity, usually on a second floor, or where individual rooms were rented out. In 14 de Febrero, Bogotá, for instance, the group of Community Mothers mentioned above highlighted rape within the home as the most serious issue affecting the community. In their focus group ranking, six women voted renters as the most serious perpetrators of rape, followed by other male family members, stepfathers and delinquents. This succinctly illustrates the fact that children are often in greater danger of abuse inside the home than outside in the street, and while housing can be used as a productive asset to generate income, this can have severe negative ramifications within the household, in terms of sexual abuse of children, and to a lesser extent, of adult women (Kellett and Tipple 2000; Moser 1998).

Children were not always passive victims of violence, however, but were also agents of violence in their own right.[9] In a minority of cases in the study communities, children lashed out and hit parents, as noted by a group of fifteen elderly people in Jericó, Bogotá. More common was violence among siblings and friends mainly in the form of physical and verbal fights. In Chinautla, Guatemala, a group of three young women (aged 14–15) discussed how they argued with their siblings, usually over tasks in the home. Sexual violence among children in the home was also mentioned. In La Merced, Guatemala City, a group of two women (aged 25 and 35) discussed how sexual relations sometimes occurred between siblings when children were left at home on their own while their mother was at work.

The causal factors underlying intra-family violence

Intra-family violence was not only considered a permanent feature of life in the communities, but also consistent over time with the underlying causes of the phenomenon perceived as deep-seated, many stretching back centuries. At the same time, the PUAs also provided the opportunity for community members to identify more immediate contextual structural causes that implicitly condoned intra-family violence. As with other types of violence these were mediated through issues of identity and agency. In this case, however, as illustrated below, the nature of gender ideologies, and especially the construction of masculinities and femininities, often underlay interpretations of factors contributing to intra-family violence in both countries. While the causes of intra-family violence were diverse, the same motives emerged in both countries.

First, and foremost, women in both countries repeatedly blamed violence perpetrated against women and children on *machismo*, with men who

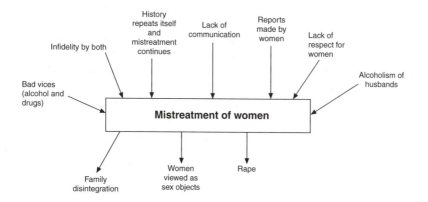

Figure 5.3 Causal flow diagram of mistreatment of women in El Carmen, Santa
Lucía Cotzumalguapa, Guatemala (drawn by a mixed sex group of four
students and one young woman aged 18–22).

perpetrated violence referred to as '*machistas*,' using physical force as an
expression of their power over women. A group of four women from La
Merced, Guatemala City, said that men often beat women when they
wanted to feel powerful, picking on those whom they saw as weaker. As
shown in Figure 5.3, drawn by a mixed gender group from Santa Lucía
Cotzumalguapa, this was also associated with a lack of respect for women,
and the fact that they were viewed simply as sex objects. Although not all
machistas were necessarily violent, most men who perpetrated violence in
the home were *machistas*. In this sense, female community members consistently associated *machismo*, in its many forms, with violence, especially
within the home. Yet, just as men, caught within the bind of the dominance of hegemonic masculinities and *machismo*, committed violence, so
too women tended to accept it because of so-called *masochismo* – referring to the manner in which women put up with continual violence or
abuse from husbands, and indeed, internalized it.[10] This was well illustrated by a group of four adult women also from Santa Lucía Cotzumalguapa, Guatemala, who said that they would expect to be abused if they
didn't look after their husband properly in terms of cooking, cleaning and
washing his clothes.

These findings are consistent with an extensive literature that has highlighted the fact that as part of patriarchal gender relations, men have
enforced their will and social control over women through violence
(Pickup *et al.* 2001; Salles and Tuirán 1997). Throughout Latin America,
entrenched structural factors underlie intra-family violence allowing abuse
in the home to flourish (Jackson 1999; Wade 1994). At the same time, it is
important not to over-emphasize the notion of 'hegemonic masculinity,'

especially in relation to the 'men as problem, women as victim' discourse (Cornwall 2000b: 22). As mentioned above, some focus groups identified women fighting back at men and beating them either in retaliation, or as a way of dealing with their partners. Finally, the fact that some people committed acts of violence and others did not, and some only engaged in violence at particular times requires acknowledgment of individual agency.[11]

A second crucial structural factor exacerbating intra-family violence, especially spouse abuse, was the fact that levels of unemployment had increased more among men than women. Often, responsibility to provide for their families then fell on women's shoulders, in that they were forced to undertake income-generating activities such as street vending, childcare, domestic service and dressmaking activities as a survival strategy. In Colombia, in particular, the macroeconomic crisis discussed in Chapter 4 had resulted in an increase in 'female-maintained' households in which women were the main economic breadwinners, although there were male spouses or partners in residence.[12] In Pórtico, Medellín, for instance, a focus group of two adult men and six adult women suggested that 80 percent of women in the community were maintaining their households. As also mentioned in Chapter 4, this was noted by a man in Cali who recounted how he took care of the home while his wife worked (see Kaztman 1992; Salles and Tuirán 1997).

The increasing prevalence of female-maintained households, as well as male unemployment and women's increasing role in the labor market – leaving men at home without their wives – resulted in frustration and loss of status in terms of masculine identities (see Chant 1997). This was cited by many focus groups in Colombia as a major reason for the perceived intensification of intra-family violence since the mid-1980s when economic crisis began to set in. This is shown in the timelines on variations in intra-family violence from the 1970s until 1999 (see Figure 5.4). In Guatemala, men similarly felt an erosion of their power within the household, effectively undermining the legitimacy of male authority (see Chant 2000; Greig 2000).

A third major factor underlying intra-family violence related to excessive alcohol consumption (and to a lesser extent drug consumption). Chapter 6 discusses the violence-related implications of both types of substance abuse, and therefore this is only briefly mentioned here. While some men beat and abused their family members when under the influence of alcohol, others did not. Nevertheless, alcohol consumption, especially in Guatemala, was identified as critically important in causing intra-family violence. Those men prone to engage in alcohol-related abuse were more likely to do so at specific times. In both Guatemala and Colombia, focus groups identified marked temporal variations over an annual cycle, with major festivals associated with high levels of alcohol consumption also associated with increasing levels of intra-family violence (see Figure 5.5). As families got together to celebrate, the resulting tensions,

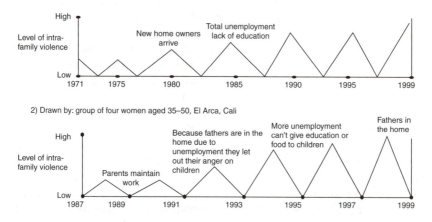

Figure 5.4 Timelines showing changes in intra-family violence, 1970–99 in 14 de Febrero, Bogotá, Colombia and El Arca, Cali, Colombia (drawn by two groups of adults).

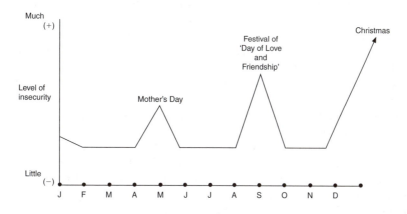

Figure 5.5 Timeline showing changes in insecurity within the home over a year in Amanecer, Bucaramanga, Colombia (drawn by five community leaders, four female and one male).

linked with consuming large amounts of alcohol, often exploded in violence. On a different time scale, violence within the home also tended to increase at weekends when people (and men in particular) received their wages and headed for the bar or brothel to spend their money. In La Merced, Guatemala City, one woman who was part of a larger focus group of five adult women reported how she hated the smell of alcohol as it always reminded her of being beaten by her husband. She knew that when she smelt it on her husband that she had to flee the house to escape his abuse.

Infidelity, or often more accurately, suspicion of infidelity, usually on the part of men, but also among women, was continually cited as a reason for intra-family abuse, and especially conjugal violence. In Guatemala, a focus group of four women from La Merced, Guatemala City, blamed what they referred to as 'third parties' as one of the main causes of conflict between spouses. They said that generally, women gave their husbands three chances to be unfaithful, after which the relationship was over. They also noted that violent arguments often erupted as a result of accusations, many of which were unfounded, between men and women. Such mistrust, jealousy and fear of infidelity are structurally ingrained aspects of gender identities and ideologies in both Colombia and Guatemala (see Wade 1994, on Colombia; also Chant 1997, on Mexico and Costa Rica).

A final common perception in both Colombian and Guatemalan communities relates to the inter-generational transfer of abuse in the home. Many people reported that those who were themselves abused, in turn, abused their own children. This was a key explanatory factor in violence against children committed by fathers, and to a lesser extent, by mothers. In Embudo, Bogotá, a 43-year-old male community leader discussed 'hereditary rape,' stating that: 'he who was raped gets converted into a rapist.' This was further identified by a group of six Community Mothers in Cali, who pointed out when drawing a causal flow diagram, that: 'an abused father abuses his son.' These patterns were similar in Guatemala. In Figure 5.3 above, a group of young people from Santa Lucía Cotzumalguapa articulated the issue as 'history repeats itself and mistreatment continues.' This reference to the cyclical nature of the inter-generational transfer of abuse showed how strongly they perceived it to be structurally embedded in cultural norms and behavior. At the same time, individual agency meant that while certain people who had been abused, became abusers themselves, not all did so (see also Chant 1997, on the importance of female-instigated single parenthood).

While each of the different causal factors have so far been explored separately, it is important to reiterate that they were all causally inter-related, with certain types of violence that originated both inside and outside the home leading to other types of intra-family violence, and vice versa (see below). For example, according to a group of Community Mothers from Cali, violence against children was partly caused by fights and problems among parents; when couples argued and felt frustrated, they took out their worries on their children. However, this same group also identified 'hooded militias' as a cause of child abuse (usually linked with political violence), in that they created fear in the community, and made people anxious. As a result, parents, in particular, were reported to be more likely to abuse their children. The role of political violence in causing intra-family conflict was also noted in Aguazul, in Colombia. Here in a focus group of four adults, two women described how their brothers had been killed by the guerrillas and paramilitaries. As a result, other siblings then wanted to seek revenge. This led to intense conflict within families, with everyone fighting each other as emotions ran high, often erupting in physical violence.

The consequences of intra-family violence

Just as the causal factors involved in intra-family violence were deep-seated, so were the ramifications. Indeed, it was often difficult to distinguish factors linked with causes and effects, and in many cases they overlapped in non-linear relationships. Nevertheless, for the sake of clarity, the following issues are each discussed separately.

The first relates to family disintegration (*desintegración familiar*). While this was sometimes cited as a cause of violence within the home in Colombia and Guatemala, it was more commonly identified as a major outcome. In some cases, the term was also used as a euphemism for intra-family violence when focus groups were reluctant to discuss violence overtly. Among community members, a key component of such disintegration was a lack of communication among family members, but especially between parents and children. In turn, this was related to 'lack of understanding' and 'lack of affection' between parents and children. One group of three girls aged 13 and 14 from Concepción, Guatemala City, felt that they received little emotional support from their parents; one felt that other relatives understood them better than their own parents – who were often fighting anyway. Similar patterns emerged in Colombia. Figure 5.6 shows how a group of ten young women from Aguazul prioritized 'lack of family communication' as the key problem in their community. Moreover, they highlighted clearly how this was closely interrelated with intra-family violence and alcohol abuse. Related with this, a focus group of 17-year-olds from Santa Lucía Cotzumpalguapa, Guatemala, identified those who benefited and those who lost out in situations of family disintegration. They said that men benefited because they usually ended up with another woman, and that the beer producing company, *Gallo*, increased its profits because men drank more beer. In addition, they suggested that *maras* benefited because their parents no longer went out to look for them when they went missing, and prostitutes were better off because they made more money. Children, wives and society all lost out – children because they were left to fend for themselves, wives because they were left with no money and more responsibilities, and society because women and children were ignored.

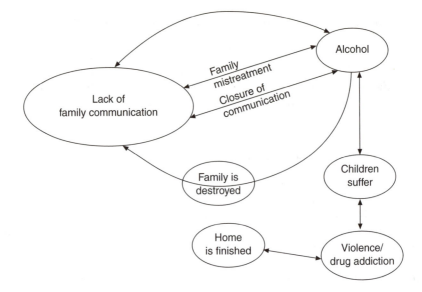

Figure 5.6 Causal flow diagram of lack of family communication in Colombia Chiquita, Aquazul, Columbia (prepared by ten girls aged 9–14).

As such, a key issue relating to family disintegration was the restructuring of households, with an increased proportion of single parent or women-headed households one of the most important outcomes of intra-family violence. According to community members in Guatemala, abusive male partners often left spouses to live with other women with whom they were having affairs. A group of adult women from El Carmen, Santa Lucía Cotzumalguapa, pointed out that single motherhood was caused by men getting tired of their wives, beating them and finding younger women who had more money. Equally, women were increasingly leaving abusive men. Another group of single mothers from La Merced, Guatemala City, noted that many women who were unable to cope with the violence, alcohol abuse and *machismo* on the part of their husbands, now left them (see Figure 5.7). Although they said that leaving their husband was a last resort, it was often the only option when women feared for their lives. Reiterating the same issue, a 28-year-old indigenous woman from Santa Lucía Cotzumalguapa, separated from her partner, described how he had beaten her since they first married when she was 13. Eventually she left him when she discovered he had another woman and two other children. Although he wanted to reunite with her, she said, 'I'm tired of all the mistreatment.' She was willing to put up with little money and not being able to send her children to school to escape his violence.

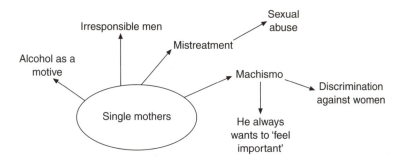

Figure 5.7 Causal flow diagram of single motherhood in La Merced, Guatemala City (drawn by four adult women aged 18–48).

These examples all illustrate the way in which the process of family disintegration was identified as involving a breakdown of relationships, norms and values learned through socialization processes in the family within the home – the so-called social capital within communities (see Chapter 8). The fact that it frequently included violence, and especially conflict between parents and children, as well as being associated with household structures and the absence of a mother or father concurs with other research in the region (see Guendel and González 1996, on Costa Rica; Kaztman 1997, on Uruguay; also Datta and McIlwaine 2000).

As discussed above, intra-family violence, coupled with family disintegration, had particularly deleterious consequences for children's welfare. While some were victims or perpetrators of violence within the home, even more witnessed violence and conflict on a daily basis. Teachers in particular were sensitive to the issue of family disintegration, parent–child conflicts and intra-family violence, primarily because they had to deal with the effects among children in the classrooms. In Guatemala, a group of teachers from San Marcos perceived that the causes of family conflict and violence were linked both to *machismo* and to infidelity among parents. According to them, male children became 'good for nothings,' alcoholics, drug addicts or joined *maras*, while female children became single mothers or prostitutes. Two groups of primary school teachers in Bogotá and Medellín, Colombia, similarly identified a wide range of consequences of intra-family violence for children that involved severe behavioral problems such as low self-esteem and aggression, with sexual abuse and rape causing the most severe problems (see Table 5.1). Violence also undermined their educational capacity – either with their achievement levels being very low, or with young people leaving school altogether. Ultimately, this eroded human capital assets and capabilities, with serious long-term consequences for both countries.

113

Table 5.1 The effects of intra-family violence on children's behavior in school, identified by primary school teachers in Colombia

Seven primary school teachers in 14 de Febrero, Bogotá	*Thirty primary school teachers in Pórtico, Medellín*
Lack of discipline	Low self-esteem
Bad vocabulary	Emotional instability
Aggression with other pupils	Verbal and physical aggression
Introverted children	Lack of respect
Low academic achievement	Aggressive games
Sexual abuse of girls	Anti-social behavior
Unhelpful attitude	Loneliness
School desertion	Absenteeism
	Low academic achievement
	Lack of conflict resolution
	Abandonment of the home
	Disarticulation within the community

However, not all children who had experienced or witnessed violence within the home had behavioral problems. A group of three women from Nuevo Horizonte, Guatemala City, in their causal impact diagram (Figure 5.8), drew a nuanced account of what might happen, outlining two alternative paths. On the one hand, they showed how the mother who left her abusive partner and cared for her offspring had children that were well adjusted. On the other, they illustrated what might happen if the mother established a home with another man. In their eyes, this could lead to a chain of negative and mutually reinforcing circumstances, with children becoming involved with gangs, drugs and ultimately being 'destroyed.' According to these women, if mothers decided, for whatever reasons, to remain alone with their children, then other forms of violence and family integration could be averted. However, if for other reasons, they established relationships with other men, there was the possibility of severe hardships for children.

The ramifications of intra-family conflict for violence outside the home

Not only did one type of intra-family violence lead to other types of intra-family violence but it also had critically important consequences in generating other types of violence outside the home. According to many focus groups in both countries, a complex system of causality and outcomes existed in which violence permeated the entire spectrum of community social relations, with households and families being the critical nexus. They discussed how intra-family violence often encouraged individuals, and especially children and youth, to engage in other types of violence

114

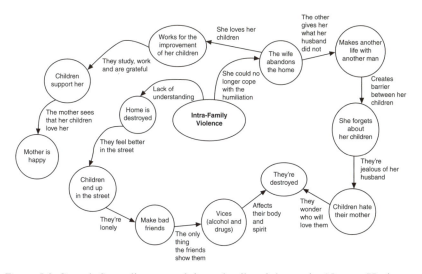

Figure 5.8 Causal flow diagram of intra-family violence in Nuevo Horizonte, Guatemala City (prepared by three women aged 18, 20 and 39).

outside the home. At a general level, a problem tree (Figure 5.9) drawn by a group of adult women from Jericó, Bogotá, reflected the severity of the situation when they noted that a major consequence of intra-household violence was 'total violence – war,' that would create a 'country without future.'

At a more specific level, probably one of the least recognized but most critical outcomes of intra-family violence related to inter-generational conflict, particularly between fathers and their sons. As channels of communication between parents and their children were broken, children turned away from their parents, and the older generation began to blame young people for the ills of society. In some cases, young people withdrew from mainstream society. Thus in 14 de Febrero, Bogotá, a group of male rock or punk musicians who dressed in black, shaved their heads, and espoused an ideology of anarchic communism, stated that, 'People don't like us. We are looked on as drug addicts and as being associated with satanic cults.'

This chapter, together with the previous one, has focused on community perceptions of the main underlying causes and consequences of violence – whether political, economic or social in nature – and the important mutually reinforcing interrelationships between all three. They have highlighted both similarities and differences in terms of the manifestations of violence in two different country contexts. One of the most important common themes that emerge from all the chapters is the fact that it was adolescents and young adults, particularly male adults, who were often at the 'apex' of a nexus of violence, and consequently most likely to

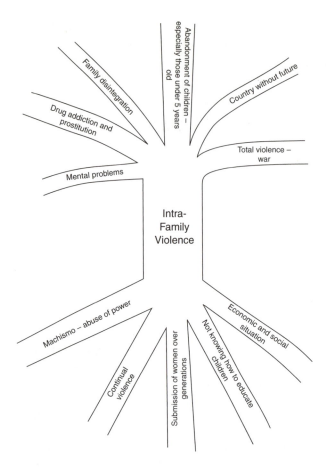

Figure 5.9 Problem tree of intra-family violence in Jericó, Bogotá, Colombia (drawn by a group of adult women aged 28–38).

experience all three types simultaneously. Associated with this were two important violence-related issues. First, was the problematic phenomenon of drug consumption, critically important in Colombia and emerging as an issue in Guatemala. Second, was the issue of gangs and other violence-associated community level institutions, with the particular phenomenon of *maras* a much voiced concern in Guatemala. Given the significance of both issues in the daily lives of poor communities, the next two chapters focus specifically on each in turn, with relative emphasis on each country associated with the level of concern as articulated by local communities.

6

SUBSTANCE ABUSE-LINKED VIOLENCE RELATING TO DRUG AND ALCOHOL CONSUMPTION

We were all born to die ... to avoid death you have to trick it.
(Male drug addict from Bogotá, Colombia)

Although neither alcohol nor drug consumption were perceived as violent in themselves, the fact that widespread substance abuse was closely linked to violence, both economic and social in nature, meant it was recognized as a problem in local communities in both countries. However, as this chapter describes, levels of preoccupation did not necessarily correlate either with the intensity of consumption, or with the associated violence levels. This in itself meant that, in many respects, substance abuse-linked violence was the most insidious manifestation of violence experienced in both countries. Although alcohol abuse-related violence in particular was highly visible both in the streets and inside the home, with fundamental daily effects in terms of fear, insecurity and well-being, people appeared unable or unwilling to confront it. Indeed, drug consumption was more of a concern, despite the fact that violence related with this was often less acute than that resulting from alcohol abuse. This was the case not only in Colombia, where drug consumption was a widespread phenomenon, particularly among young men in the larger cities, but also in Guatemala where, comparatively speaking, levels of drug abuse were much lower than Colombia.

In both countries, the level of preoccupation with drug consumption shown by local communities differed markedly from the level and focus of concern shown by most policymakers or academics in their respective countries. Alarm over the production and trans-shipment of drugs such as cocaine and marijuana has served to obscure the growing problem of drug consumption-related violence in Latin America as a whole. As Pérez Gómez (1998: 56) has commented: 'Most Latin American countries do have a drug consumption problem, a condition that is often denied or ignored in international discussions.' In contrast, alcohol has long been recognized as the substance most used across the continent, with abuse a major problem affecting both urban and rural communities (Garrard-Burnett 2000).

Differences in interpretations of drug and alcohol consumption-related violence were further complicated by contradictory attitudes toward the phenomena, as perceived by community members themselves. On the one hand, such consumption, particularly of alcohol, was regarded as having an important function in generating social cohesion – with an associated degree of acceptability. On the other hand, it was regarded as a 'problem' when socially accepted boundaries were crossed, particularly associated with violence (see Harvey 1994). In addition, not everyone consumed drugs, and of those that did, not all were violent. Perceptions of drug and alcohol-related violence therefore depended on context-specific factors, both in terms of the consumption choices made by individual social agents, as well as the manner in which the phenomenon was viewed. In exploring this issue, the chapter begins by describing the scale and characteristics of both drug and alcohol-related violence before examining the causes and consequences of each.

The phenomenon of drug and alcohol-related violence

In Colombia, concern with drug-related problems was associated with drug consumption and local small-scale trafficking. General problem listings in the nine communities revealed that overall, an average of 23 percent of all violence-related problems were perceived as linked to drugs. This varied among communities. In Rosario, Girón, for instance, they represented one-third of violence problems, while in Colombia Chiquita, Aguazul, they were not perceived as affecting the community at all. In terms of listings of types of violence, drug-related violence represented 15 percent of all types across the nine communities, with Rosario and 14 de Febrero, Bogotá, the communities most affected. This percentage was lower than the general problem listings, explained by the fact that community members tended to be more specific in violence listings. Therefore, they were less likely to identify drugs as an issue *per se*, than to mention the types of violence associated with them. In Embudo, Bogotá, for example, which was notorious both for consumption and sale of a diversity of substances, violence listings illustrated that 'fights' – which often revolved around drugs – rather than drugs as a category, were the single most important type of violence listed.

In contrast, in Guatemala, drug-related problems were not prioritized to the same extent. In terms of problem listings, an overall average of 13 percent of all violence-related problems were perceived as drug-related. Again, this varied across communities with concerns higher in urban areas such as Nuevo Horizonte, Guatemala City – where they related to one-fifth of violence problems – than in smaller towns with larger indigenous populations, such as El Carmen, Santa Lucía Cotzumalguapa, where drugs were perceived to be related to only 6 percent of problems.

Turning to alcohol-related problems, in neither Colombia nor Guatemala were they perceived as severe as those relating to drugs. In Colombia, they represented on average 2 percent of violence-related problems in the general problem listings and only emerged as significant in five of the nine communities. In contrast, in Guatemala they represented an average of 10 percent of all violence-related problems. Again, there were variations among communities with alcohol-related violence reported as most common in Limoncito, San Marcos, and in El Carmen, Santa Lucía Cotzumalguapa.

These significant differences in prioritization of drug and alcohol-related violence – ranging from a perception that it did not affect the community at all to a view that it posed a significant problem – showed the importance of context-specific cultural constructions of perceptions of drug use. As McDonald (1994: 1) states: 'a problem does not exist until perceived as a problem and defined as such.' This position emphasizes individual and collective agency with two factors of particular significance. First, drugs (and associated trafficking activities) were perceived as more threatening to the social and political order, and consequently identified as more dangerous than alcohol. Second, where consumption levels were so high as to be endemic it had become a way of life and gained a level of social acceptability. For instance, in most contexts heavy drinking was viewed as a normal activity, and much of its associated violence took place inside the home. As such, there was considerable under-reporting of the problem, particularly in Colombia. This evidence is supported by Madrigal (1998: 245) whose policy-focused research notes that while the prevalence of excessive drinking is high in Latin America, self-awareness or perceptions by others of this pattern are low: 'indicating that the region enjoys a permissive environment for drinking.'

Types and nature of drug and alcohol-related violence

As noted earlier, while drugs themselves were not perceived as violent, a range of drug-related violence was identified as linked to the behavior of drug addicts. In Colombia, for instance, people showed a remarkable knowledge of drug-related violence, identifying a total of twenty-four different types of violence and/or problems related to drugs (see Appendix 9), while in Guatemala listings revealed ten types.[1] The need to feed addicts' drug habits was closely linked to economic violence, most frequently robbery. In Girón, Colombia, a 13-year-old girl noted: 'The people who take marijuana rob; they rob from houses.' However, drugs also permeated intra-family violence, and sexual violence. Young women in particular frequently blamed drug addicts for rapes in their *barrio*, both in the street and at home. Drug consumption was also closely linked to death. Some people killed to obtain drugs, murdered when under the influence of drugs, or were killed by the physiological or psychological effects of consumption. Community members in Embudo, Bogotá, identified two *basureros de muertos* (rubbish dumps for the dead), while a focus group of drug addicts used a causal flow diagram to describe the inevitability and acceptance of death (Figure 6.1). In Guatemala, violence related with drug consumption ranged from sexual violence, such as rape, to delinquency and gang fights. Drug distribution was frequently mentioned, especially the so-called *narcotraficantes* (drug dealers). Again, drug-related problems were perceived as more serious in large urban areas, especially in the *colonias* in Guatemala City, and in the border towns of Huehuetenango and Esquipulas, than in the smaller towns.

In both countries, drug consumption was a relatively new problem, especially when compared with alcohol. In most Colombian communities, consumption generally began in the 1980s, increasing in the 1990s when it also became more visible in public. This was illustrated by a timeline drawn by four adults in 14 de Febrero, Bogotá, that showed how, before 1980, drugs were consumed either within homes or 'hidden', with violence linked to police actions relating to 'social cleansing.' Since the 1990s, however, there had been huge increases in drug consumption, which in turn was linked to rising levels of insecurity (see Figure 6.2).

Not surprisingly, drug consumption in Colombia cannot be understood without reference to the drug trafficking cartels that fundamentally influenced the accessibility of drugs and attitudes toward them. A variety of focus groups noted that the growth of large drug cartels had contributed to more widespread drug distribution, and hence consumption. In Embudo, Bogotá, people commented that on the death of Pablo Escobar, the sale of

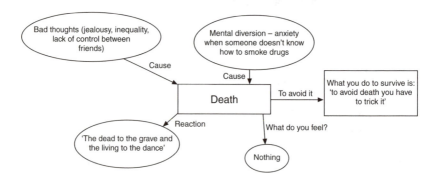

Figure 6.1 Causal flow diagram of death due to drug consumption in Embudo, Bogotá, Colombia (drawn by one man and one woman).

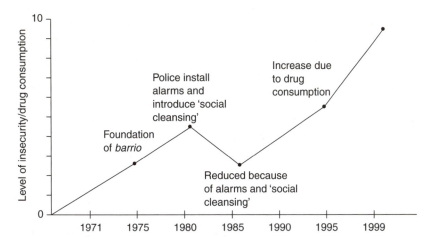

Figure 6.2 Timeline showing drug consumption and insecurity, 1971–99 in 14 de Febrero, Bogotá, Colombia (drawn by four women and two men).

drugs decreased. At the same time, in both Medellín and Cali, the drug cartels were often seen in a very positive light, especially during the 1980s when they were most active. Pórtico, Medellín, for example, benefited from a basketball court built with money donated by Pablo Escobar. Yet, as one man from Medellín pointed out: 'When the drug traffickers left, the situation became very difficult; everyone was left worse off.' In Cali, a marked decrease in the economic fortunes of the community El Arca occurred with the capture of 'Los Rodriguez' of the Cali cartel. One community leader stated: 'The drug traffickers helped us to a certain extent; they produced an increase in employment and allowed the people to build their own homes.' This perception challenges the broadly stereo-typical view that drug cartels uniformly bring negative effects to communities. As Leeds (1996) notes in the context of Brazil, the relation-ship between drug barons and communities is a complex, reciprocal, and to a degree, mutually beneficial one.

In Guatemala, the problem was significantly different. As a drug ship-ment and trafficking rather than drug-producing country, drug consump-tion was more recent in origin, and first perceived of as a serious issue in the 1990s.[2] Although drug consumption had a longer history in Guatemala City, in many cases, its arrival was purported to be linked to the signing of the Peace Accords in 1996. Thus, while in Concepción, Guatemala City, a focus group maintained that drug consumption had been increasing steadily since 1989, in contrast, in El Carmen, Santa Lucía Cotzumalguapa, another focus group of six men noted that the '*narcos*' had emerged as a

121

new phenomenon in 1999 when traffickers paid local farmers to use their sugarcane fields as landing strips. The most obvious manifestation were the new cars in town – even a Porsche. Because of trafficking activity, local consumption had also increased. Similarly, in Santa Cruz del Quiché, a group of adults noted that drug traffickers had arrived since the Peace Accords, coming from the United States to sell cocaine to the local gangs. This growth in drug consumption in both countries is supported by regional level data that shows the increase to be associated in particular with a surplus production of coca paste and cocaine. Difficulties selling the final product on international markets due to tighter controls on distribution channels, have meant that domestic markets are becoming increasingly exploited (ADE/GTZ 2001).

As was the case with drugs, alcohol was closely associated with violent behavior both within households and in the local community. The fact that alcohol-linked violence was perceived as far more of a problem in Guatemala than Colombia meant that little information was elicited on this issue in Colombia. In Guatemala, overall, people identified sixteen alcohol-related problems. Among these, alcohol abuse as a form of social violence outside the home was associated with fist-fights or occasionally gun fights in local *cantinas* or streets (especially in Villa Real, Esquipulas). Generally, they involved men, although arguments were often over women. The other widely identified problem was that of drunken men raping women and girls, both in the streets and in the home (see Chapter 5). In some cases it was economic in nature, such as when inebriated people stole money to buy alcohol. In El Carmen, Santa Lucía Cotzumalguapa, for instance, a focus group noted how people avoided walking near the bar where men often robbed them to obtain money to buy more alcohol.

For as long as people could remember, heavy alcohol consumption had been widespread in most communities in Guatemala. As in many other parts of Latin America, social drinking, particularly by men, played an important role in the formation and maintenance of social relationships within the community. In this sense, alcohol consumption contributed to community-level social cohesion in a complex process which shaped community perceptions and attitudes to the phenomenon (see Harvey 1994, on Peru). But drinking could be both socially acceptable and unacceptable depending on whether it was consumed excessively (ibid.).[3] The extent to which some viewed alcohol consumption as a problem was partially reflected in the fact that all the study communities had at least one Alcoholics Anonymous located within the *colonia* (see Chapter 8). With heavy consumption more or less constant in the long term, people nevertheless noted variations across shorter time frames. Over the period of a year, for instance, peak times for alcohol consumption and associated violence were festivals and holidays, as a timeline drawn by a very elderly man

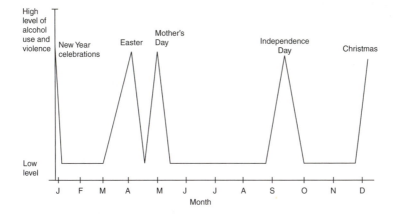

Figure 6.3 Timeline showing changes in alcohol consumption and related violence over the period of one year in San Jorge, Chinautla, Guatemala (prepared by an 83-year-old man).

in San Jorge, Chinautla, showed (Figure 6.3). As noted in Chapter 5, these celebration times were intimately associated with the consumption of large quantities of alcohol, with intra-family violence varying directly according to the levels of alcohol consumed. For example, a group of four women from La Merced, Guatemala City, made a direct link between the days of the week when men were more likely to drink – Friday, Saturday and Sundays, and sometimes Mondays – and the days when most intra-family violence occurred. It was reported that men were paid on Fridays or Saturdays, after which they started drinking until the following Monday.[4] In all the communities, the most important drinking day was Sunday. Not only did intra-family, bar and street violence increase on these days, so too did robbery and assaults because of the knowledge not only that these were paydays, but also that people were less careful when under the influence of alcohol.

The range of drugs and alcohol available and the nature of consumers

Turning to the availability of drugs and alcohol, there were interesting comparisons between the two countries. In Colombia, for instance, some seventeen different types were identified (some of which were different names for the same drug). Marijuana was most commonly mentioned, followed by *bazuco* and *perico/a*, both forms of crack with a cocaine base, and usually smoked rather than injected. It also included various types of pills, such as *roche* (epilepsy pills) often taken in conjunction with other types of drugs. Some also turned to solvents such as paint thinner, known by the English *tiner*, or glue, often referred to by a brand-name – Boxer. Others inhaled petrol, or drank antiseptic alcohol consumed with Coca-Cola or another type of soft drink – sometimes known as *chamberlai*. Although different drugs were often associated with particular consumers, some drug users would mix together various types (including alcohol) in a given day.

Regional level data from Colombia show that marijuana (cannabis) became increasingly popular in the 1990s, especially among young people, as well as the use of solvents. The use of cocaine among young people still remains relatively low, although it has been increasing. Also significant is the growing popularity of tranquilizers. In Latin America as a whole, cannabis and cocaine are more common among middle to upper income groups, with coca paste and solvents more prevalent among lower income, marginalized groups, although this divide is blurring. Similarly, while drugs have until now been seen as a male domain, with women often accounting for less than 10 percent of consumption, women and girls are becoming increasingly significant consumers (ADE/GTZ 2001: 13–15).

Such was the extent of drug consumption, that many young people immediately identified themselves according to whether or not they consumed drugs, especially in Colombia. For instance, those not consuming drugs called themselves *sanos* (healthy) or *zanahórios* (carrots), while they referred to drug users as *viciosos* (people with vices), *marihuaneros* (marijuana smokers), *colinos*, or *sopladores*. Of particular significance were differences in tolerance levels which fundamentally influenced estimates of the proportion of consumers, highlighting city-specific differences. Table 6.1 summarizes information from four Colombian communities that differed markedly in terms of levels of drug tolerance, and associated levels of consumption and visibility. Thus, for instance, in 14 de Febrero, Bogotá, where a moderate level of tolerance existed, community members noted a rate of drug consumption of around 40–50 percent. A group of seven community leaders estimated that there were 500 users of which only fifty were 'open,' with the rest 'closed' users – usually adults who consumed drugs in their home. The *cerrados* were often drug distributors, known as '*mulas de los abiertos*' (mules of the open ones) and dependent on the *abiertos* for their supply, and sometimes the sale of drugs. Drug addicts themselves, from the same community, estimated there were 30–40 hardcore (*más llevados*) users and 100 young people who also took drugs on a more irregular basis, getting the permanent users to buy drugs for them.[5] In total contrast, in Pórtico, Medellín, which had the highest levels of tolerance and drug visibility, an estimated 60 percent of the population smoked marijuana. This was not seen as substance abuse but rather as a hobby and a way, according to one young man, to 'relax, sleep, pass the time and keep your mind elsewhere.' In contrast to other communities

Table 6.1 Levels of tolerance and visibility of drug consumption in four Colombian communities

Community	Level of tolerance	Percentage of population consuming and type of consumer	Level of visibility	Main type of drug
14 de Febrero, Bogotá	Medium	40–50 percent Youth and adults	Visible among youth	Marijuana and *bazuco* among youth
			Hidden among adults	Marijuana and cocaine among adults
Pórtico, Medellín	High	60 percent Youth and adults	Visible	Cocaine, marijuana and 'roches'
Cachicamo, Yopal	Very low	Floating population of 3–4 people; Youth	Visible	Marijuana and *bazuco*
Rosario, Girón	Very low	5 percent Youth	Visible	Marijuana and *bazuco*

Source: Focus groups in nine communities. Adapted from Moser and McIlwaine (2000).

though, *bazuco* was rarely consumed because it was associated with the 'war' from which the city was just emerging.

Of critical importance in relation to consumption was the fact that drugs were considerably cheaper than alcohol. For example, one joint of marijuana cost between 300 and 500 *pesos* (U.S.$0.19 and U.S.$0.3 respectively), yet a small bottle of beer cost 800 *pesos* (U.S.$0.5). Moreover, a bottle of brandy (at 9,000 *pesos*) (U.S.$5.6) cost more than a gram of the most expensive hard drugs – cocaine and *perico* (8,000 *pesos* for good quality – U.S.$5). One gram of *bazuco* was not much more expensive than a bottle of beer. Drug consumption levels were also calculated. For example, in 14 de Febrero a young male drug addict estimated that he spent between 10,000 and 20,000 *pesos* (U.S.$6.2 and 12.5) per day, while another group of three consumers spent an average of 15,000 *pesos* (U.S.$9.4) daily. Finally, in Pórtico, nine young men from the gang, 'Los Muchachos,' estimated that they smoked ten joints of marijuana a day at a cost of between 3,000 and 5,000 *pesos* (U.S.$1.9 and 3.1).

Drug consumption across all communities was most commonly associated with youth aged between 15–30 years, and primarily with young men, with women representing around one-third of consumers. In 14 de Febrero, Bogotá, a focus group of seven community leaders estimated that 20 percent were aged between 10–20 years, 50 percent between 21–30 years,

20 percent between 31–40 years, and only 10 percent over 50 years. Not only did parents commonly consume drugs, but children as young as 8 years of age were also identified as drug users. Different drugs were taken at different ages depending on costs. It was said that some children began with marijuana at the age of 8, moving on to petrol and glue at the age of 12. The use of *bazuco* came later at the age of 14, with *perico,* as the most expensive, the last to be consumed.

Turning to Guatemala, the situation was less complex. Although a variety of drugs were available, glue sniffing was the most common type used, followed by marijuana. There were also spatial variations, with people in the capital more likely to consume hard drugs such as crack and cocaine, although marijuana was also popular. When glue was not available, people sniffed paint thinner or white spirits. Figure 6.4, drawn by an 18-year-old young man in Nuevo Horizonte, Guatemala City, shows the types and usage of different types of drugs, reflecting a widely held knowledge of such issues.

In terms of the drug costs, as in Colombia, some types were cheaper than alcohol. In Gucumatz, Santa Cruz del Quiché, for instance, a focus group of three young people reported that a cigarette of marijuana cost 30 *centavos*, compared with 10 *quetzales* for a litre of beer.[6] Similarly, glue was only 25 *centavos* for a tube. Crack and cocaine were much more expensive at 300 *quetzales* for a stone of crack and 100 *quetzales* for an ounce of cocaine. Indeed, a police official in Santa Cruz del Quiché

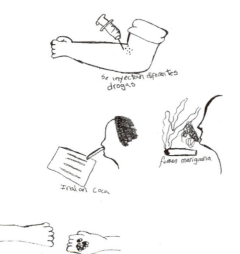

Figure 6.4 Drawing of types of drugs available in Neuvo Horizonte, Guatemala City (drawn by an 18-year-old young man).

Note
Se inyectan diferentes drogas, they inject different drugs; *fuman mariguana*, they smoke marijuana; *inhalan coca*, they inhale cocaine; *lo venden*, they sell it.

reported that cocaine was mainly a drug for the middle and upper classes in the region because of its expense. In La Merced, Guatemala City, drugs were much cheaper than in the departments. For instance, crack cost 15 *quetzales* per stone, while cocaine cost 25 *quetzales* per ounce.

As in Colombia, drug consumption was associated with men rather than women, except in the Guatemala City communities. In La Merced, Guatemala City, where consumption was widespread, a 40-year-old man stated that about 10 percent of all women in the *colonia* smoked marijuana. Outside Guatemala City, levels of reported consumption were lower. For example, in Villa Real, Esquipulas, a group of male adolescents stated that only 10 percent of the male youth were involved in drug taking, while some parents were clandestine glue sniffers. Similarly, in Limoncito, San Marcos, around 15 percent of the male youth were said to be taking drugs. Drug usage also depended on age, with most drug addicts being young men. A group of adolescent women in La Merced said that most drug addicts were male and aged between 17 and 22, and became alcoholics once they reached 30. Another group of adult women from the same community reported that boys began to sniff glue at the age of 10 and then moved on to marijuana at around 15, before turning to harder drugs such as cocaine and crack. Outside Guatemala City, young men tended to start later, at around 15 years.

Different types of alcohol were also commonly consumed. While beer was most widespread, heavy drinkers or alcoholics usually drank various types of rum or, if desperate, antiseptic alcohol. In La Merced, Guatemala City, a woman who owned a street stall selling beer noted this distinction between alcoholics who consumed *guaro* (rum) or chemicals, and the rest who were social drinkers and drank beer. Illegal or clandestine alcohol, made from fermented fruit, was also mentioned in three communities – known variously as *kuto*, *kuxa* and *kusha*. This was particularly prevalent in Santa Cruz del Quiché where it was easily available in local *cantinas*. Here, a police official reported that this was an extremely cheap, traditional drink, especially among the Mayan population. A group of fourteen adults from the community ranked clandestine alcohol as their greatest problem, blaming its prevalence particularly on poverty because it was the most affordable.[7]

In Guatemala, alcohol consumers were called a range of names beyond *alcohólicos*, such as *borachos*, *bolos*, *charamileros* or *charamilas* and *chibolas*. While some Guatemalan indigenous groups reported especially high levels of alcohol use linked with trauma and poverty, alcohol abuse was widespread, regardless of ethnic identity. All age groups drank alcohol, with many boys starting at 12, 13 or 14 years of age (according to a 17-year-old in Santa Cruz del Quiché). When compared with drug use, however, alcohol was again associated with the more mature, while drugs were linked with youth (see below).

As in Colombia, the majority of heavy drinkers in the communities were male. In El Carmen, Santa Lucía Cotzumalguapa, three young women noted that 90 percent of men drank heavily, while in La Merced, Guatemala City, a woman whose husband had been killed in a traffic accident while drunk, put the figure at 75 percent. The only effective constraint identified was the Evangelical faiths that required a vow of abstinence. While some women also drank heavily, generally they were less likely to have drinking problems. Thus, a 40-year-old man in La Merced, Guatemala City, noted that for every 100 adult women, 60 drank. While men were more likely to drink publicly in *cantinas*, women tended to drink privately at home.

The causes of drug and alcohol consumption and their associated violence

In seeking to identify the causal factors underlying drug and alcohol-related violence, issues of individual agency and identity were both important. As mentioned above, in both countries gender and age were critical factors in determining the type of substance abuse. At the same time, not all men and women were involved in high levels of drug and/or alcohol consumption, and among those that were, not all were perpetrators of abuse-related violence. In turn, drug and alcohol consumption was influenced by a complex set of issues relating to human agency including values, attitudes, life experience and social identity. Thus, as Madrigal (1998: 234) points out: 'Problems emerge[d] not from an inert substance, but from the interaction between it, the user, and the context.' As such, the association between violence and alcohol consumption, and especially drunkenness is thought to be learnt as part of the dominant mode of drunken behavior (McDonald 1994: 14). Similarly, there are also different behavioral patterns and meanings linked with drugs such as cocaine and cannabis (ibid.). As this section shows, the underlying causal factors were often similar to those identified in previous chapters. In addition, the consequences of substance abuse were often interrelated in a seemingly spiraling vicious circle, which meant it was not always possible to distinguish between cause and effect.

As discussed in Chapter 5, drug consumption among youth in both Colombia and Guatemala was frequently perceived as the direct outcome of intra-family violence and conflict. For example, a problem tree drawn by Community Mothers from Rosario, Girón, in Colombia, identified how conflict within the home could precipitate youth turning to drugs (Figure 6.5). The women also noted a gender difference, maintaining that while young men were more likely to turn to drugs and gangs when family life became untenable, young women tended to get involved in early sexual relationships, ending up becoming pregnant, or turning to prostitution.[8]

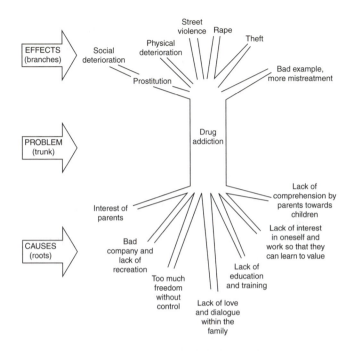

Figure 6.5 Problem tree of drug addiction in Rosario, Girón, Colombia (drawn by seven Community Mothers).

Similarly in Guatemala, one of the most commonly mentioned causes of drug addiction was intra-family violence and family disintegration. This referred to a lack of love and communication between parents and children, as well as lack of parental discipline. In Sacuma, Huehuetenango, a group of four teachers identified this as the primary cause of drug addiction in their school, along with the influence of television and, according to one: 'a loss of moral values in society.' In addition, mothers were also blamed for their children's drug use when they abandoned them in order to go out to work. Children left alone without discipline were reported to be easy prey for drug addicts to recruit new consumers. Indeed, one woman in La Merced, Guatemala City, went so far as to suggest that all drug addicts were originally abandoned children, either because their parents had separated, or because their mother went out to work.

Focus groups also identified clear linkages between the alcohol-related abuses of fathers and the drug abuses of their sons. In Nuevo Horizonte, Guatemala City, a middle-aged woman discussed the cause of drug addiction as deriving from: 'the bad example of the parents getting drunk and hitting them on a daily basis.' Other people maintained that children were

129

likely to learn to drink when their parents drank in front of them. Finally, marital conflict or disappointment in a romantic affair was also seen as inducing men to drink heavily. A focus group from Nuevo Horizonte, Guatemala City, described such causal factors as 'because your wife treats you badly' and 'marriage without love or premature marriage.'

Another important cause of drug consumption was the daily peer pressure that children and youth experienced, from as young as 10 years. In Colombia, in Jericó, Bogotá, for instance, a group of four 11-year-old girls said that they had been pressured to smoke cigarettes (the first step), and then drugs (starting with Boxer glue). Often, gangs of drug pushers stood outside the school gates trying to make students try drugs, offering the first consignment for free, and thereafter charging. Pressure also came from friends with one commonly cited reason in all communities for getting involved in drugs being *malas amistades* (bad friendships) or *malas companias* (bad company). Finally, some parents not only provided a bad example to their children by their own behavior but actually taught them to smoke marijuana. In El Arca, Cali, for instance, a group of three adults said that with so many parents consuming drugs, children learnt to accept it as normal. Peer pressure and a desire to belong were also important among youth in Guatemala. In Nuevo Horizonte, Guatemala City, one women at a women's group meeting pointed out: 'Children begin to take drugs when they're young, they look at young men who do it, and then they want to do it as well.'

Alcohol consumption was also associated with 'bad company' and peer pressure to drink, clearly identified by an adult group in Nuevo Horizonte, Guatemala City (Figure 6.6). As mentioned earlier, drinking alcohol was a major leisure pursuit in most communities, revolving primarily around *cantinas*, and to a lesser extent, brothels. Men were reported as going directly to the *cantina* after work, and spending all their free time with their friends drinking. This perception of the normality and low level of importance of problem drinking in Latin America also contributes to social pressure to drink, as 'everyone thinks that it is the thing to do' (Madrigal 1998: 245).

In both countries, poverty and unemployment were linked to desperation that made some men drink heavily. In Guatemala, for instance, two women in Sacuma, Huehuetenango, noted that there were lots of drunks in the streets because there was no work, commenting that in the past the government had cleared the streets by sending them to public works schemes. Similarly, in Gucumatz, Santa Cruz del Quiché, three young men cited poverty, disillusion and not being able to find jobs as the key causes of alcoholism (see also Figure 6.6). Some young indigenous people reported that they turned to drugs when they experienced discrimination. Overall, however, rather than desperation or depression, it was reported that young people tended to take drugs when they were unemployed, as a means of passing the time.

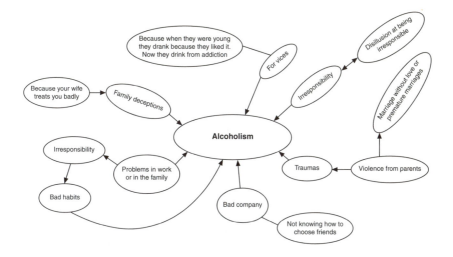

Figure 6.6 Causal flow diagram of alcoholism in Nuevo Horizonte, Guatemala City (prepared by five adult women and one man).

Increased drug consumption was also blamed on the unprecedented growth of trafficking, with drug consumers then becoming pushers to feed their habit. In Sacuma, Huehuetenango, for instance, two women in their thirties stated that young people started to deal because of a desire for power and money, and also because one could make easy money.[9] They also noted that this should be understood in light of the fact that few young people could earn a good living without turning to the sale of drugs. A similar situation was found in Colombia, where it was said that people became desperate and turn to drugs as a way either to fill their time, or to soften the edge of their despair. For example, three Communist Party founder members of the community of 14 de Febrero, Bogotá, noted that stress related to not working could lead people to take drugs (Figure 6.7). Lack of education was also commonly cited as both a cause and a consequence of drug consumption.

The consequences of drug and alcohol comsumption and their associated violence

The outcomes of high levels of substance abuse and their associated violence were forcefully articulated by community members, supporting the assessment of Pérez Gómez (1998) who noted that drug use is related to an increase in social disintegration, violence and criminality, threatens physical and mental health, and, along with the use of alcohol, may bring

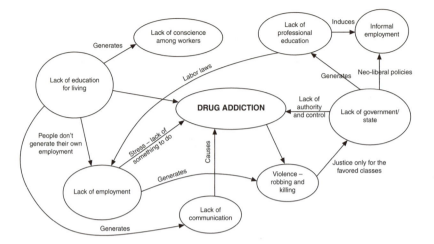

Figure 6.7 Causal flow diagram of drug addiction in 14 de Febrero, Bogotá, Colombia (drawn by three adult founders of the community).

health problems, domestic instability and economic insecurity. Yet, again these were shaped by context-specific experiences.

In Guatemala, the most commonly cited consequence of alcohol consumption was economic hardship within households caused by breadwinners using the family budget to buy alcohol. Women in particular noted how they were often left without food for their children because their husbands had drunk the family budget, as noted in Figure 6.8. In San Jorge, Chinautla, a middle-aged man noted that: 'Rum kills everything; many sell all they own in order to be able to drink.' Alcoholism was also associated with indebtedness within communities. Two carpenters in Villa Real, Esquipulas, noted that there were very few carpenters that didn't drink heavily, and as a result, all of them owed money. They often developed networks of debt relief among themselves – many regularly spent 100 percent of their weekly earnings on alcohol. If they didn't spend on their own alcohol consumption, they bought drinks for their friends. One of the carpenters noted that many women had to go out to work because their husbands drank all their wages. The extraordinary impact of this expenditure, an issue usually ignored by policy-focused researchers, was best illustrated in Colombia by the household expenditure provided by a mother from Pórtico, Medellín. This showed that almost half the household earnings were spent on alcohol, drugs and gambling. Another aggregate household expenditure from same community revealed that expenditure on drugs exceeded expenditure on education. Drugs and alcohol combined were the second largest expenditure item after food (see

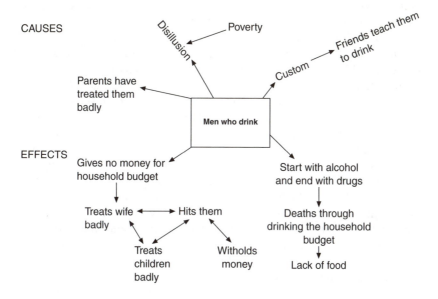

Figure 6.8 Causal flow diagram of men who drink in La Merced, Guatemala City (drawn by three women aged 16, 34 and 40).

Appendix 10). Such expenditure analyses revealed the extent to which substance abuse habits drained critical resources required for food and educational needs, in both cases reducing human capital assets.

One of the main violence-related consequences of heavy drinking in Guatemala was an increase in intra-family violence. Although conjugal conflict was sometimes perceived as a cause of alcoholism, as noted above, it was more commonly seen as an outcome (see Chapter 5). This was not only associated with verbal, physical and sexual violence against women, but also against children. A young boy from La Merced, Guatemala City, noted that because his father was a drunk, he hid from him when he came home from the *cantina*. Again, the health impacts of such abuse had implications for human capital of both the women and the children who were victims of such abuse.

In Guatemala, drugs were also linked with sexual violence, especially with rape, as noted above. An adult man from Nuevo Horizonte, Guatemala City, discussed how drug addicts were more prone to rape girls when they walked around the streets in 'provocative clothing,' because men under the influence of drugs 'were less able to prevent themselves.' This was repeated many times, often in conjunction with the phrase: 'they don't feel anything they're doing while taking drugs.' As mentioned earlier, death was also discussed as a frequent outcome of drug taking, resulting from illnesses, overdoses or from drug-linked violence. Fighting also occurred over drug sale territories among *maras* within communities, leading to gang deaths, especially in Guatemala City (see Chapter 7).

Similar patterns were reported in relation to alcohol abuse and sexual violence outside the home. In Concepción, Guatemala City, five mothers identified the main problem in the community as rapes of girls by drunks, linked with men urinating in the streets, and exposing themselves. Indeed, women and children tended to be afraid to go near bars, because of the threat of rape. For example, an 11-year-old girl in El Carmen, Santa Lucía Cotzumalguapa, said that she didn't like going near the *cantina* because of the drunks who 'touched her.' Also related to this were fights among men in and around the *cantinas*. In Villa Real, Esquipulas, in particular, street fighting linked with alcohol was especially widespread. Here, a major problem affecting the community was that drunken men went around shooting their guns indiscriminately. Another problem was 'crimes of passion' with men killing each other in bars or brothels. For example, one woman reported how her husband had been shot the previous year in the local brothel during a drunken fight over a prostitute.

In Colombia, a particularly grave outcome of the involvement of young people with drugs was that they usually left school once they became users. In all communities it was mainly teachers who linked drug consumption among students with the operation of gangs that lobbied schools. For example, a group of thirty teachers in 14 de Febrero, Bogotá, described how students who had joined gangs automatically got involved in drugs. Indeed, one of them complained that teachers were unable to cope with these types of problems: 'We are not trained to deal with drug addiction nor with gang culture; for this we need special training, and also the gangs are very frightening.' Therefore, while drugs affected all spectrums of society, it was among youth that the ramifications were most severe. Once addicted, it was said that they were rarely able to secure employment beyond drug dealing and robbery.

In both countries, another important consequence of drug consumption and, to a lesser extent, drunkenness, was the generation of insecurity and fear in communities. People were afraid of drug addicts in particular, both because they were perceived as the perpetrators of assaults and robbery, and also because drugs were illegal, and therefore feared, at least by older generations. In discussing *marihuaneros*, an adult woman from Girón, Colombia, pointed out: 'People can't go out in the evening . . . one can't send a girl or even a boy out alone because they'll get caught up with them.' Another woman from Concepción, Guatemala City, similarly pointed out that: 'The drug addicts are a problem because when they're drugged they will do anything, they are violent and dangerous.'

Fear was interpreted spatially through mapping, and, as noted in Chapter 3, was often equated with areas where drugs were sold or consumed. For example, the most commonly cited dangerous places in six maps drawn in 14 de Febrero, Bogotá, were the basketball courts where young people consumed drugs, the banks of the river where young women had reportedly been raped by drug addicts, a park which was dark and where drug addicts congregated, a street where crack was sold, and a house where drugs were sold (Figure 6.9 provides one such example). In Guatemala, the most commonly feared areas were river banks, cemeteries and bridges because this was where drug addicts congregated. In Limoncito, San Marcos, for instance, the local cemetery was avoided by everyone in the evenings because of the association with drug addicts, and in turn with *maras* and rapes. In this respect there were important contradictions in the provision of open spaces such as basketball courts and football pitches. The fact that these were the most common place for drugs to be consumed made them very unsafe for the rest of the community. Yet many youth argued that it was precisely the lack of organized sports clubs or youth clubs that generated the boredom and discontent which led them to take drugs in the first place. This reduced mobility due to fear also eroded social cohesion and a sense of union within the community (see Chapter 8). There was also a strong gender dimension to fear. While men of all ages were afraid of robbery and mugging, levels of fear among women of all ages was higher and related to fear of attack and especially

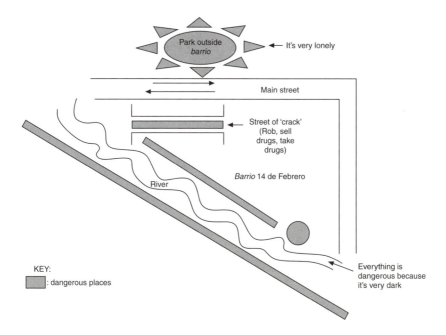

Figure 6.9 Map of dangerous places in 14 de Febrero, Bogotá, Colombia (drawn by six young women aged 12–22).

rape by drug addicts (a pattern widely noted elsewhere – see Koskela 1999; Pain 1991; Winton 2003, on Guatemala).

The ultimate irony of substance abuse-related violence, particularly related to alcohol, was that it pervaded the daily life of all community members to such an extent that for the majority it had become 'normalized.' The fact that so many community members themselves indulged in alcohol or drug consumption, which for the majority was a recreational pleasure, and for a smaller number as a means of dulling the pain of a bleak existence, made them unwilling to confront this as a problem pervading their communities. Yet communities themselves articulated an important distinction between alcohol and drug consumption where they felt powerless to confront the problem. In addition, a highly significant link to drug-related violence was the increasing threat that gangs and gang violence posed to local communities in both countries, as discussed in the following chapter.

7

ORGANIZED VIOLENCE AT THE COMMUNITY LEVEL

> The wars among the gangs cause many deaths; they carry out many massacres.
>
> (Young man from Medellín, Colombia)

While the nature of organized violence in Colombia and Guatemala has been given considerable attention at the national level (see Chapter 3), there remains little understanding at the local level as to how such group violence is organized. Yet this is essential for comprehending both the multiple realities of violence in communities, as well as the processes of the 'democratization' of violence, discussed in Chapter 1. Along with the 'normalization' of violence in both Colombia and Guatemala (Pecaut 1999; Torres-Rivas 1999), a plethora of local-level violence-focused organizations and groupings have emerged.

This chapter focuses on the nature of organized violence within communities in terms of the manner in which different groups function, the factors underlying the dramatic multiplication of organized violence, and the ramifications of group membership for its members. In the case of Colombia, in particular, it highlights both the diversity and range of organizations involved in perpetrating violence, while in the case of Guatemala it focuses on the dominance of the *maras* in perceptions of violence among community members. It also illustrates the ways in which group membership has tended to become intertwined with the creation of masculine spaces, where men adhere broadly to hegemonic masculine identities. Chapter 8, then, turns to the broader implications of organized violence, as well as other types of violence, for community members themselves. This is explored analytically in terms of their impact on social institutions and social capital.

The nature of organized violence in communities

The diversity of organized violence groups in Colombia

In Cali, Colombia, community members identified a total of thirty-seven armed groups involved in the perpetration of violence in the *barrio*. This clearly demonstrated the critical role organized violence groups played in the institutional landscape in El Arca, as in other communities. Figure 7.1, an institutional map drawn by four community leaders from Cali illustrate this dominance in terms of the size of the circles drawn, showing that the popular militias were the most influential groups, along with gangs, the 'guerrilla front' (the ELN), and a social cleansing group. It shows that around one-quarter of the organizations identified were related to the perpetration of violence. Figure 7.1 also highlights the complexity of relationships between the various organizations. For instance, the militias were linked with the guerrillas, while the social cleansing group was associated with the state security forces (see also Jimeno 2001; Chapter 1).

Considering the enormous diversity of organizations involved in the use of force, it was useful to analyze these in a systematic manner. Table 7.1 summarizes the main groups identified by community members, broadly categorized by the predominant type of violence in which they were involved, and listed in descending order by level and sophistication of organization.[1] It should be emphasized that the categorization by type of violence is purely heuristic and that any groups might have been simultaneously involved in other types of violence. Although specific meanings varied according to city, all the definitions were based on information from community members.

Given the armed conflict in Colombia, it was not surprising to find a wide range of armed actors involved primarily, although not exclusively, in

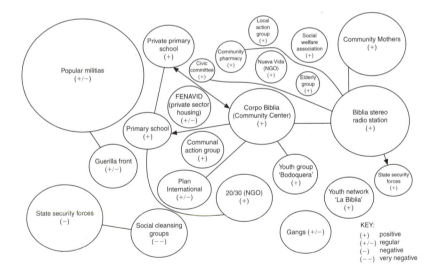

Figure 7.1 Institutional mapping of El Arca, Cali, Colombia (prepared by four community leaders).

Table 7.1 The nature of organized violence groups in Colombia

Dominant type of group violence	*Type of group and activities*
Mainly political	***Guerrilla/gatos***: Guerrilla organizations known locally at 'cats.' Includes the FARC (*Fuerzas Armadas Revolucionarias de Colombia –* Armed Revolutionary Forces of Colombia), a pro-Soviet guerrilla group, and the ELN (*Ejército de Liberación Nacional* – National Liberation Army), a pro-Cuban guerrilla group. Highly sophisticated organizations that control large areas of the national territory. ***Paramilitares/pájaros***: Paramilitary organizations known locally as 'birds.' Usually linked with the extreme Right. Includes a range of civil defense groups funded by landowners, emerald magnates, drug traffickers and thought to be linked with military. Ostensibly aim to protect civilians and eradicate the two main guerrilla organizations. Highly organized, male-dominated structure. ***Grupos de limpieza social***: Social cleansing groups. Also known as *paperos* in Cali, *rayas* in Bogotá, and *capuchos* in Medellín. Highly organized male professional killers. Target groups are delinquents, beggars, drug addicts, petty thieves, street children, and prostitutes. Usually have links with the police, the military or other state security forces (DAS). ***Milicias populares***: Popular militias that commit violence, mainly through control of delinquency. Usually informal protection/justice forces. Some linked with guerrillas. ***Sicarios***: Paid assassins, usually contracted to kill for revenge. Often linked with social cleansing. ***Encapuchados***: Literally, hooded people. Generic name for those who commit acts of crime and violence. May be *sicarios*, militia members or guerillas. There may be good and bad *encapuchados*.
Mainly economic	***Oficina***: Group of organized male drug dealers or business people that hires others to commit acts of crime or violence. ***Banda***: Group of male delinquents organized to commit crimes, primarily robbery and other acts of violence. A *banda* may offer its criminal services to others. May specialize in a particular good, such as jewellery. ***Apartamenteros***: Thieves who specialize in theft from apartments. ***Ladrones***: Generic name for thieves. May specialize in particular types. ***Atracadores***: Thieves armed with guns or knives. Usually mug people in the streets, although may specialize in particular types of attacks, such as attacks on taxis. Less organized than *ladrones*. ***Raponeros***: Petty thieves or 'snatchers.' Operate individually or in groups and mainly comprising male children or adolescents.
Mainly social	***Pandilla***: A gang with a closed internal organizational structure. Uses symbols and markings to denote gang identity. Comprises mainly men (usually in early 20s) involved in delinquency, territorial disputes and drug consumption. ***Gallada***: A gang of primarily male teenagers or adolescents that congregates in a *parche*. May commit crimes and acts of violence. May form into a *pandilla* if an identity and symbolism is developed. ***Combo***: A place or group that commits acts of violence. Less open and more organized than a *parche*. Male-dominated, but may have female members. ***Parche***: A place or group of teenagers that meet to converse, drink or consume drugs. May also involve acts of crime and violence. Usually based on flexible association and spontaneous congregation. Male-dominated, but may have female members.

Source: Descriptions of community members. Adapted from Moser and McIlwaine (2000).

politically-motivated violence in local communities. Both the ELN and FARC were identified in Cali, as well as in several other communities, most notably Yopal and Aguazul (see Chapter 4). Of all the groups, those involved in political conflict were the most organized. They also had the most far-reaching consequences for communities in terms of the severe nature of violence committed, such as murders and violent extortion (see Chernick 1998).

The militias also had links with the guerrillas. In Medellín, a 19-year-old man who was a member of the Los Muchachos gang recounted how the *barrio* previously had been dominated by a militia comprising 'reinserted ex-guerrilla members' (from the M-19). He discussed how they had a monopoly over extortion activities, and never consulted with the community. Together with various friends, he had run the militias out of the *barrio* by forming Los Muchachos whose primary aim, in his opinion, was protection. However, he also explained how the disappearance of the militias also led to the formation of a wide range of *combos* (see below), some comprising former militia members. This example illustrated the fluidity of different armed actors operating in communities, many of whom were simultaneously involved in multiple violent activities that were political, economic and social in nature.

Social cleansing groups functioned in similar ways to militias. Their primary aim was to kill delinquents, drug addicts and street children, as a way of controlling crime and violence. Sometimes, victims of delinquency hired social cleansing groups or *sicarios* to kill those who had attacked them. In communities, such as Jericó, Bogotá, people talked of the *carros fantásmas* arriving (cars with tinted glass) – a euphemism for the arrival of any illegal or informal violence-related group, but most often social cleansing groups. In Cali, a group of adult women noted how their fear of social cleansing groups made them constantly caution their children not to hang around street corners in case the social cleansers found them. Social cleansing groups were reportedly associated with the police, military and other state security forces such as the Administrative Department of Security (*Departamento Administrativo de Seguridad*, DAS) as well as self-defense groups and paramilitaries (see Salazar 1990, 1994, on *sicarios*).

When they could not define the exact group to which they belonged, community members also used the term '*encapuchado*' to refer to 'hooded men' that committed violent crimes. While many had links with the guerrillas, others were involved in petty crime and robbery. Several people made the distinction between *capuchos buenos* (good hoods) and *capuchos malos* (bad hoods); in Cali, an adult woman noted that: 'the good hoods have large guns and protect the community,' while, 'the bad hoods have small guns, are badly dressed and they're the ones that rob.'

The most organized robbers were the *bandas* and *oficinas* who functioned in a mafia-style manner, with the former involved in drug distribution as well as robbery. While the *bandas* sold their 'services,' the *oficinas* contracted others to do the work for them. There was a high level of conflict among the *bandas*, as a man from Medellín pointed out: 'The wars among the *bandas* cause many deaths, they are involved in many massacres over drugs and debts.' Again, some were more specialized, such as the *bandas de joyeros* (jewellery gangs), and the *apartamenteros* (involved in property theft). Also engaging in robbery were the *raponeros*, who were usually children or adolescents – often street children (*gamines*) – involved in *ad hoc* 'snatching' in the streets.

To a lesser extent, youth gangs were also involved in robbery, usually to fund their activities. More common was their involvement in delinquency, the exercise of power through fighting over territory, and the assertion of a specific youth identity. The most organized form of youth gang was the *pandilla* (a generic term used throughout Latin America). *Combos* and *galladas* were basically incipient forms of the more formal *pandillas*. Their identities, reflected through the use of symbols and territorial markers, such as clothing, tattoos, and graffiti, were not as developed as the *pandillas*. This sophistication was linked mainly with the age of the members, with membership of a *gallada* or *combo* often being a form of informal apprenticeship for forming a *pandilla* (although the process was not necessarily linear). The *pandillas* were more likely to have names than the *combos* and *galladas* (such as *El Tanque* and *Los Conejos* in Jericó and *El King* in Medellín). The *parches* (literally meaning 'patch') were the least organized, often based on spontaneous groupings within a given space. They comprised teenagers 'hanging out,' involved in vandalism and delinquency. This was one of the few groups to have female members, although they were usually the girlfriends of male *parche* members rather than participants in their own right (see Peréz and Mejía 1996; Rodgers, forthcoming).

Discussing the *combos* in Medellín, an adult man noted that: 'The *combos* kill among themselves and in this way, 40–50 young men have been killed in the last few years.' He went on to say that since the *combos* were involved in gunfights, people feared that they might get caught in the crossfire. Similarly, in Jericó, Bogotá, the *pandillas* and *bandas* were the focus of social cleansing. Indeed, there had been a number of *escarmientos públicos* (public punishments) conducted by social cleansing groups involving the killing of *pandilla* leaders. This highlighted the conflict among different types of organized violence groups, especially the militias and social cleansing groups (see Riaño-Alcalá 1991).

Spatial and temporal variations in the diversity of organized violence groups

In Colombia, the diversity of groups also varied by community and context. In general, the larger the urban area was, the more complex the nature of organized violence. For example, in Bogotá, the *parches*, *combos*, *galladas* and *pandillas* were widespread. In Jericó, thirteen *pandillas* were identified, while in 14 de Febrero, there were several *bandas*, *oficinas* and *pandillas*. However, Cali and Medellín, with histories of drug cartels, had the most developed organized violence culture. In El Arca, Cali, with its enormous diversity of armed actors, the most common were the *encapuchados*, guerrillas and social cleansing groups. Until 1999, Pórtico, Medellín, had been overrun with *parches*, *combos*, *bandas*, *pandillas* and militias, although the creation of the peace process had reduced their operation by this time (see Chapter 2). In 1999, the community was dominated by Los Muchachos, who had been transformed into a conflict mediator and protector of the community.

The frontier communities of Casanare were associated primarily with guerrilla and paramilitary activity. Both Colombia Chiquita, Aguazul, and Cachicamo, Yopal, were dominated by guerrilla and paramilitary groups, although there were also *bandas* in the latter. Organized violence groups were the least prevalent in the Santander communities. This may have been related to the fact that until recently, Bucaramanga had a fairly buoyant economy with youth able to secure employment in local industry. Nevertheless, people in these communities consistently complained of the *vagancia* among young men and women who hung around street corners, taking drugs and involved in robbery.

Most community members noted an increase in the proliferation in organized violence groups over time, not only in number but also in the diversity of types. In Jericó, Bogotá, for instance, a female community leader discussed the interrelation between the *pandillas*, who had grown dramatically since 1987, and the social cleansing groups who had tried to control them. Although the latter were having some effect, especially between 1995 and 1996, the *pandillas* were still growing by 1999. She noted: 'It's a vicious circle, they're wiped out yet they grow again.' However, at the time of the research in Medellín, people had noted a decline in the number of *combos* and militias due to the local conflict resolution efforts.

Organized violence in Colombia was thus highly complex and diverse. While some groups overlapped and multiplied, others operated in isolation. Levels of conflict among the groups were high with the youth gangs in particular being the object of control and derision from other groups, especially the militias and social cleansers. While the politically organized groups such as the guerrillas and paramilitaries were involved in the most serious types of violence and crime, reflecting this sophistication, even the loosely organized groups such as the *parches* were involved in murders and rapes (see Aboutanos 1997, on Cali). In terms of the people most likely to be involved in organized violence groups, young men predominated, with the result that they were the most likely not only to perpetrate, but also to be victims of violence (see Restrepo 1997, on Cali).

The dominance and functioning of organized violence groups in Guatemala

In La Merced, Guatemala City, one young woman pointed out that: 'The community is full of *maras*. All the youth are integrated into the *maras* simply for solidarity.' Another man from Limoncito, San Marcos, said: 'The *maras* and delinquents have ruined the community; they're round every corner waiting to rob you.' While there was less diversity of organized violence in terms of the number of distinct groups in Guatemala, they still dominated people's lives in communities, especially in terms of the three main types – the *maras*, robbers and delinquents. This is reflected in the listings of different types of violence in that these three together constituted the most important perpetrators of violence, representing over half of the violence identified in the nine communities – with each community having at least four or five *maras* (see Appendix 11). In addition, much of the rape outside the home, constituting 8 percent of all violence, was attributed to gangs.

Figure 7.2 from La Merced, Guatemala City, shows the complicated links between delinquency, robbery and *mara* activity. As was the case in Colombia, the activities of different organized violence groups overlapped such that it was often difficult to distinguish between them, particularly as the term '*maras*' had increasingly become a catch-all term for male street violence. Listings of general problems and types of violence demonstrated numerous interchangeable categories within which individuals or groups

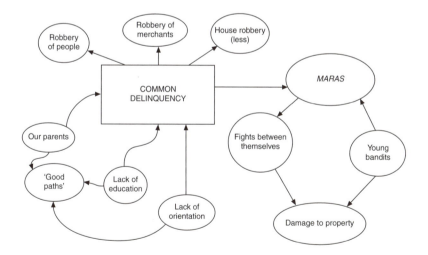

Figure 7.2 Causal flow diagram of linkages between delinquency and *maras* in La Merced, Guatemala City (identified by Deputy Chief of local police station).

were often perceived as synonymous, or very closely interrelated (see Appendix 12).

However, distinctions could be made according to the main type of violence perpetrated and whether they constituted a social institution. Thus, thieves and delinquents could be categorized together on grounds that both perpetrated economic violence and were not members of a specific social institution. However, they were still viewed as an important element of organized violence by community members. As an adult woman from Nuevo Horizonte, Guatemala City, noted in relation to thieves: 'Now they join together in groups and they rob the young people in the schools and the night college and they hit them.' Delinquents were usually identified as boys and young men who had dropped out of school and hung around on street corners. Out of boredom, forced idleness and frequent involvement in the consumption of drugs (such as marijuana), they were often involved in petty crimes such as stealing handbags. Thieves, in contrast, were more likely to be older men and far more violent. An elderly woman in Villa Real, Esquipulas, noted: 'They [robbers] bother us a lot in the community. They steal everything, even shoes.' In Nuevo Horizonte, Guatemala City, some thieves were also reported carrying machetes when stealing, especially while robbing from houses.

Maras, on the other hand, formed a distinct category on two counts. First, although they were involved in robbery and assault, they engaged primarily in various types of social violence. Figure 7.3, drawn by a group of young people from Gucumatz, Santa Cruz del Quiché, highlights the range of their activities. In another community in Huehuetenango, a mother and her daughter stated: 'There is vengeance between *maras*, they fight between themselves. If one does something against the *maras* they take revenge.' As a group of 17–22-year-old young men in La Merced, Guatemala City, described, it could be the result of differences of opinion over types of music (rap or rock), rivalry over women or levels of alcohol drunk (see Figure 7.3). Above all, they were concerned with the ownership, control and defense of 'turf,' the physical space within communities. Such intra-gang warfare conflicts were an integral component of gang life, with groups often forming and reforming alliances between themselves. In addition, *maras* were consistently accused of rape. As a young woman from El Carmen, Santa Lucía Cotzumalguapa, pointed out: 'The *maras* grab young girls and rape them...the girls are then left pregnant and single mothers' (see Figure 7.4 and Figure 7.5 on pp. 147 and 149).

The second main difference was that *maras* were usually fairly cohesive social units from the perspective of the members themselves, who actively cultivated a common identity. This was reflected in their names, clothing and tattoos. In all communities the two most common names were the MS (Mara Salvatrucha) and the M18 or La 18 (both of which derived from *latino* gangs in Los Angeles) with a range of other names such as the

- Drink alcohol
- Look for problems with other *maras* – to see who wins, which is the better *mara*
- Fight with other *maras* for girlfriends or for vengeance
- Paint walls – to let people know who they are, mark their territory and insult other *maras*
- Consume drugs – when they have money (including paint thinner, glue, cocaine and marijuana)
- Rob when necessary
- Drug trafficking
- Attend dances where they start fights with other gangs

Figure 7.3 Activities of *maras* in Gucumatz, Santa Cruz de Quiché, Guatemala (identified by a mixed group of nine young people aged 14–20).

White Fence, Rockers, Calambres, Escorpiones and Los Duendes.[2] While some were common names inspired by gangs elsewhere, others were context-specific, such as the Asovaq or AVQ (*Asociación de Vagos Quichelenses* – Association of Lazy Guys from Quiché) from the community in Santa Cruz del Quiché. In terms of their clothing, the most common signifiers were baggy jeans, use of bandanas and sometimes wearing special color combinations. Thus in La Merced, Guatemala City, three out of four gangs wore red and white clothing. Many people recognized the external influences of *mara* identity. The eldest son of an elderly couple, who formed a focus group in Sacuma, Huehuetenango, stated: 'The *maras* are not from here, they come from over there, they are Salvadorian by their clothing' (see also AVANCSO 1996; Winton 2003).

Although primarily a male social institution, a small number of female *maras* also existed. For example, a group of indigenous people from Gucumatz, Santa Cruz del Quiché, comprising a young man and two young women, described the two groups of indigenous girl *maras* in their community as adolescents who had abandoned their *traje* (traditional clothing) for large trousers. Some were the girlfriends of members of male *maras*, and many had become pregnant. Of the two groups identified, Las Chicas Big (literally the Big Girls), with more than twenty members, were the girlfriends of members of the male gang, Los Calambres, while the other, Las Chicas (the Girls) was a female gang in its own right.[3]

Spatial and temporal variations in the dominance of organized violence groups

Although thieves and delinquents were found throughout the Guatemalan communities there were significant differences in the levels of violence they committed, with these tending to be more serious in Guatemala City than in the smaller towns in the departments. People generally felt that robbery had always existed, but that over time it had increased in public areas with attacks on people and on trucks, theft from street markets, and in some areas kidnapping for financial extortion. There were also variations according to community. While delinquency and robbery were thought to have increased in Santa Cruz del Quiché and Huehuetenango, in Esquipulas and La Merced, Guatemala City, it was reported to have declined. In La Merced, a 35-year-old women reported how robbery had decreased between 1996 and 1999: 'Before, the thieves weren't afraid of the police, the army had to come... now with the new police, I feel more secure and there is less robbery.' The role of the new police force was similarly cited as the main reason for the decline in Esquipulas (see Chapter 4).

The nature of *mara* activity also varied geographically. The *maras* in Guatemala City were reported to be much more organized than those in the departments, enforcing stricter norms concerning gang-specific clothing and tattoos. They also committed more serious violence, and were involved in much larger-scale territorial disputes. *Maras* in San Marcos, Santa Cruz del Quiché and Esquipulas, while using the same names as the larger gangs in the City, were generally (but not exclusively) perceived as less threatening, and more commonly were involved in activities such as throwing stones, painting graffiti on walls, and robbery. Despite some variations, it was felt that the *maras* had increased dramatically, especially since the signing of the Peace Accords. In Sacuma, Huehuetenango, an area of the country that had been seriously affected by the civil war, an adult woman from a group of six noted with reference to the *maras*: 'instead of signing peace, they signed violence,' continuing to say: 'now it is intolerable' (see below).[4]

Mara activity was also interpreted differently according to with whom they were being discussed. At one end of the spectrum, many young people considered *maras* to be informal groups that provided people with a sense of identity and mutual support (see below). At the other end, older people in particular described the *maras* as dangerous robbers, drug addicts and killers. Thus an elderly man from Concepción, Guatemala City, said of the *maras*: 'They're all thieves who enjoy frightening people, they also kill.'

Therefore, while organized violence groups lacked the diversity of Colombia, violence in communities was linked in one way or another with delinquents, thieves, and especially the *maras* whose identity was based on male-dominated inter-gang warfare (Winton 2003). Indeed, there was widespread public panic about the upsurge of youth gangs, which, while certainly a reality, was not as severe as the media sensationalization maintained (De Orrellana 1997; Smutt and Miranda 1998, on El Salvador). The overlaps between the groups were also important, with boundaries between them often viewed as fluid.

The causes of the emergence of organized violence groups

Despite the huge variations in the nature of organized violence groups both within and between countries, it is possible to identify a number of factors underlying the emergence and proliferation of such groups shared by Colombia and Guatemala alike. At the same time, it is important to emphasize the difficulty of separating causes and effects, as most were intricately connected.[5]

Figure 7.4, drawn by three primary school teachers from Sacuma, Huehuetenango, Guatemala, shows that one of the most commonly cited reasons for people joining gangs were family problems. Reinforcing this, a 16-year-old young woman from La Merced, Guatemala City, said that although joining a *mara* was a part of growing up, family problems were usually to blame: 'Those who actually join *maras* are more likely to be young boys who have suffered at home, and been badly treated by their fathers.' Similarly, a group of four teachers from Cali, Colombia, identified intra-family violence and lack of affection as the main reasons for joining *pandillas*, while an adult woman from Jericó, Bogotá, pointed out that: 'For young people who are mistreated in the home, they go into the street and do the same thing there as part of a *pandilla*.'

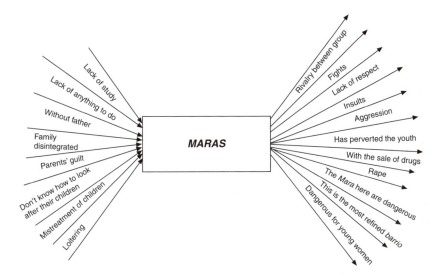

Figure 7.4 Causal flow diagram of *maras* in Sacuma, Huehuetenango, Guatemala (drawn by three primary school teachers aged 20–40).

Throughout all the communities parental neglect or lack of guidance was repeatedly identified as a major factor in becoming involved in organized violence. A 30-year-old *ladino* woman in La Merced, Guatemala City, identified the roots of parental irresponsibility in alcohol abuse on the part of mothers and fathers, as well as mothers going out to work and leaving their children at home alone. Without this parental care, children became afraid, were often undernourished, and as a result, many dropped out of school. Ultimately, this led them to spend their days hanging around street corners. She argued that it usually wasn't long until they got involved in organized violence in some form. In Jericó, Bogotá, a couple in their forties reiterated the detrimental effect of working parents: 'The problem of *pandillas* is because the parents work and abandon the children; you see cases of *pandilleros* [pandilla members] at 9 years of age ... no wonder the street is converted into an alternative attraction for young people.' Similarly, an elderly man in Limoncito, San Marcos, described how his 14-year-old grandson was a member of a *mara* because of the bad example set by his parents. His father smoked marijuana, his mother was an alcoholic, and the young boy himself was also apparently addicted to marijuana. In blaming parents, a teacher from Cali, Colombia, pointed out: 'It's [joining *pandillas*] related to a lack of culture on the part of parents in terms of educating their children properly ... many are rude and uneducated and so their children have no alternative.'

In response to this combination of family-related factors, gangs and delinquency provided an alternative space and refuge for young people. In 14 de Febrero, Bogotá, a 34-year-old woman pointed out that: 'Problems inside the family cause drug consumption among children and youth and, linked with this, turns them toward the *parches* as they search for the tranquillity that they don't have in the home.' In similar vein, a young woman from a group of four in San Jorge, Chinautla, noted that: 'Children grow up without love so they stay in the streets and look for love from the *maras*; what their families don't give them, the *maras* do.' With the family losing its support and socialization function, young people searched and found it in organized violence groups instead, a phenomenon widely supported by other gang studies (AVANCSO 1996, on Guatemala; Smutt and Miranda 1998, on El Salvador; also Kramer 2000, on the U.S.A.).

There were also gender differences in joining gangs. Although as noted above, most gangs were male-dominated, a young woman from La Merced, Guatemala City, discussed how the motivations for joining gangs differed between women and men. Figure 7.5 shows the importance of intra-family violence, especially violence perpetrated by fathers. When girls were mistreated by their fathers, their friends encouraged them to leave home and join a *mara*: 'It's better to be with the *mara* than with the family,' she concluded.[6] The major gender difference was that girls, as against boys, often joined a gang to find a boyfriend. However, once they

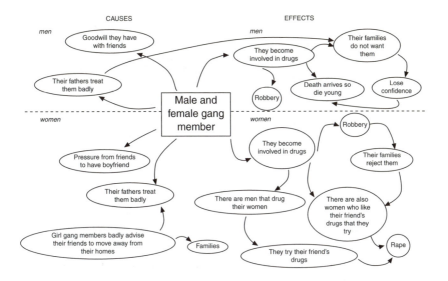

Figure 7.5 Causal flow diagram of being a male and female gang member in La Merced, Guatemala City (drawn by one girl aged 16).

had found a partner, such young men would often 'take advantage of them.' This was reiterated by a group of five young women in Girón, Colombia, who also reported how 'wild girls' (*muchachas vagas*) involved in male-dominated gangs, were often sexually abused once they joined. Indeed, many of the organizing principles of gang membership were based on machismo, power and the subjugation of women.[7]

Another significant issue highlighted in Figure 7.5 was the important influence of peer pressure in young people's decision to become involved in organized violence. In both countries older generations referred to this as 'bad friendships' (*malas amistades*). As the young woman from La Merced identified in her diagram, men joined gangs because of the 'good-will that they have with friends' to whom they would be introduced in the gang. In Pórtico, Medellín, an adult woman reported how she was afraid of her sons being recruited by friends because of their links with the *pandillas* and militias.

Closely linked with both family issues and peer pressure was the perva-sive sense of exclusion experienced by young people in communities. Figure 7.6, drawn by a group of six young men from Girón in Colombia, identified the fact that 'we're not recognized or taken into account' as a major issue in encouraging young people to get involved in drugs, *vagancia* and delinquency. They associated their exclusion with lack of educational and recreational opportunities, which ultimately was linked with their lack

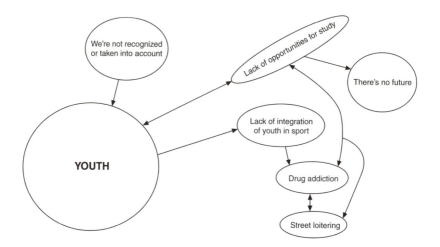

Figure 7.6 Problems faced by young people in Rosario, Girón, Colombia (identified by a group of six young men age 14–18).

of a future. A group of five 14- to 17-year-old girls from the same community in Girón identified exclusion, together with inter-generational conflict as their main problem with 'people talking badly of young people,' especially young unmarried women who did not work. They discussed how a group of elderly women in the *barrio* called them *muchachas vagas* implying that they took drugs and hung around with men. Although they themselves were not involved in organized violence, they reported that many young women and men got involved because people thought so badly of them anyway.

Organized violence also gave people a means of livelihood (see Chapter 4). For those with few employment opportunities, particularly the young, membership provided an income. In Girón, Colombia, a 46-year-old woman pointed out that people became delinquents: 'Because they have nothing to do, because there's no work, and because they have no marked role in society.' Some also suggested that young people found it easier to rob than to work. A 64-year-old man from La Merced, Guatemala City, whose 17-year-old son was a *mara* member, said of the *maras*: 'They don't work because they don't like it. They need money to buy drugs. They don't want to work.' Some organizations had more sophisticated career structures than others; neighborhood gangs such as the *maras*, *pandillas* and *combos*, provided mainly casual earnings while the guerrilla and para-military organizations offered a regular income and career prospects (Suárez 2000, on Colombia).[8] However, a group of five young men from Medellín, Colombia, all members of a *combo*, recounted their involvement in organized violence began when they got bored with school and an older guy, who told them that high school was really bad, taught them how to rob. They then joined a *parche*. At this time, they stole watches, shoes, and bicycles inside and outside the *barrio* (but not in their own block), for both a hobby and to support themselves. They then formed a *combo* and after the murder of many of their co-members, they began robbing goods vehicles in order to fund their war with the militias: 'we robbed everything that gave more money.' More recently, some in the *combo* began to rob cars (outside the *barrio*). This highlighted how robbery evolved as the organization became more sophisticated and as their needs changed. Robbery also became an issue of power for some. For instance, the same *combo* members, whose idol was Che Guevara, felt robbing the rich could be justified. A group of teachers from 14 de Febero, Bogotá, reiterated this when discussing *pandillas*, when one of them stated: 'Unemployment causes resentment with those who have and because of that they rob.' In a similar vein, a 40-year-old indigenous woman from Santa Lucía Cotzumalguapa, Guatemala, commented that the *maras*: 'Kill those who have money.'[9]

Lack of education was also identified as a reason for people joining organized violence groups (see also Chapter 4). Figure 7.7 from Pórtico, Medellín, which highlights many of the factors raised so far, stressed lack of schools and education as underlying causal factors. Linked to this, *combo* members viewed as important a dislike of studying. Indeed, the

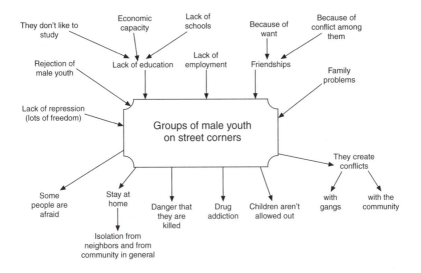

Figure 7.7 Causal flow diagram of groups of male youth on street corners in Pórtico, Medellín, Colombia (prepared by a mixed group of eight adults aged over 40).

fact that many young people in Latin America have few employment opportunities, together with generally poor quality education, means that they often suffer high levels of economic exclusion, which is thought to place them at heightened social risk (FLACSO n.d.).[10]

In some cases, involvement in organized violence groups was a means for young people to protect themselves at school. In Santa Cruz del Quiché, Guatemala, three young indigenous women described how children as young as 10 or 12 years joined the *maras* when they had problems with school companions. They were then able to call on older members to defend them.[11] This in turn, was linked with the search for power and respect. For example, a female community leader in Jericó, Bogotá, in discussing the reasons for joining a *pandilla*, stated 'often it is not economic nor is it hunger, it's the desire for leadership, the force of power.'

Finally, it is important to note that once people were members of organized violence groups, it was often difficult to leave. However, this depended on the nature of the group. Membership in certain types of *maras* and *parches*, for instance, were viewed as rites of passage by young people, and especially men. An elderly woman from La Merced, Guatemala City, recounted how each of her three sons had been a member of the *maras* as an automatic stage of growing up, but as each in turn had found a girlfriend and settled down with a regular job and children, they had systematically left the *maras* (see Moser and Winton 2002).[12] Other groups were not so easy to leave. These included certain types of *maras* in Guatemala, as well as some of the *combos* and militias, not to mention the guerrilla and paramilitary groups in Colombia. In El Arca, Cali, a young man noted of the *combos*: 'So many young people have been murdered, few get out alive.' A 14-year-old schoolboy from La Merced, Guatemala City, stated that there were only two ways of safely leaving the *maras*, either by marrying or by leaving the community.

It should be reiterated that the factors underlying the emergence and proliferation of organized violence groups were intricately interrelated, and that each community and each group were also influenced by context-specific issues. At the same time it is important to emphasize that organized violence groups were primarily male domains. Although many of the causes outlined affected women as well as men, the need to assert or adhere to notions of hegemonic masculinity appeared to encourage men to join these groups rather than women (with exceptions – see Figure 7.5). Indeed, as mentioned in Chapter 5, it was often suggested that young women, rather than turning to gangs, would often enter prostitution if, for example, they had family problems, or needed to earn a living. A community leader from Jericó, Bogotá, in Colombia, talking about how the young had lost their way, noted: 'The young men go off to the *pandillas*; for the young women, it's prostitution.'

The consequences of membership in an organized violence group

A recurrent consequence of organized violence group membership voiced by members of groups and community members alike was the exclusion it engendered in the young people themselves. In La Merced, Guatemala City, the 17-year-old women who drew Figure 7.5 showed how both women and men experienced rejection from their families, as well as a loss of confidence as a result. Similarly, a member of the Los Muchachos gang in Medellín, Colombia, said that he felt alienated by the community because people ran away when he passed by their houses. The association between gangs and drug abuse compounded this (see Figures 7.5 and 7.7). For instance, a young man from Pórtico, Medellín, bemoaned the fact that: 'just by being with Los Muchachos, people call you a *marijuanero* [user of marijuana].' Therefore, while involvement in an organized violence group provided young people with a common cultural identity, and a sense of belonging in situations of exclusion, ironically at the same time this further contributed to their exclusion (see Winton 2003; also Chapter 8).[13]

Equally serious was the widespread revenge fighting between gangs using arms, which sometimes resulted in killings (see earlier). A community leader from Jericó, Bogotá, for example, noted that people joined *pandillas* in order to learn how to kill, which they did through their gang fights. The *combo* members from Pórtico, Medellín, also reported widespread murders among their ranks mainly as a result of fights with the militias and other *combos*, with one noting: 'Many young people from here were killed; three were killed behind the school.' In El Arca, Cali, a community leader said that the *galladas* and *combos*: 'had killed three or four young men to steal their shoes.' This was also reflected in drawings from children, especially in Colombia, which indicated a high awareness and fear of firearms, with some children even writing details about the guns such as 'this is a 38.' Figure 7.8 highlights how all three groups identified were drawn with guns. Although murder among warring *maras* in Guatemala was less common than in Colombia, it was still an issue. An elderly man from San Jorge, Chinautla, for instance, reported that: 'The *maras* kill among themselves; that's why they are so dangerous.'

The relatively high incidence of murder using firearms was linked with the high circulation of weapons throughout Latin America, particularly in the wake of widespread political conflict. In Colombia, the types of weapons used by violent groups had reportedly become more serious over time. According to a focus group of young men in El Arca, Cali, while bottles, stones and machetes were predominant in the early 1980s, this changed to knives and guns by the early 1990s, and firearms alone by 1999. *Maras* in Central America also reportedly have access to a range of weapons, including high calibre military weapons such as M-16s, AK-47s

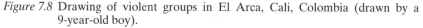

Figure 7.8 Drawing of violent groups in El Arca, Cali, Colombia (drawn by a 9-year-old boy).

Note
ELN, guerrilla; *ladrones*, thieves; *pandillas*, gangs.

and RPG-2 rocket launchers (Choloros *et al.* 1997). In this environment, it was perhaps not surprising that death was a likely outcome of involvement in an organized violence group in both countries. For example, in the neighborhoods of Cali, the homicide rate in 1995 stood at a staggering 800 per 100,000 inhabitants, with the majority of victims young men under the age of 24 (Restrepo 1997: 65). Similarly, the most common cause of death among 15–24-year-old Guatemalans in 1997 (30.5 percent) was firearms (Poitevín *et al.* 2000).

It is also important to highlight the positive role played by membership of many organized violence groups, especially for young men. In Jericó, Bogotá, for instance, a group of Community Mothers viewed the *parches* in a favorable light, saying they were not armed, not involved in drug consumption, and that they gave young people a focus to their lives. Similarly, a young man from Esquipulas, Guatemala, pointed out that: 'some *maras* provide a guide for young people that they don't have in the family.' Furthermore, the protection function was significant in making some people more lenient in their attitudes toward such groups. Such positive benefits were felt particularly by members themselves, especially for the young men who predominated in these groups; organized violence groups provided them with a sense of identity and belonging, an income, and protection in the face of widespread exclusion. The fact that some people exercised their agency in choosing to become involved in violent organizations as a means of coping with their problems must be viewed in the context of the limited opportunities open to them, in other words, the conditions which led to the proliferation of such groups in the first place.

As more and more people become involved in organized violence and use violence as the primary way of dealing with the problems in their lives, so the phenomenon has become increasingly democratized in both countries. Yet it is important to conclude by noting that the vast majority of people in the communities were not involved in organized violence, and indeed, perceived such groups to be the source of many societal ills. As such, they were seen to have severe deleterious effects on communities. The following chapter explores this issue from the perspective of community members themselves, utilizing the concept of social capital to facilitate this analysis.

8

VIOLENCE, SOCIAL INSTITUTIONS AND SOCIAL CAPITAL IN COMMUNITIES

> I feel abandoned. No-one helps you anymore and I can't go
> out much because of the *maras*.
> > (Adult woman from La Merced, Guatemala City)

While Chapters 4 to 7 foregrounded the perceptions of violence among local Colombian and Guatemalan community members, this penultimate chapter comes full circle by re-introducing an analytical perspective, in this case of the relationship between violence, trust and social institutions. Violence and fear not only affect the ability of individuals and households to function, they also influence the nature of social relations within communities themselves. To analyze the impact of violence on social institutions, this chapter utilizes the concept of social capital. From the extensive literature on social capital, it introduces two interrelated categories that are particularly relevant for the analysis of violence. First, the distinction between structural and cognitive social capital, and second, between productive and perverse social capital.

The chapter highlights how violence is intricately interrelated with social capital in local communities. Violence erodes cognitive social capital in terms of undermining prevailing levels of trust, while also generating widespread fear. It also transforms the nature of structural social capital, changing the function of productive social institutions, as well as creating or strengthening perverse organizations. But social capital can also be reconstituted to address the problem of violence. Perceptions of trusted social institutions in Colombia, for instance, show that local community-based women's organizations may have the potential for reconstituting productive social capital in communities. In drawing together many of the issues identified in previous chapters, this chapter also provides a concluding summary of key themes relating to the profound impacts of the multiple and intersecting types of violence on the lives of people in Colombian and Guatemalan urban communities, before turning to the more practical solutions discussed in Chapter 9.

Conceptualizing violence and social capital

Although people in local communities did not discuss social capital as an issue in itself, they frequently made reference to 'social fabric' (*tejido social*), 'social union' (*unión social*) or 'social unity' (*unidad social*), relating these concepts to the nature of violence. Furthermore, through the use of institutional mapping tools, they discussed and assessed the social institutions in their communities. On the basis of this information, the concept of social capital is introduced as an analytical construct for better understanding the impact of violence on social relations in local poor urban communities. A set of interrelated categories is identified which aims to contribute to ongoing academic debates on social capital.[1]

While the literature on social capital is vast and burgeoning (see Mohan and Mohan 2002; Portes and Landolt 2000), rather than detailing the origins and various conceptualizations,[2] this chapter focuses on the relationship between social capital and violence. As noted in Chapter 1, the definition of social capital used in the current study refers to the norms, obligations and reciprocity incorporated in the institutional arrangements of communities, while acknowledging that it is one of the most intangible forms of capital (Bebbington 1999; Moser 1998). Thus, social capital is identified as generating and providing benefits through the membership of social networks or organizations (Portes 1998).

Widespread criticisms of social capital exist. These relate not only to whether it actually constitutes 'capital,' but also how the concept has come to serve neoliberal ideologies of the 'Washington consensus' (Fine 1999, 2001). Of particular interest in this context is the critique that identifies social capital as having exclusionary and detrimental effects, as much as beneficial outcomes (Putzel 1997). Some people have greater access to social capital than others, and can actively exclude people from its benefits (Harriss and De Renzio 1997; Portes 1998). This has most commonly been discussed empirically in relation to ethnicity, with the finding that some ethnic groups generate social capital for exclusive use among their own people (see Kyle 1999). The potential for conflict through the associated exclusion has been most marked in relation to 'linking social capital,' which refers to vertical ties among people of different social standing (World Bank 2000: 128).[3]

Preliminary research on the relationships between violence and social capital has also identified negative dimensions. To date, most studies have focused on the United States (see Kawachi *et al.* 1999), or have used quantitative measures of social capital and violence (through for example, victimization surveys) (ibid.; Lederman *et al.* 1999). One of the few qualitative studies that examines the relationship between social capital and violent political conflict in Cambodia, Rwanda, Guatemala and Somalia (Colletta and Cullen 2000), argues that violent conflict can undermine as well as reconstitute social capital. This suggests that social capital can mitigate conflict as well as generate further social fragmentation and violence (see also Auyero 2000, on Argentina; Moser and Holland 1998, on Jamaica). Finally, of particular relevance in the current context, is recent research on gangs, mafia organizations and drug cartels that identifies how such institutions generate 'perverse' social capital (Rubio 1997a).

Drawing on this nascent work, the current study identifies a set of inter-related categories for analyzing the relationships between social capital and violence. Critical in this are the distinctions between productive and perverse social capital, structural and cognitive social capital, and vertical and horizontal social capital. The productive and perverse categorization draws on Rubio's (1997a) research. He defines 'productive social capital' as the social relations that may generate institutional change and favor economic growth. In contrast, 'perverse social capital' refers to the networks and reward systems that encourage rent-seeking behavior and criminal activity. Rubio further suggests that criminal activities may depend on sophisticated economic and social structures that provide viable alternatives to legitimate activities, particularly for young people. In contextualizing Rubio's work, this study defines productive social capital as social relations that generate favorable outcomes, especially for those belonging to an organization and for the community at large. Perverse social capital denotes social relations that may have positive benefits for those involved in organizations, but negative outcomes for wider communities. Perverse social capital is also premised on the use of force, as well as illegal, criminal activities.

A second interrelated categorization, first developed by Uphoff (1997, 2000), distinguishes between structural and cognitive social capital. Structural social capital deals with the arena of roles and denotes the interpersonal relationships operating within the realm of formal or informal organizations or networks. Cognitive social capital, in contrast, concentrates on ideas and attitudes, denoting instrumental ideas (such as routines) as well as normative ideas, revolving around values, norms and beliefs. Structural and cognitive are closely interlinked and can be identified along a continuum of levels from societal, local to individual (Krishna and Uphoff 1999).

The final interrelated categorization concerns the differentiation between horizontal and vertical or hierarchical organizations (Putnam 1993; see also World Bank 2000). Horizontal social capital refers primarily to relations between close friends and neighbors within communities (as in the World Bank's, 2000, bonding social capital) or to community-based organizations operating from within the community itself. Vertical or hierarchical social capital refers to relations between community members and people outside the *barrio* (as in the World Bank's, 2000, linking social capital) or to external organizations operating within the community.

In reality, the operationalization of such conceptual distinctions is diffi-cult since it requires identifying effectively intangible attributes of social relations. This has led many to rely on what Bebbington (1999: 2036) refers to as surrogate indicators. For analysis purposes, this study also adopts such 'surrogate indicators;' thus, structural social capital refers to social organizations and networks of trust and cohesion, while cognitive social capital denotes invisible, informal elements of trust, altruism and solidarity experienced among individuals. Horizontal organizations are usually membership based while hierarchical institutions are mainly service providers. As outlined below, there were important interrelations between these categorizations.

Cognitive social capital and violence in communities

In both Colombian and Guatemalan communities a common concern was the nature of trust and feelings of unity and solidarity, a key dimension of cognitive social capital. Community listings identified lack of trust, mani-fested in complaints about the 'lack of union' (*falta de unión*), and 'lack of social fabric' (*falta de tejido social*). These constituted 14 percent of total problems in Colombia and 10 percent in Guatemala (see Chapter 3). Com-ments by community members provided further reflections. In Esquipulas, Guatemala, an adult man noted that: 'we live like cats and dogs,' while an elderly woman in San Marcos, Guatemala, stated: 'no-one gets involved in the lives of others.' In Bucaramanga, Colombia, an adult woman bemoaned a similar situation: 'no-one trusts their neighbors... we are like strangers.'

As noted in previous chapters, lack of cognitive social capital was closely linked to the fear that dominated all the communities in both coun-tries. The roots of fear lay in the widespread prevalence of violence. As highlighted by three young men from Bucaramanga, Colombia, fear was often the outcome of the simultaneous experience of various types of viol-ence (see Figure 3.8 on p. 64). They identified how intra-family violence was linked to insecurity which in turn was linked to gang activity, drug taking, robbery, killing and delinquency. The outcomes were identified as 'social mistrust,' 'lack of unity' and 'fear,' as well as the 'lack of social insti-tutions,' referring to structural social capital discussed below (see also Jimeno 2001, on Colombia; ODHAG 1999, on Guatemala).

Although the construction of fear was influenced by the interrelation of all types of violence, political conflict had particularly severe ramifications. In Colombia, this was especially marked in Aguazul and Yopal where it was associated with high levels of guerrilla and paramilitary activity (see Chapter 4). Both communities were terrorized by the guerrillas and the paramili-taries who threatened to kill people who spoke with the 'enemy.' Figure 8.1, prepared by four adults from Aguazul, illustrates the deep-seated effects of

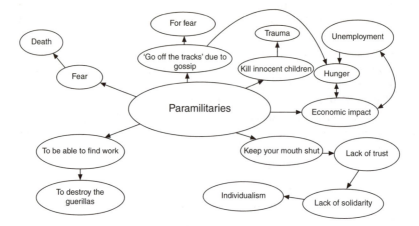

Figure 8.1 Causal flow diagram of the effects of paramilitary groups on Colombia Chiquita, Aguazul, Colombia (prepared by a mixed group of four adults).

paramilitary activity on social capital. Living under constant threat, they reiterated the importance of remaining silent, since even the suspicion of talking to the guerrillas could lead to assassination by the paramilitaries. Ultimately, this resulted in lack of trust, erosion of solidarity and a shift toward individualism. Summarizing this sentiment a man from the community said:

> The war between the paramilitaries and guerrillas is killing everyone because of the distrust among the people who constantly accuse each other – with the extortion everyone has to give money and, besides that, one has to remain silent. This generates mistrust among everyone. There is lots of death and confusion.

In the Guatemalan communities the legacy of political violence had similarly severe effects. As mentioned in Chapter 2, armed conflict had practically decimated trust especially in communities with predominant indigenous populations. An indigenous man from Gucumatz, Santa Cruz del Quiché, remembered how in the past a gathering of two or more people was regarded as subversive and could lead to murder by the security forces, recounting that they couldn't even hold a funeral without fear of being killed. The erosion of cognitive social capital had left a legacy of widespread social fragmentation, and people still found it difficult to trust each other. As a woman from San Marcos complained: 'Everyone lives their own lives.'

160

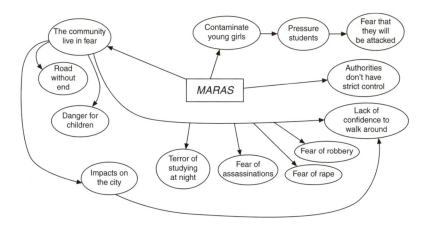

Figure 8.2 Diagram of the effects of *maras* in Sacuma, Huehuetenango, Guatemala (identified by three primary school teachers aged 20–35).

Although in the Mayan-dominated communities some people still discussed their fear of political violence, in most communities this had been replaced by fear of delinquency, robbery and the *maras*, as discussed in Chapter 7. Figure 8.2, drawn by a group of primary school teachers in Sacuma, Huehuetenango, shows the different dimensions of fear including being afraid of attack, robbery, rape, assassination and of studying at night. This would ultimately lead to a 'road without end.' As highlighted in Figure 8.2, gender and age, as well as ethnicity, influenced perceptions of fear. Women and young people were particularly afraid of *maras*, primarily linked to their perpetration of rape. In addition, indigenous women reported that the continuing rampant levels of rape were a legacy of the past use of rape as a military tool (see Chapter 4; Lira 1998). In this context, among certain organized violence groups such as the *maras*, rape had become an integral, normalized element in the use of force.

Fear generated by economic and social violence was also important in Colombia, particularly in relation to gang warfare, organized delinquency and drug users. A woman from 14 de Febrero, Bogotá, noted that 'before' people were more united and: 'one didn't see young people smoking [marijuana] because there was more communication.' Now, there was no collaboration, people no longer respected one another, and they were afraid to confront others about the problems of the *barrio*. In Jericó, Bogotá, a group of 10-year-olds discussed the *pandillas*, saying that they were destroying the *barrio*, the family, young people and even: 'all of Colombia ... and the planet.' In the context of widespread fighting between gangs and militias, an adult woman in Medellín pointed out: 'A serious problem is the lack of union in the community, with the result that there's not enough communication.'

Fear in the private sphere of the home generated by intra-family violence was also extremely important, with the consequent level of trust among family members often minimal or non-existent (see Chapter 5). Such fear and mistrust was frequently gender-based, given that women and girls were most likely to be victims of abuse. Yet this was not entirely the case since it was young men who were most likely to desert their families for organized violence groups (see Chapter 7).

Not surprisingly, this widespread climate of fear generated other conflicts within communities, some of which were violent in nature. In Guatemala, this was manifest in ubiquitous neighborhood conflicts; because people didn't trust one another, there were few channels of communication among them. Consequently, conflicts erupted continuously around such issues as land tenure. In La Merced, Guatemala City, for instance, an urbanization program which involved the distribution and legalization of land plots[4] resulted in one woman who challenged the community leaders having her house set on fire, her family nearly burned and receiving lynching threats. Conflict over water was also common, with accusations of stealing between neighbors. In Santa Lucía Cotzumalguapa, a protest about water shortages led a group to set the municipality on fire. In San Marcos, arguments erupted over market stalls, both among stallholders and between them and the mayor, when he tried to relocate them nearer the center of town. In Colombia, insecurity had reportedly led to increased murders and killing in Medellín; as one of a group of four women aged between 20 and 25 complained: 'Before the *barrio* was secure, the young people were beautiful and healthy but now they've gone off the rails and they're killing.'

Gossip also generated further conflict, thereby further contributing to the erosion of cognitive social capital. In Colombia, as identified in Figure 8.1, gossip was perceived to lead to assassination by the paramilitaries. More commonly, however, gossip led to arguments among community members. As noted in Chapters 5 and 6, young people complained about being on the receiving end of gossip that led to severe inter-generational conflicts. In Girón, Colombia, a group of three 15–16-year-old women described how adult gossip made them feel excluded, generating conflicts with their parents. Gossip was usually gender-based and associated with women rather than men.

Restrictions in spatial mobility were also closely associated with the erosion of cognitive social. Figure 8.3, drawn by a mother and daughter in La Merced, Guatemala City, outlined various aspects of fear and showed the way their mobility was particularly limited by fear of robbery and rape. Reinforcing fear was gossip about the types of crimes committed in the *colonia*. This highlighted how people were often afraid of potential rather

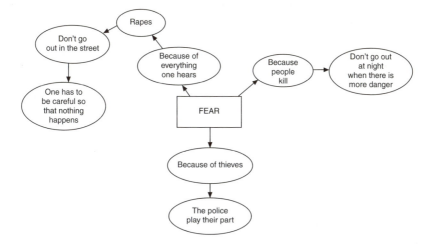

Figure 8.3 Causal flow diagram of fear in La Merced, Guatemala City (identified by a mother (aged 38) and daughter (aged 16) in a tortilla-making enterprise).

than actual violence. The views of the two women from La Merced were reiterated by another woman from Nuevo Horizonte, Guatemala City, who said: 'People cannot walk in safety; you can't go out feeling at ease.' Similarly, in discussing drug addicts, an adult woman from Girón, Colombia, pointed out: 'People can't go out in the evening . . . you can't send a girl or even a boy out alone because they'll get caught up with them.' Also, in Medellín, Colombia, an adult man noted: 'You have to stay at home so as not to get involved with the groups of gangs on the street corners, you can't let your children out.' He went on to say that one of the main dangers was from stray gunfire.

This widespread reduction in people's mobility meant that social interaction in public decreased, a sense of union within the community was lost, and social cohesion was eroded. When young people were afraid of traveling at night, they were unable to participate in evening education activities. Equally, people were less likely to participate in community groups that met at night (see Figure 8.2 on the effects of *maras*; also Chapter 9 on the places associated with fear and violence).

Another spatial dimension of the erosion of cognitive social capital was the dislocation of the *barrios* and *colonias* from the wider urban areas in which they were located. Known as 'area stigma,' most of the communities were invariably associated with crime, organized violence and drug consumption (see Chapter 4). In several, people reported that taxis and some bus routes from the center of town no longer served their area, while some shop owners complained that they could no longer get delivery of goods because of widespread theft from their lorries. In Medellín, Colombia, an adult man reported: 'people say that they can't enter the *barrio* because of all the killing.' Similarly, a young man from Bucaramanga, pointed out: 'This zone is blamed as the main generator of violence in the city... it affects the self-esteem and confidence of people.' In the same community, another man said that: 'just because we live here they think we're thieves or delinquents.' Thus, not only was the social fabric within communities severely eroded, the communities themselves were separated from the urban area as a whole, which in turn, reduced levels of cohesion (see also Auyero 2000; Moser and Holland 1998).

Overall, the blurring between different types of violence meant that the sources of fear and insecurity had become less distinct, while at the same time more insidious. This heightened the sense of vulnerability, suspicion and isolation felt by many community members in both countries, especially in communities dominated by a range of violent groups. As Torres-Rivas (1999: 294) states: 'to live in insecurity, with the sensation of a permanent threat, or close to pain or death, all contribute to the breakdown of basic solidarity.'

Structural social capital and violence in communities

The widespread prevalence of fear and violence not only fragmented cognitive social capital but also affected social organizations in local communities and networks – the structural social capital. Violence affected the institutional landscape of communities in two deep-seated ways: first, it transformed how productive organizations and networks functioned, and second, it led to the establishment or reinforcement of perverse organizations and networks.

Information about the prevalence and importance of social institutions was gathered using institutional listings, maps and matrices.[5] In Colombia, people identified 371 organizations in total across the nine communities, while in Guatemala they identified 322. These were divided into service delivery organizations (in which community members did not make decisions and which were usually run by an outside agency) and membership groups (in which community members participated in the functioning of the organization) (see Appendices 13 and 14).

In both countries, the vast majority of social organizations were productive, and were linked to or run by the state. In Colombia, for instance, focus groups commonly identified central government institutions, such as the Colombian Institute of Family Welfare (*Instituto Colombiano de Bienestar Familiar*, ICBF) linked with the Community Mothers, and especially, the partly state-funded Communal Action Boards (*Juntas de Acción Comunal*, JACs). Figure 8.4 from Medellín shows how most of the organi-

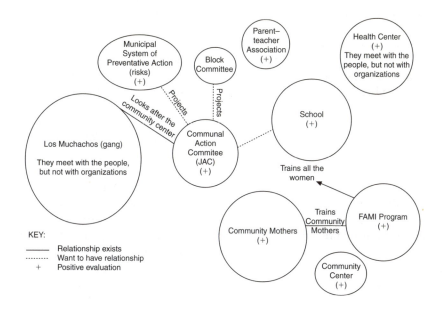

Figure 8.4 Institutional mapping of Porticó, Medellín, Colombia (drawn by a mixed group of 20 people).

zations this group identified were influenced by the state. In Guatemala, frequently mentioned productive institutions included schools, hospitals and churches, as well as NGOs. The NGOs were usually externally funded and managed, such as Medicine without Borders, UNICEF and World Vision. While NGOs also existed in Colombia, they were less widespread.

Perverse social organizations were identified in both Colombia and Guatemala, fostering perverse social capital, reinforced through the use of force. As described in Chapter 7, these included guerrilla and paramilitary groups, a host of different types of neighborhood gangs, thieves, drug dealers and users, as well as bars and brothels (the latter were perceived as organizations only in Guatemala). In Colombia, violence-related groups were viewed as the most important membership organization in three communities in Yopal, Medellín and Bogotá (see Appendix 15). In light of this, Figure 8.4 highlights the overwhelming importance of Los Muchachos in the Medellín community – the gang discussed in Chapter 7. While perverse organizations were less frequently identified in Guatemala – only 13 percent of all membership groups – there were as many violence-related organizations as youth, sports and recreational organizations. There were also differences between communities. For instance, perverse groups in La Merced, Guatemala City, San Jorge, Chinautla and Villa Real, Esquipulas, constituted roughly one quarter of all membership organizations, while in three other communities no such institutions were identified (see Appendix 14).

Analysis of social institutions in terms of whether they were formal service delivery or membership based showed revealing differences between the two countries. Formal state-run service delivery institutions, such as education and health services, were perceived as most widespread and important, constituting around one-third of all organizations in both countries. However, in Guatemala, service delivery organizations were much more prevalent than membership organizations (74 percent as against 26 percent) suggesting that local social organizations had been eroded by decades of political conflict. In contrast, in Colombia the difference was not as marked (52 percent compared with 48 percent). At the same time, probably the gravest finding from Colombia was the fact that the most prevalent membership organizations were those related to the perpetration or prevention of violence (over one quarter). The fact that more than one in every five local social organization was violence-focused is illustrative of the predominant level of conflict engulfing the country. In contrast, in the post-conflict situation of Guatemala, it was churches and religious groups that were the most prevalent membership group (Appendices 13 and 14).

The transformation of structural social capital and violence: the reconstitution of productive organizations

The perpetration of different types of violence transformed productive social organizations in two main ways: first, service delivery rather than membership organizations were more likely to predominate in communities with high levels of violence; and, second, externally run, often hierarchical organizations were often more trusted than locally-based membership organizations.

With reference to the first, communities with a history or contemporary experience of high levels of political conflict were likely to have fewer productive membership organizations. For instance, in Colombia, the communities with low proportions of membership organizations were Aguazul (36 percent of all organizations), Yopal (25 percent) and Girón (38 percent). The two former communities were particularly affected by guerrilla and paramilitary activity, while the latter was home to a large displaced population. Moreover, in Yopal and Aguazul, many of these organizations were perverse – almost half in Yopal. Similar patterns were identified in Guatemala, with the lowest proportions of membership organizations in Santa Cruz del Quiché (9 percent of the total), and in Sacuma, Huehuetenango (21 percent) – both departments previously affected by the civil conflict and with high composition of indigenous populations (Appendices 15 and 16).

In both countries this pattern reflected a widespread reluctance to participate in membership organizations for fear of reprisals. In the case of Guatemala, this was the result of a legacy of persecution and in Colombia, of a continuing threat. In contrast, service delivery organizations involved less danger for those receiving services. Unwillingness to participate in community activities was highlighted by one woman in La Merced, Guatemala City, who complained: 'We don't like to participate because there are neighbors who talk about us, and we don't want to get involved in problems because people will talk about us.' On a more practical level, fear of violence prevented people from attending community meetings held in the evenings.

Lack of involvement was also associated with lack of leadership. In Santa Cruz del Quiché, Guatemala, where this was linked to the armed conflict, one man pointed out that community leaders had either been killed or had disappeared in the 1980s. Similarly, in Aguazul, Colombia, a focus group noted how the violent death of community leaders had led to the absence of organizational management which, in turn, resulted in lack of union and dialog replaced by mistrust (see below).

People's willingness to join community organizations was also affected by levels of confidence in the organizations themselves.[6] In Colombia, membership organizations were less trusted than service delivery organizations. Indeed, a quarter of people did not trust Colombian neighborhood committees, while one-third mistrusted them in Guatemala. Commenting on this, a woman from Medellín, Colombia, said: 'The Communal Action Board [JAC] ran a meeting with their supporters in order to get help with fixing the houses, but it was all lies.' In 14 de Febrero, Bogotá, a young man held similar views about the local JAC : 'we don't trust them; they're very closed.' In La Merced, Guatemala City, a woman similarly reported: 'The people from the committee promise but don't meet their promises, because of this nobody believes them' (see Appendices 17 and 18).

The prevalence and importance of national or international NGOs reflected another dimension of the transformation of structural social capital. Not only did NGOs usually provide services rather than involve membership, they were often run externally in a hierarchical manner, and in some cases, from abroad – although the latter was much more common in Guatemala. In Colombia, NGOs were the most trusted institution after the drug and alcohol rehabilitation centers and were especially important in Jericó, Bogotá (identified in one-third of cases) (see Appendix 17). According to a Community Mother, Jericó had been used as a pilot area for national and international NGOs (as well as the state) since 1988. There were also numerous NGOs in Cali (identified in over one-third of cases), especially Plan International – an 'adopt a child' organization. In the Casanare communities, there were also several NGOs linked to the oil companies such as *Fundación Amanecer* in Aguazul established by BP (see Figure 8.9 on p. 175) (see Appendix 13).

NGOs were even more widespread in Guatemala, especially in Santa Cruz del Quiché and in Guatemala City (see Appendix 14). In the former, they constituted one-third of all institutions, reportedly linked with the influx of organizations in the aftermath of the civil war. Figure 8.5 from Concepción, Guatemala City, shows how three international organizations – Medicine Without Borders, the Norwegian church and World Vision – had played a crucial role in the development of community infrastructure, especially during the early phases of securing a water supply, and buying and legalizing plots. Another focus group, comprising an elderly man and a young woman, elaborated further on the role of international organizations in Concepción. They pointed out that Care International assisted the municipality in the provision of drainage between 1986 and 1987, and that together with Medicine Without Borders, UNICEF provided the first drinking water supply in 1994. Many focus groups felt that international organizations were more trustworthy than local membership or national institutions because they were not involved in neighborhood politics, vote-buying or corruption. A similar situation was found in Villa Real, Esquipulas, where the Spanish bilateral agency, Cooperación Española, was considered much more important and trustworthy than the local neighborhood committee; according to a carpenter, only 50 percent of people trusted the committee, compared with 65 percent who trusted Cooperación Española.

This orientation toward external, especially foreign organizations, reinforced paternalism. Although some created local improvement committees,

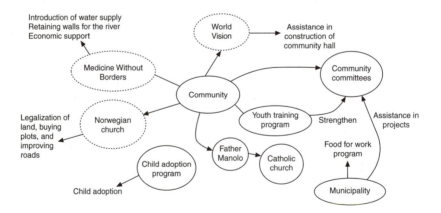

Figure 8.5 Institutional mapping of Concepción, Guatemala City (drawn by a group of six adult men).

Note
Dotted circles are institutions that have worked in the community in the past and had a large impact.

such as Cooperación Española in Esquipulas, Guatemala, in other places, their presence discouraged grassroots organizations. In San Jorge, Chinautla, one woman, said that: 'the people in San Jorge want everything to fall from the sky,' referring to their inability to organize for themselves. In Gucumatz, Santa Cruz del Quiché, another man noted: 'Before, everything was given away and the people grew accustomed to it, now nobody collaborates unless they are given something in exchange, now there is no community participation.'

Erosion of productive networks

Violence affected formal links between social institutions as much as informal networks among people. At a formal level, few linkages other than basic functional ties were identified between institutions. Organizations rarely co-ordinated activities with each other, and little effort was made by people working within membership organizations to develop close links with other groups. The tendency was to view ties merely as conduits for funding or as basic extensions of their operating functions, such as a link between a drug rehabilitation center and a hospital. Figure 8.6 from San Marcos, Guatemala, drawn by a shoemaker, highlights not only the severe lack of institutional diversity in this community (with few membership organizations at all), but also the limited nature of ties among organizations. It shows the positive ties among different evangelical schools, and between the schools and hospitals, and negative relations between the *cantinas* and Alcoholics Anonymous or between the brothels and the police. Similarly, in Cali, Colombia, a group of four adult men and one woman discussed how the Center for Community Development only got involved with other organizations through 'lending space,' with one noting: 'there's no coordination or integration between organizations.' Thus, most links among institutions were between service delivery rather than membership organizations (see Figure 8.6).

Informal networks were much more common with people in all communities reporting some form of relations with others, even if only with a single neighbor or family who lived close by. However, in general, they were not extensive and tended to revolve around credit and loans rather than fostering social relations among neighbors. In Girón, Colombia, several groups identified the importance of the local money-lender and the shops in the community for providing loans and credit, while others discussed the sharing of clothes among neighbors and family. Similarly in Esquipulas, Guatemala, a carpenter described a loan network he had developed with other artisans in the community to lend and borrow money on a weekly basis (see Chapter 7).

This focus of formal links on functional ties and informal networks on survival and economic matters rather than social support had its roots in the erosion of cognitive social capital associated with high levels of fear.

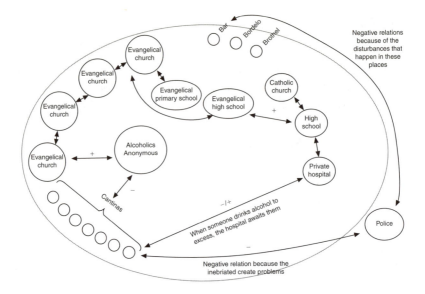

Figure 8.6 Institutional mapping of Limoncito, San Marcos, Guatemala (prepared by two shoemakers aged 28 and 50).

People only engaged with others institutionally or individually if necessary, and usually only with those very close to them. For instance, a female shop-owner from San Marcos, Guatemala, said that there were no formal support networks in the community and she had no links with any organizations. However, she did have informal ties with her sister-in-law who lent her money, she confided in a neighbor about problems with her husband, and a stall holder in the market gave her credit.

Overall, productive social institutions and networks in both countries were transformed in contexts of violence. People generally were more likely to trust service delivery organizations, and, in the case of Guatemala, NGOs, especially foreign ones rather than membership organizations. Hierarchical institutions were often preferred to those structured more horizontally, reflecting levels of high social fragmentation and lack of trust. This was further manifested in formal and informal networks functioning through necessity rather than for social support.

The transformation of structural social capital and violence: the emergence of perverse organizations

While the reconstitution of productive social organizations was a negative outcome of high levels of violence, even more deleterious to communities was the emergence and importance of perverse organizations. Chapter 7 provided a detailed description of the characteristics of the different groups involved in organized violence, and so this section turns to their impact on the community as a whole.

In communities where people lived in fear, felt excluded and trusted no-one, joining a perverse organization gave them a sense of identity and focus otherwise absent from their lives (see Chapter 7). However, as perverse groups proliferated, levels of violence increased and in a cyclical process as fear became further entrenched, so cognitive social capital was additionally eroded. In this sense, it could be argued that while perverse organizations were internally productive, they were externally perverse because of their detrimental effects on social relations within communities.

Although perverse organizations were generally reviled within communities, some also viewed them favorably. Evaluations of trust in institutions in Colombia, for example, revealed that 18 percent of people thought that perverse groups were positive, primarily because of their informal vigilance roles (see Appendix 17). Figure 8.4 from Medellín highlights the importance of the gang, Los Muchachos in looking after the community center, as one man noted: 'Los Muchachos look after the *barrio* and they collaborate with people.' One of the gang members themselves reported: 'If it wasn't for us, the school would have been broken into and the children would have been robbed.' However, they also attracted negative views; one woman stated that most insecurity in the *barrio* was the fault of the gang: 'It's generated by Los Muchachos, no-one ever feels peaceful because of their shooting.' These perceptions prevailed in other communities. For instance, a woman from El Arca, Cali, pointed out that the 'good *capuchos* [hooded gun-men]' looked after the community, while the 'bad *capuchos*' robbed them. Also in Cali, a man commented that it was the guerrillas that protected them from theft: 'The guerrillas don't allow robbery; in some parts of the *barrio* you can sleep with your windows open.' Figure 8.7 summarizes this contradictory, ambiguous attitude in which social cleansing groups and the police were viewed negatively (and often perceived to be one and the same institution), yet the militias were thought to be positive.

In Guatemala, however, none of the communities perceived the *maras* as fulfilling a protective role, reflected in the totally negative evaluations of violence-related organizations (see Appendix 18). Indeed, they were universally disliked and feared (see Figure 8.2). In marked contrast, however, there was widespread support for social cleansing groups that were praised for their efforts in curbing delinquency and *mara* activity (see Chapters 4 and 9).

Because of their protective role, perverse organizations flourished in contexts where state security forces were seen as weak, corrupt and ineffective (see Chapter 4). As such, in Colombia, the second least trusted

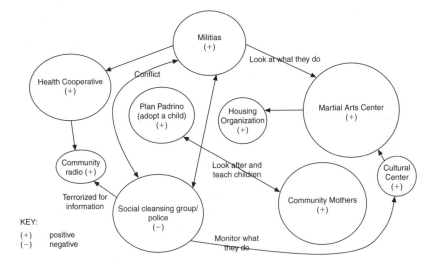

Figure 8.7 Institutional mapping of El Arca, Cali, Colombia (drawn by five young men).

organizations – following those involved in the perpetration of violence – were the state security and justice institutions such as the police, army and the judicial system (see Appendix 17). Similarly, there was a marked lack of trust in the state security institutions in Guatemala, particularly among the indigenous population. Again, aside from violence-related groups, state security organizations, such as the police and army, received the highest percentage of negative rankings (61 percent) (Appendix 18). In Guatemala, it was, however, noted that a level of trust was slowly being rebuilt with the creation of a new police force (see Chapter 4).

In light of this mistrust, the state security forces were therefore not perceived as productive organizations, but as perverse; they functioned for the benefit of their members, often using violence to reinforce their power. Indeed, in both countries, the police were accused of corruption, and of creating further violence rather than preventing it. In Concepción, Guatemala City, a young man reported: 'After 1995, violence increased because of the aggression of the police … the police hit us without a motive.' In Bucaramanga, Colombia, a young man pointed out that: 'the police cause more problems than they solve.'

Creation of perverse networks

Some of the networks within communities were also perverse, multiplying as perverse institutions grew. Generally, they were hierarchical in structure, and maintained through violence. The drug network, established for sale and distribution purposes within the community and found most frequently in Colombia, was one such network. These operated with strict rules of contract, and authority patterns rigidly and violently enforced. At the same time, they were extremely cohesive, even if this was not undertaken on a voluntary basis. Figure 8.8 from Embudo, Bogotá, an area notorious for the sale and consumption of drugs, was drawn by a 34-year-old woman whose two children were involved in drug distribution as *taquilleros* (see below). It shows how the drug networks were organized in a vertical, gendered manner with men in positions of authority and women playing supportive roles. Each street invariably had two male *cabezas* (heads) who were the main source of drugs, controlled their sale, but did not live in the *barrio*. Each head distributed drugs through male or female intermediaries called *jibaros*. These were sometimes called *los duros* (the hard people) primarily because they forcefully maintained their authority. A male drug addict and thief noted that the *jibaros* killed those who didn't keep to their contracts. The *jibaros* controlled one or two *taquilleros* who conducted the actual sale of drugs. *Taquilleros* rarely consumed drugs themselves, and were usually friends or relatives of the *jibaros*. While *taquilleros* rarely killed, they often punched or hit consumers who didn't pay up on time. *Taquilleros* worked with other friends, mainly women and children, who acted as 'lookouts,' advising them of police movements or the arrival of strangers (see Figure 8.8).[7]

This perverse drug distribution network was also linked to a network of *ollas* (literally, kitchen pot), which were distinct 'spaces' where drugs were sold and consumed. Two female sex workers from Embudo, Bogotá, noted that *ollas* were not just linked with drugs, but also associated with attacks,

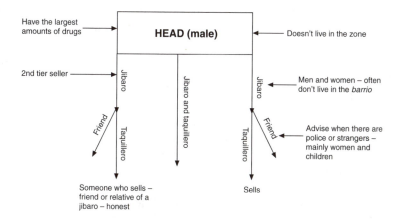

Figure 8.8 Diagram of drug sale and distribution in Embudo, Bogotá, Colombia (prepared by 34 year-old woman).

murder, sexual violence and prostitution. Families sometimes lived in them, but usually they were inhabited by individuals – robbers, drug addicts and prostitutes. In Embudo, there were approximately thirty *ollas*, although there were fewer in other communities. Despite their negative functions, *ollas* were firmly established in the institutional structure of Embudo in particular, providing a core function for the maintenance of community unity, albeit perverse in nature.

While communities benefited in some respects from the presence of perverse social organizations, particularly from the protection provided in the absence or inefficiency of state efforts, ultimately such organizations and networks created high levels of insecurity among the population. This perverse social capital not only reduced both formal and informal social interaction, but also further delegitimized the role of the state.

Rebuilding social capital: the role of productive institutions

While explicit interventions to 'reconstruct' social capital to reduce violence are discussed in Chapter 9, it is nevertheless important to identify here which organizations were identified as contributing to community level cohesion – even in the midst of violence, fear and mistrust. In both countries women-led community groups were found to play an important role in rebuilding social capital. In Colombia, women's organizations and childcare groups were the most trusted of all membership groups (see Appendix 17). Overall, 88 percent of people trusted these organizations, and in five of the eight communities where they existed (excluding Cachicamo, Yopal), all were evaluated positively.

Childcare groups, referred to state-supported 'Community Homes' (*Hogares Comunitarios*), that were managed and organized entirely by local women, and were based on a horizontal management structure. Women known as Community Mothers ran such childcare groups from their homes, with as many as eight or nine groups in each community. Levels of trust were associated with their horizontal patterns of organization, their physical location within the community and the fact that they were seen as an essential part of the community itself. Unlike the community committees, which were broadly mistrusted (see above), they were not involved in decision-making and had far less potential for corruption. As such, levels of trust in such organizations were high among both women and men, and young and old (see Figure 8.7 drawn by five young men).

While not as widespread as Community Homes, women's organizations were also extremely important in some Colombian communities, especially those experiencing high levels of violence. Figure 8.9, drawn by a group of adult men and women in Colombia Chiquita, illustrates how the

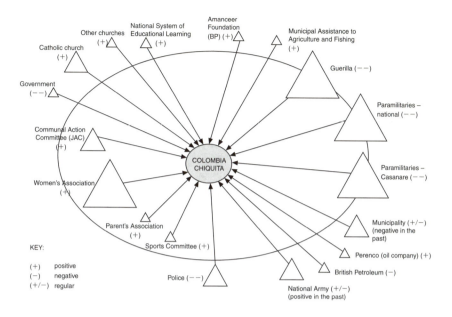

Figure 8.9 Institutional mapping of Colombia Chiquita, Aguazul, Colombia (drawn by four adult men and three adult women).

Women's Association was seen as the most important productive institution; while the paramilitaries and the guerrillas were perceived as equally important, they were negative. The only other influential organization was the Communal Action Board, run by men in a hierarchical manner, which reportedly no longer kept its promises (see earlier). In contrast, focus groups described the Women's Association as 'successful,' 'trustworthy' and 'well-functioning,' providing a positive example of successful community organization and co-operation. Founded by a woman, displaced from another violent area, its aim was to re-unite a community whose social fabric had been destroyed by paramilitary and guerrilla violence. This was done through training women so they could maintain their families when male members of their households were assassinated – mainly by setting up their own small businesses. In her view, women were more likely to be heard by the authorities because: 'there is always truth and sincerity in the eyes of women.' Tragically, this woman leader, caught in the middle of the war between guerrillas and paramilitaries, has since been assassinated.

In Guatemala, although women's organizations and childcare groups were only identified in three of the research communities – Nuevo Horizonte and La Merced, Guatemala City, and Gucumatz, Santa Cruz del

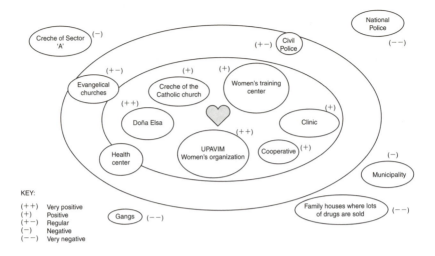

Figure 8.10 Institutional mapping of La Merced, Guatemala City (drawn by an adult woman).

Quiché – they also played an important role. In La Merced, for example, there were six of these organizations, outnumbered only by churches and neighborhood committees. One of these organizations, called UPAVIM (*Unidas para Vivir Mejor* – United to Live Better), provided a wide range of services to its women members, including income-generating activities, childcare, health care and training courses. Figure 8.10 illustrates how this and other women's organizations played a fundamental role in the community. In addition to UPAVIM, the focus group identified a crèche, another women's training center, and a prominent local woman called Doña Elsa who was perceived as an institution herself.

However, overall levels of trust in these institutions were lower than in Colombia (see Appendices 17 and 18). For instance, while for those involved, UPAVIM was referred to as a 'lifeline,' others who were still on waiting lists and could not get access to the center were disparaging about it. In communities with lamentably poor public services, it is perhaps not surprising that membership organizations providing services should attract some degree of envy. Yet, this situation highlights the importance of institutional openness and transparency (see also Moser and McIlwaine 2001b).

This chapter has highlighted how violence had a profound effect on social capital within communities. It is too simplistic to argue that violence eroded social capital; rather, it eroded, transformed and reconstituted social capital in different ways, depending as much on the type of social capital as on the configuration and intersection of different types of viol-ence. Not only did violence reduce cognitive social capital through under-mining trust and generating fear, but it also influenced how structural social capital operated; the functions of productive social organizations were curtailed while those of perverse organizations multiplied. This, in turn, contributed to increased insecurity, and often exacerbated further violence. However, some positive processes were also identified, especially in relation to the rebuilding of trust and cohesion – the essential social capital – through non-threatening organizations such as women's groups. Thus, the relationships between social capital and violence are central not only to understanding people's experiences of violence, but also to achiev-ing its reduction. The final chapter of the book focuses on this, discussing strategies, solutions and interventions for coping with, and reducing, violence.

9

AVOIDING OR CONFRONTING VIOLENCE?

Community perceptions of strategies and solutions

Living daily with the diversity of types of routinized, banalized violence, discussed in detail in previous chapters, meant that community members constantly confronted the problem as to how to survive or manage the phenomenon. Here, an important distinction needs to be made between strategies to cope with violence as against specific solutions to resolve the problem. While there is a common tendency to view coping strategies and proactive solutions as one and the same, despite obvious interrelationships between the two, they are markedly different. Thus this final chapter addresses each in turn. In giving voice to people's individual and communal responses, while recognizing their agency, it shows that avoidance rather than confrontation was the more common strategy. Lack of trust in outside institutions, highlighted in Chapter 8, and the resource constraint situation they confronted were both influential in reaching this conclusion. This discussion of coping strategies and solutions also pulls together many of the ideas and experiences of violence in both countries, as discussed in earlier chapters.

Indeed, local community members had very clear ideas of potential solutions that could prevent or reduce, if not eliminate, the high levels of violence. As described in Chapters 1 and 2, over the past decade there has been a growing preoccupation among policymakers with violence as a development concern. Therefore, the second part of this chapter concludes the book by coming full circle and returning to the policy-focused debate. This is achieved by comparing local community perceptions of solutions to violence with those of policymakers. The relevance of such a comparison is assisted by two issues. First, is the introduction of an integrated framework for intervention, and, second, quantification of perception data in terms of different types of capital assets. While a simplification of reality, this is intended to make the research results more accessible to policymakers both in the research countries as well as in a broader context.

Strategies for coping with violence

In Colombia and Guatemala, community focus group listings identified strategies to cope with violence that revealed surprising similarities. These fell into the four distinct categories: avoidance, confrontation, conciliation and other strategies (Appendix 19 provides details of the results discussed in this section).[1] As noted above, in both countries, community members reported *avoidance* as the most common strategy adopted. In Colombia, this comprised three-quarters of the strategies identified, while in Guatemala it was just over half. Within this category, the 'law of silence,' or ignoring the situation, was the single most practised mechanism in Colombian communities, used by one-fifth of community members, while in Guatemala the comparable figure was around one tenth.

Avoidance strategies

As discussed in earlier chapters, widespread fear of retribution, powerlessness and concern not to exacerbate the situation induced such responses. The fact that Colombia was in the middle of a rapidly escalating civil war meant that reactions to political violence were dominated by silence. Thus three women in Aguazul identified that their strategy to avoid being killed was to 'keep your mouth shut' (Figure 9.1). In Guatemala, maintaining silence had become a way of life after the lengthy civil war, but in the post-conflict context also extended to economic crime, such as robbery and gang violence as well as social violence such as rape, as noted by young women in Concepción, Guatemala City.

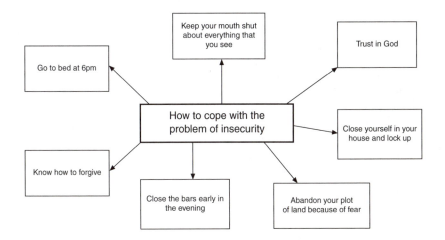

Figure 9.1 Flow diagram of how to cope with the problem of insecurity in Colombia Chiquita, Aguazul, Colombia (drawn by three women aged 25–63).

In both countries, the silence surrounding intra-family violence was particularly marked (see Chapter 5). Not only did neighbors and friends not intervene in this type of conflict, but also family members themselves maintained silence. For instance, in Colombia a young man from Pórtico, Medellín, noted how he 'watched television' when his father was beating his mother, mainly because he felt he could do little to help. In a community in Chinautla, Guatemala, one woman stated: 'often we just stay silent, do nothing, when there's violence in the family.'

The other predominant avoidance strategy, also reported in Chapters 3 and 8, entailed changing mobility patterns within communities, both temporarily and permanently. In Guatemalan as in Colombian communities, people avoided places where gangs and drug addicts congregated, including particular street corners, river banks, and parks, changing their walking routes to avoid such places and seeking areas with streetlights. For instance, two *'jóvenes sanos'* (healthy young men, i.e. not drug addicts) from 14 de Febrero, Bogotá, noted how they avoided the 'hang-outs' of drug addicts by taking a 'long route' home. In the case of Huehuetenango, Guatemala, this strategy was operationalized in response to rape on the part of women. Again in Aguazul, Colombia, women identified how they severely restricted their activities after dark, locking themselves in their houses from as early as six o'clock, but in most cases after nine o'clock when the incidence of violence dramatically increased (see Figure 9.1). Women were most likely to report these responses, although both men and women explained how they avoided going out alone. In Colombia, a group of young women from Girón identified this as a major restriction in their lives. They wanted to continue education at night school, but felt it too dangerous to use public transport after dark. In La Merced and Concepción, Guatemala City, community members explained how they attempted to ensure their children stayed in at night in order to keep them away from gangs and drugs. An adult male from Concepción stated: 'We have to keep our children entertained and teach them skills so that they don't get involved in gangs.'

Other strategies included avoiding people involved in crime and violence-related activities, as well as the places where they met. Young people kept away from people who sold drugs or from friends who had become involved in gangs or delinquency and whom they feared would lead them astray. This was especially important with reference to drug consumption, where peer pressure was particularly problematic (see Chapter 6). Parents from Nuevo Horizonte, Guatemala City, reported how they tried to keep their children busy at weekends to reduce the likelihood that they would come into contact with drugs. Other people described how, as a means of coping, they would flee from violent situations, particularly from gang and drug-related violence, whether they were witnesses or victims. This was especially relevant to robbery and gang violence, where people ran away from thieves or gangs. Flight was also significant in relation to intra-family violence; deserting the family home was the most important response to this type of violence, whether victims or witnesses. Participants also changed the way they looked in order to evade violence, with women in both countries emphasizing how they avoided robbery by not wearing jewellery. In Colombia, a group of three adults from Cali noted that one had to go out: 'without rings, without a watch, without luxury shoes, and without brand names clothes.' Similarly, a young woman from Santa Lucía Cotzumalguapa, Guatemala, pointed out: 'You have to take care of yourself to deal with rape and one way is by dressing decently and not wearing skirts.'

Confrontation and conciliation strategies

Fear of violent repercussions meant that strategies involving confrontation and conciliation were less common (10 and 12 percent of responses in Colombia and Guatemala respectively). Indeed, in Colombia the few focus groups who cited confrontation as a response were either gang members or drug consumers. For instance, a member of the gang Los Muchachos in Medellín said that they dealt with murder in the community by 'killing them first.' Similarly, a group of two men and one woman from Concepción, Guatemala City, reported how they carried firearms or other weapons to defend themselves against robberies and assaults. A similar strategy was reported by a focus group of four youths in Chinautla, Guatemala, who described how they would use arms to protect themselves against gangs. Several women in Nuevo Horizonte, Guatemala City, noted that self-defense was a form of response to rape, with one adult woman stating that it was important to: 'bite or scream in response to rape.' A minority of people in Colombia also suggested that 'hitting back' was an appropriate way of dealing with intra-family violence.

Most people were afraid of the perpetrators of crime and would avoid conciliation strategies. Occasionally people reported the strategy of getting to know those involved in crime as a means of protecting themselves. But it was only young people who considered this an option since most were afraid of groups such as gangs or guerrillas, especially women and the elderly. The predominant conciliation strategy, however, involved religion. Participants prayed both for those involved in crime and for their victims and, as a way of protecting the community and individuals from harm. In Guatemalan communities, Protestant evangelical religion in particular was practiced as a means of responding to violent and unstable circumstances. In Santa Cruz del Quiché this tendency was especially notable, with an adult woman stating that 'religious sects are important for solving violence' as 'thieves are scared of God.' Similarly, several women in Aguazul, Colombia, identified 'trust in God' as a strategy. As this community was severely affected by political violence, fear of murder meant confrontation was not an option.

Other strategies

Finally, among other strategies, was the mechanism of reporting conflicts or violent events to the authorities. Here, there were important differences between the two countries, reflecting very different levels of trust in formal institutions. For instance, in Guatemala, community members noted that people reported 15 percent of offenses, particularly robbery or gang-related crime, while only 2 percent were reported in Colombia. Two other important differences need to be noted. First, in Guatemala, where the incidence of intra-family violence and rape was especially high, children and young people often turned to school teachers as well as the local judge and doctor, as responsible authorities to which to report such offenses. However, this was not always the case. Frequently, as in Colombia, fear of reporting cases of intra-family sexual abuse meant that people coped privately with their problems. Second, again in Guatemala but not in Colombia, crimes were reported to human rights organizations. A man from Huehuetenango, Guatemala, identified that when a violent event took place: 'We go to a human rights organization that will investigate the crime or sometimes to the police that follow up the report through the Public Ministry.' In Santa Cruz del Quiché and La Merced, Guatemala City, strategies to deal with intra-family violence also included going to human rights institutions. The latter case demonstrated how organizations that had mainly represented the indigenous population in the past were now beginning to be utilized by the *ladino* population to address non-political violence.[2]

A final strategy in both countries was simply to submit. In this way it was safer to allow a thief to rob, as they were less likely to cause harm. Submission to intra-family violence was also noted; a number of women considered that nothing could be done about this mistreatment. In Colombia for instance, a group of four 11-year-old girls in Jericó, Bogotá, when discussing how to deal with rape, noted that they were afraid to tell their parents for fear of rejection, and could only talk about it with their friends. Their main strategy was to have an abortion and, as one stated: 'be brave and deal with it as it comes.'

Community perceptions of interventions to prevent or reduce violence

Background on recent policy approaches to violence reduction

Facing the complexity of violence on a daily basis, local communities were extremely concerned to identify ways in which to address the problem, despite the fact that they often felt powerless to achieve change. Given the severity of the situation described throughout this book, perspectives on this issue as articulated by women, men, youth and children are obviously of intrinsic importance in themselves. In addition, 'bottom-up' perceptions of potential solutions can make an important contribution to ongoing policy debates on violence reduction, the majority of which comprise 'top-down' prescriptions by professional experts. Probably the greatest challenge relates to identifying mechanisms that can reconcile the multiplicity of interrelated layering of violence, which community members identified, with the sector or violence-specific solutions that policymakers have tended to prioritize.

By way of contextual background, it is useful to outline very briefly recent changes in dominant approaches to violence reduction. As with the policy analysis of violence itself, interventions to reduce violence have tended to be dominated by a particular policy approach and its associated professional discipline. Commonly, each has prioritized a specific type of violence and focuses on a particular target group. In this way, there are clear distinctions between policies focusing on economic, social and political violence as separate domains. However, with growing recognition of the interrelationships between different types of violence and conflict, this is gradually changing.

Over the past decades violence reduction initiatives have shifted from a focus on the control of violence, to those that concentrate on prevention (Vanderschueren 1996). At the same time, recent approaches to armed conflict reduction emphasize the negotiation of peaceful conflict resolution, as well as the legal enforcement of conflict reduction through the promotion of human rights. Current perspectives with an integrative approach include top-down foci on citizen security and infrastructure renewal, as well as bottom-up community driven development strategies to strengthen or reconstruct levels of social capital. Table 9.1 outlines these policy approaches as 'ideal types.'

As background it is useful to briefly describe each in turn. One of the earliest and most widely established violence reduction approaches is criminal justice. This top-down approach focuses on deterrence and control of violence through higher rates of arrest, conviction and punishment, facilitated by judicial, police and penal reform. It is often particularly popular among politicians seeking short-term solutions to the symptoms of violence. Both the justice and police systems tend to be male-dominated elite institutions frequently resulting in constraints in access for groups excluded on the basis of gender, age or ethnicity. Equally, gender stereotyping of crime perpetrators means that young men are more susceptible to arrest and conviction. This approach has been more successful in reducing economic violence than social violence relating to gender and age-based domestic violence, and has rarely been used as a mechanism to

Table 9.1 Different 'ideal type' policy approaches to violence reduction

Approach	Objective	Violence category addressed	Intervention	Limitations
Criminal justice	Violence deterrence and control through higher arrest, conviction rates and more severe punishment	Economic	Top-down strengthening of judicial, penal, and police systems and their associated institutions	Limited applicability to contexts of political and social violence; success dependent on enforcement
Public health	Violence prevention through the reduction of individual risk factors that focus particularly on human capital	Economic Social	Top-down surveillance; risk factor identification; resultant behavior modification; scaling up of successful interventions	Almost exclusive focus on individual; often imposed top-down; sensitive to quality of surveillance data
Conflict transformation	Non-violent conflict resolution through negotiated terms between conflicting parties	Political Social	Top-down or bottom-up conflict reduction negotiations between different social actors	Often long-term in its impact; faces challenges in bringing parties to the table and in mediating conflict
Human rights	Legal enforcement of human rights by states, and other social actors	Political Social	Top-down legal enforcement, reinforced by bottom-up participation and NGO lobbying	Legal framework often difficult to enforce in lawlessness contexts with corruption and impunity
Infrastructure renewal	Reduction in violence opportunities through environmental, spatial interventions	Economic Social	Top-down municipal level interventions to improve community level physical infrastructure	Does not address underlying causes of spatially manifested violence such as robbery and rape
Citizen security	Composite set of measures to prevent and/or reduce violence	Economic Social	Top-down multi-sector government-directed approach	Very popular with governments seeking to address country concerns
Social capital	Building social capital through community level informal and formal social institutions	Political Economic Social	Bottom-up participatory appraisal; institutional mapping; community level reduction measures	Less well articulated than other approaches

Source: Adapted from Moser et al. (2000).

reduce political violence. Having said this, there have been increasing attempts to make the criminal justice system more gender-aware and community based. This can be seen, for example, in the establishment of Women's Police Stations, such as those founded in São Paulo, Brazil, in 1985 (Pickup *et al.* 2001) and in the development of local justice systems (Vanderschueren 1996).

Today, the most popular and widely used approach is still the well-established public health perspective that focuses on economic and social violence. This aims to prevent violence by reducing individual risk factors. It draws on epidemiological surveillance – especially homicide rates – to develop risk reduction strategies for modifying individual behavior, the social and physical environment, or both. In focusing on specific 'at risk' target groups it has the potential to address women and girls as much as men and boys, and in some contexts has become widely associated with addressing the problems of gangs. Over time, it has broadened its focus to include not only prevention but also rehabilitation. One of the most important examples of public health interventions is DESEPAZ in Cali, Colombia (see Moser *et al.* 2000).

The conflict transformation approach aims primarily to reduce armed conflict and to rebuild the fabric of societies, although it is increasingly also associated with violence more generally. Influenced by the work of Galtung (1985), historically small pacifist groups, such as the Quakers, have played an important role in conflict transformation. More recently, international institutions, such as the United Nations, have also begun to address political violence through non-violent negotiation among conflicting parties, often relying on third-party mediation. However, since excluded groups often do not participate in international or national conflict transformation and peace talks, their legitimate interests and needs are often not recognized in peace negotiations. This said, conflict transformation approaches have also been implemented at the local level.

The human rights approach focuses on the role of the state in protecting citizens' rights to be free from the threat or victimization of violence. Drawing on the documentation of abuse in relation to international human rights conventions, it addresses armed conflict and political and social violence. While early uses of this perspective were targeted toward governments that violated human rights, more recent formulations have focused on all social actors who deny or abuse rights, including guerrilla and paramilitary groups. Civil society institutions have played a critical role in the contestation of rights. In particular, this focuses on currently excluded groups, such as women, children and indigenous people.

Given the multiple layering of violence, and associated identity of different social actors experiencing violence, policymakers are beginning to shift away from menu-like checklists of single-sector interventions toward more integrated approaches. The citizen security approach is one such integrated approach that incorporates interventions that prevent and reduce violence through a menu of different initiatives. As the name implies, the overall objective is to provide better security for citizens rather than tackling the underlying causes of violence themselves. Interventions tend to be top-down in focus and vary according to government prioritization.

Another more integrated approach is that of infrastructure and environmental renewal that focuses on the reduction of opportunities for perpetration of violence through spatially identified upgrading to improve the living environment. Top-down municipal level interventions to improve communities' physical infrastructure, particularly in urban areas, include roads and other transport facilities, lighting in open public spaces, community sanitary facilities and the location of bank cash dispensers. As with the citizen security perspective, it addresses the physical manifestations of daily economic and social violence rather than its underlying causes.

Finally, the community-driven social capital approach, still in the process of formulation and development, focuses most directly on rebuilding social cohesion in informal and formal institutions such as families, gangs and community organizations. Using bottom-up, participatory processes, it aims to create trust by building on community identification of needs, and focuses on the strengths and assets of communities affected by violence. It also provides the potential for community needs to be scaled up to public sector interventions (see for example, Moser and Holland 1998, on Jamaica).

In reality, different policy approaches, described above as ideal types, are integrated together, with well-established approaches often combined with more innovative ones. The resulting integrated framework for intervention are increasingly recognized as essential if policymakers are to recognize the multiplicity of violence as well as the agency and identities of different social actors.

Community-level perceptions of interventions to address violence

What, if any, of the solutions identified by community members in Colombia or Guatemala coincided with those of policymakers identified above? Analysis of responses from both countries provides the opportunity to identify any lessons that community perceptions can contribute to the redefinition of violence reduction policies.

In order to provide quantitatively relevant data, both existing and potential solutions to violence-related problems were identified within communities, and then categorized according to types of capital assets. As shown in Table 9.2, in total, around half the solutions to all types of violence identified by the urban poor were associated with social capital assets, representing 47 percent in Colombian communities, and 58 percent

Table 9.2 Interventions for reducing violence by type of capital asset, in Colombia and Guatemala

Intervention by type of capital assets	% of all solutions		
	Colombia	*Guatemala*	*Total*
Increase social capital assets	47	58	52.5
Productive	35	33	34
Perverse	12	25	18.5
Increase human capital assets	29	31	30
Increase physical capital assets	23	12	17.5
Total ≈	**100**	**100**	**100**

Source: 133 focus group listings in Colombia, 176 listings in Guatemala. Adapted from Moser and McIlwaine (2000, 2001a).

in Guatemala (see also Appendices 20 and 21). Solutions relating to human capital assets represented almost one-third in both countries, while physical capital solutions were the least cited, constituting only 23 percent in Colombia and 12 percent in Guatemala.

Despite the significant prioritization of solutions to strengthen social capital, it was widely recognized that, on their own, such solutions were unsustainable, and that integrated or combined strategies were essential if various forms were to be confronted simultaneously. This was well illustrated by Figure 9.2, in which a woman from Esquipulas, Guatemala,

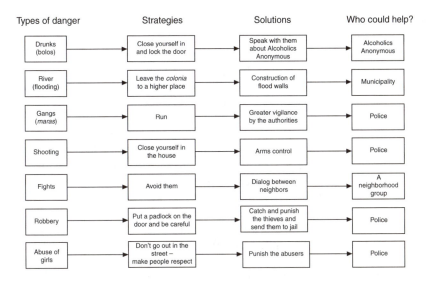

Figure 9.2 Diagram of interventions for reducing violence in Villa Real, Esquipulas, Guatemala (identified by one adult woman aged 38).

showed her opinion of a series of joint solutions needed to reduce violence. Interventions identified brought together dialog between people and community mobilization (social capital), human capital (especially talks concerning alcoholism) and physical capital (the construction of floodwalls and increased security in the home). In addition, she clarified the distinction between strategies to avoid the problem adopted by people themselves, and the ranges of informal and informal institutions whose assistance was essential to confront the problem.

Increasing social capital assets

Solutions focusing on social capital were by far the most important type of intervention identified. Such solutions were identified as the most important in all communities in Guatemala, and in seven of the nine communities in Colombia. At the same time, there were important distinctions between interventions relative to productive as against perverse social capital (see Chapter 8). The former referred to generating trust and peace, as well as a series of interventions to integrate youth into society, and positive police reform through human rights training; the latter dealt with repressive solutions that were more likely to generate negative social capital. These included social cleansing or negative police reform – demands for the police to be more severe with criminals, and greater military presence. Productive social capital interventions outnumbered perverse social capital interventions in both countries, with three-quarters of all social capital solutions denoting positive options in Colombia, and almost 60 percent in Guatemala (see Table 9.2).

Interventions to generate productive social capital assets addressed both cognitive and structural social capital. Within this category, the promotion of dialog, unity and family values within communities were the most widely cited interventions identified to strengthen cognitive social capital. As a young woman from Concepción, Guatemala City, stated: 'We need to communicate well and advise each other and we have to treat our children well to create trust in the community.' Interventions to strengthen structural social capital related to forming or strengthening local community organizations. In Jericó, Bogotá, for instance, a mother of a family group felt that the most appropriate solution was: 'to unite the community to make everyone alert.' A similar sentiment was expressed throughout Guatemala, where many participants focused on the reactivation and/or creation of community organizations that had disappeared along with the high levels of distrust associated with the civil war (see Chapter 8), as well as fostering community-wide participation in local development committees and neighborhood watch schemes. A woman from Nuevo Horizonte, Guatemala City, explained that: 'we have to organize ourselves and raise awareness in the community' in order to reduce violence. Similarly, a young woman in Esquipulas, Guatemala, explained the need: 'to generate dialog and form a group of neighbors that will take care of the community.' Some communities, including Gucumatz, Santa Cruz del Quiché, emphasized the importance of religion, in particular evangelical Protestantism, in generating trust and social capital.[3]

In Colombia, participants suggested increasing the resources of existing organizations, such as the Communal Action Boards (JACs), while in other cases, external assistance was sought to establish new organizations. Although it was accepted that external funding had to come from outside the *barrio*, community members repeated the need to control and run such organizations themselves. In Jericó, Bogotá, a group of seven 'Community Mothers,' in discussing the problem of the 'culture of violence' as a chain passed from one generation to the next, identified a series of solutions to build both structural social capital – through community-based organizations – as well as cognitive social capital through trust building among those involved in violence. Of particular significance was their demand for a bottom-up solution. As one commented: 'Peace is not to throw resources around without constructing projects from below, from the families and community organizations.' As noted in Chapter 8, however, the extent to which organizations were trusted was as important as their existence. On its own, it was not enough for local community members to take responsibility for running local institutions; in addition, it was important to develop transparency, accessibility and accountability in order to generate the necessary confidence in any such organization.

Despite widespread lack of confidence in state institutions, the most widely recurrent top-down solutions concerned strengthening the presence of state security forces, as well as the military forces, to tackle the violence. For example, an adult man from Huehuetenango, Guatemala, stated that: 'We need more control by the authorities and they need to practice better justice in the communities.' In Yopal, Colombia, greater military presence was suggested, coupled with the state providing arms for ordinary citizens to defend themselves. A small-scale cattle farmer, for example, called for: 'paid official protection from the state' as well as training the army in international humanitarian laws and human rights.

In parallel with demands for 'more authority,' were suggestions for greater social cleansing – a repressive negative social capital solution responding to the absence or ineffectiveness of state institutions and the judicial system (see Chapter 4). This was favored by the many who were disillusioned with the police and army, and felt there was no alternative. A community leader from Cali, Colombia, explained his positive attitude toward social cleansing groups: 'often the people are in favor of social euthanasia because the state doesn't respond.' Social cleansing was prioritized as a means to address both economic and social violence that included killing drug addicts, thieves, prostitutes and delinquents. Perverse

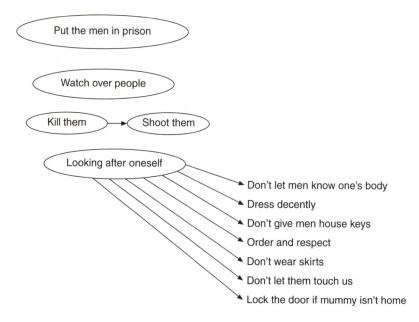

Figure 9.3 Diagram of interventions for reducing rape in El Carmen, Santa Lucía Cotzumalguapa, Guatemala (identified by 38 young women aged 12–17).

solutions were extremely widely identified in Guatemala, particularly in Huehuetenango, Esquipulas, Chinautla and Santa Lucía Cotzumalguapa, where in the latter, a focus group of women stated how rapists should be killed and shot (see Figure 9.3). However, they also suggested that such measures should be combined with less repressive interventions including prison sentences for offenders and strategies for taking care of oneself, such as keeping doors locked in the home and 'dressing decently.'

In both countries, solutions identified had a gender dimension, with men far more likely than women to favor repressive perverse social capital interventions, other than the case of rape. Since it was women who were most likely to experience rape in the absence of police intervention, they too supported such measures. In Colombia, among the female-only and male-only focus groups that discussed solutions, only one group of women favored social cleansing. Furthermore, of eleven single-sex focus groups that suggested various types of repressive solutions, nine were all-male groups.

Nevertheless, it is important not to overemphasize gender-stereotyping in attitudes to rape. Figure 9.4 illustrates male perceptions of solutions to rape, in this case from Chinautla, Guatemala. Here, a group of young men

Figure 9.4 Flow diagram of interventions for reducing rape in San Jorge, Chinaulta, Guatemala (identified by three young men aged 14–17).

emphasized the importance of combining avoidance mechanisms (not going out at night or to lonely places) with solutions designed to generate productive social capital (more police presence in the community) and physical capital solutions (the installation of streetlights and security in unlit places). This was augmented with repressive social capital interventions (increased military presence in the community).

Increasing human capital assets

Human capital solutions represented almost one-third of the total interventions, among which drug and alcohol rehabilitation programs focusing on the young were the most commonly cited area of preoccupation in both countries by all community members, regardless of age or gender. For example, an indigenous teacher from Chinautla, Guatemala, stated that: 'We need educational and rehabilitation programs in our community to reduce alcoholism, but these are hard to organize because people lack motivation.' A group of young women from La Merced, Guatemala City, not only identified a number of different solutions but also listed a

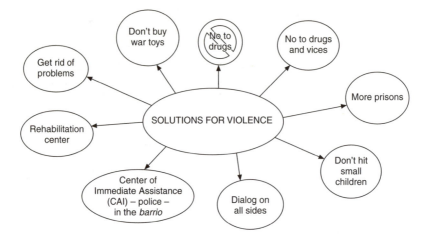

Figure 9.5 Flow diagram of solutions to address violence in 14 de Febrero, Bogotá, Colombia (prepared by seven boys aged 12–15).

diversity of social actors and institutions that should implement them. These ranged from formal institutions such as the government, church and school to informal local institutions and networks such as parents, friends and young people themselves (see also Figure 9.2). In Cali, Colombia, human capital solutions were viewed as significant, relating primarily to academic and vocational education (see Appendix 20), including activities such as woodwork and mechanics. These were suggested as a way of preventing young men from joining the many perverse social institutions in the community. A focus group of boys aged between 12 and 15 years in 14 de Febrero, Bogotá, reflected the 'no to drugs' campaign in their local school in identifying a range of solutions (Figure 9.5). They suggested interventions by both formal institutions such as the police and state rehabilitation centers, as well as preventative measures by families themselves including the message: 'don't hit small children.' In Colombia, far more than in Guatemala, youth themselves – particularly in the large cities such as Bogotá (in Embudo) and Medellín – called for drug and alcohol rehabilitation programs as well as sex education for youth (the only identified link to HIV/AIDS).

Increasing physical capital assets

Increasing physical capital was perceived as less important than increasing social or human capital in most of the communities, although it was considerably more important in Colombia, because of the severe ongoing economic crisis. In both countries, participants focused in particular on the need to generate employment as a means of addressing violence. In Colombia, physical capital interventions were most prevalent in Aguazul, associated with the acute unemployment linked with the collapse of the oil boom. Here, 24 percent of all solutions related explicitly to job creation (see Appendix 20). Physical capital solutions were also important in Girón, where they represented 28 percent of all solutions. In Guatemala, job creation was identified as most important in the predominantly indigenous community of Gucumatz, Santa Cruz del Quiché, where an adult man explained how: 'it is necessary to create work and share it throughout society as a way of confronting violence.' With the indigenous population particularly excluded from the labor market (see Chapter 4), this is perhaps not surprising.

Also important was the need for the development of community infrastructure. In Colombian communities, this especially referred to the creation of community centers, while in Guatemala, participants most notably mentioned the need for streetlights (see Figure 9.4), and the regulation of the sale of alcohol and firearms.

In summary, in both Colombia and Guatemala, the natural, understandable response to dealing with violence on a daily basis was to avoid it, rather than to confront it. Nevertheless, the dominant sense of powerlessness that pervaded their lives did not mean they were without suggestions as to how to address the problem. The diversity of responses reflected variations in gender and age-based identities, as well as community-level differences associated with contextual histories and ongoing levels of violence, together with country-level distinctions. Colombian communities showed less trust in formal state institutions than did Guatemalan communities, as noted in Chapter 8. The reverse was also true in so far as trust in local community-level institutions was higher in Colombia than Guatemala.

Despite such differentiation there was a remarkable degree of uniformity across communities in identifying the need to strengthen trust and cohesion – cognitive social capital. While interventions to strengthen structural social capital through formal institutions such as the judiciary and police service were similar to criminal justice approaches identified in Table 9.1, those relating to community-level informal institutions had more in common with bottom-up community-driven approaches, which to date have received far less attention by policymakers. An important implication of this finding concerns the identification of entry points for rebuilding local communities. As discussed in Chapter 8, women's organizations frequently played a critical, largely invisible role in rebuilding the social fabric of local communities, as well as in rebuilding trust between civil society and the state.

Above all, the data reveal that just as the causes and manifestations of violence in both Guatemala and Colombia ultimately were context-specific, so too violence-related solutions require the development of integrated intervention frameworks that move away from generalized prototype blueprints to context-specific flexible solutions tailor-made to the requirements of specific situations.

Conclusion

Throughout the book, as in this chapter, people's perceptions of their own reality have been at the forefront of the description and analysis, rather than those of the researchers. PUA methodology has provided essential analytical tools to give agency and identity to local perceptions of the multiple complexities and positioning of everyday violence, fear and insecurity. In so doing, it has shown how violence is constructed, negotiated, shaped and changed as different social actors try to control, resist or redefine the world in which they find themselves.

PUA methodology has also been invaluable in seeking to bridge the divide between the context-specific 'emic' research approaches of academics and the more 'etic' focus of policymakers that seek to systematize and classify complex realities – the so-called 'purity' of research and 'impure' domains of operational solutions. While a series of categorizations, developed through the course of the book, may assist policymakers grappling with difficult solutions, they also clearly demonstrate the limitations of not recognizing the interconnectedness that creates the fabric of fear and insecurity pervading local communities in both countries.

Such categorizations include the differentiation between political, economic and social violence and, associated with this, the critical relationships among these types of violence. The causal framework, outlined in Chapter 4, that seeks to analyze the causes, costs and consequences of violence shows that the multiple causal realities of violence can only be understood through the simultaneous analysis of structure, agency and identities. This in turn, can affect the nature of people's well-being and livelihoods from the perspective of capital assets. Finally, the review of different policy approaches to violence reduction, outlined in this chapter, locates within such dominant approaches the urgent, complex demands of local communities, particularly in terms of rebuilding trust, cohesion and social capital – essentially very new challenges for policymakers.

Each chapter in turn, as it addresses such issues as intra-family violence, substance abuse-related violence or organized violence groups, shows not only the differences, but also the remarkable similarities in endemic, routinized daily violence in both Colombia and Guatemala, despite significant contrasts in economic and political contexts. As different types of violence intersect and multiply, generating widespread fear and insecurity, it undermines human, physical, natural and social capital asset bases in communities, with experiences varying according to gender, ethnic group and age. In particular, as highlighted in Chapter 8, violence erodes, transforms and reconstitutes both productive and perverse social capital. While the gangs, paramilitary or delinquent groups are highly destructive to daily life, local people perceived that the transformation of such groups ultimately might be one of the most constructive ways of coping with violence, and preventing its further 'normalization.'

This book describes the perceptions of women and men, girls and boys in local poor urban communities. While their perception is partial and subjective, it is nevertheless overwhelming. Encounters with daily violence dominate the lives of all age groups. Youth and young are particularly susceptible to experiencing violence whether as the perpetrators of gang attacks or victims of rape. In contrast, women, children and older people are far more vulnerable to the fear and insecurity that reduce their mobility and paralyze their social relationships, trust and friendships. Is this a new phenomenon, exacerbated by contexts such as conflict, as in Colombia, or post-conflict fragility, as in Guatemala? Or is this an insidious phenomenon in cities throughout the world that has too long been ignored by researchers and policymakers alike? The identity and agency of the remarkable, proud and courageous people whose voices we have tried to represent in this book bear witness to the gravity of this issue not only for researchers but also for those concerned with addressing global poverty reduction.

APPENDICES

APPENDIX 1

The research locations and communities

Colombia

With reference to the first urban category of 'large metropolitan area/capital city,' the city of Bogotá experienced a decline in economic growth of 4.4 percent in the first quarter of 1999, with the unemployment rate during the same period standing at 18 percent of the economically active population (DANE 1999: 89–92). In terms of violence character-istics, the homicide rate in Bogotá in 1994 was 714 per million inhabitants (Newman 1998), with higher rates than most other cities except Cali and Medellín. In addition, there is widespread violence associated with drug consumption and trade, as well as gangs, especially among youth, and rob-beries and attacks, particularly against property. As elsewhere in the country, intra-family violence is also widespread in Bogotá (Klevens et al. 2000).

This category includes the three fieldwork communities of Embudo, Jericó and 14 de Febrero. Embudo, dating back to the colonial period, is located in the central area of Santa Fe, while Jericó and 14 de Febrero, both established in the 1970s and 1980s, are in the south of the city. The community of Embudo dates back to 1598, although it was not a residen-tial area until the eighteenth century, and a low-income area until the 1950s. It is sometimes referred to as a *zona de tolerancia* (zone of toler-ance) because of the concentration of the drug trade and high levels of crime and violence (murders, robberies and attacks). Indeed, this area has the highest murder rate in the city (Camacho and Guzmán 1997). Although the area has changed considerably as a result of widespread ren-ovation since 1998, when the research was conducted in 1999, the area was still a *zona de tolerancia*. 14 de Febrero was founded in 1971 by the Central Nacional Provivienda, a left-wing organization linked with the Communist Party (*Partido Comunista Colombiano*) that orchestrated land invasions and the subsequent development of the community. Provivienda remains important in the running of this now consolidated community. The other settlement in the south of the city, Jericó, was founded in 1980 by three families of night watchmen who invaded the land of a large hacienda. They subsequently sold off sub-plots illegally, organizing committees and lobbying for services. As with 14 de Febrero, Jericó is now well consolidated in terms of housing and infrastructure, as well as a huge diversity of different community-based organizations (CBOs) (see Niño Murcia and Chaparro Valderrama 1998 for an analysis of poor marginalized urban communities in southern Bogotá).

As part of the second category of 'large metropolitan areas with drug cartel history' both Medellín and Cali have large local economies, especially Medellín which is the main manufacturing city in Colombia, yet they are perhaps best known internationally as centers of drug cartels, especially during their height in the 1980s. Despite the capture of Pablo Escobar and leaders of the Cali cartels, both cities remain centers of the global drug trade now run by smaller and more fragmented cartels. While in the past, the local economies of Medellín and Cali were bolstered by the drug trade, especially through the construction industry, recent economic slowdown has hit both cities. For instance, Medellín demonstrated a negative growth rate of 8.3 percent in the first quarter of 1999, with the unemployment rate standing at 22.6 percent (DANE 1999: 92). In Cali, although the negative growth rate was much lower at 1.8 percent, unemployment remained high for the same period at 21.4 percent (ibid.). In terms of violence, the two cities are dominated by drug cartel-related violence, although political violence on the part of guerrillas and paramilitary groups has also contributed to high levels of crime and violence. In the early 1990s, homicide rates in Medellín in particular were among the highest in the world peaking in 1991; since then, the rate has declined yet remains high (Ceballos Melguizo 2001). The city also proliferates with gangs, militias and the *sicarios* (paid assassins) dating back to the 1970s (ibid.; Salazar 1994). By 1990, there were 120 youth gangs in Medellín, involving approximately 3,000 youths with an average age of 16 years (Rodgers 1998). Medellín is also home to many displaced people who have fled the political violence of surrounding areas of Antioquia and Urabá. Similar patterns prevail in Cali, with high rates of violent deaths and a city dominated by gangs and militias.

This category refers to the two research communities of Pórtico (Medellín) and El Arca (Cali). The community (or '*comuna*' as they are known locally) of Pórtico is located in the northern section of Medellín. A well-consolidated settlement, the *comuna* was founded in 1972 on land belonging to a large land-owning family who initially sold off lots to neighbors and employees, although most of the land remains illegally owned. In 1983, the settlement was extended through a land invasion with the assistance of a credit organization that assisted in building houses and infrastructure. Pablo Escobar also played a role in the *comuna*, financing the basketball pitch. El Arca, the research community in Cali, was established in 1980 through an invasion organized by a small group of M-19 (the now disbanded guerrilla organization – Movimiento 19 de Abril) which caused conflict with the police for the first few years of settlement. The community is now well serviced with water, electricity and even telephones for about 10 percent of the population.

The third category of 'intermediate cities and small towns with high levels of displaced populations' describes Metropolitan Bucaramanga (including the city of Bucaramanga and Girón). Bucaramanga experienced a decline in economic growth of 7 percent in the first quarter of 1999, and had an unemployment rate of 19.7 percent (DANE 1999: 91–92). The socio-economic situation in Girón is broadly similar. As well as having to cope with the pressures of accommodating a large proportion of displaced people, both urban areas also experience widespread delinquency, in the form of robberies and attacks, coupled with problems linked with drug consumption and intra-family violence.

This area is home to the research communities of Amanecer and Rosario. Amanecer is located in the north of the city in the area known as Ciudad Norte (a large area of low-income settlements). Established in the 1980s through the sale of lots from a local landowner, Amanecer is a small and relatively well-consolidated community. Rosario, in contrast, was established in 1991 by a land invasion of around eighty-four families on the banks of Río del Oro, which floods every year. Between 30 and 50 percent of the population are displaced from rural areas due to the violent conflict. The settlement comprises a mixture of more permanent and makeshift housing, and has regular access only to electricity and a basic water supply.

The final category in Colombia of 'frontier towns in natural resource rich areas' comprises Yopal and Aguazul, in the Department of Casanare, which are located in the country's oil-producing region. Since the mid-1980s their economies have experienced extremely high levels of activity, linked with the so-called '*Boom Petrolera*' (oil boom). However, despite initial prosperity related to the arrival of multinational oil companies, this has been followed by more recent economic collapse as labor demand fell with the completion of the construction of oil installations. Many of the benefits of the oil boom have been offset by the intensity of political violence in the department, especially between the ELN and to a lesser extent, the FARC, and the paramilitaries and Colombian armed forces. Indeed, the region remains one of the most violent in the country (Dudley and Murillo 1998).

The communities of Cachicamo and Colombia Chiquita are located in Yopal and Aguazul respectively. The community of Cachicamo is a well-established settlement located in the center of the town. Established in 1935 as the first registered settlement in the municipality, the area comprises both poor and middle-income groups. Colombia Chiquita, in contrast, was established in 1994 through a land invasion of private farm land, and is home to many displaced people as well as people who migrated to the area to take advantage of the oil boom. Colombia Chiquita in particular has experienced at first hand the violence of the paramilitaries and guerrillas who regularly enter the community and threaten and/or kill the community leaders and inhabitants.

Guatemala

As the capital and the main part of the first urban category 'capital city and towns in central Guatemala,' Guatemala City and the surrounding department has a population of around 2.3 million people which represents around 40 percent of the total population in the country (PNUD 1998: 54). Ethnically, the city is dominated by the *ladino* population, with only 19.3 percent comprising indigenous people (PNUD 2000: 58). In terms of the economy, in 1998, 57.4 percent of the population was excluded from the labor force, with an official unemployment rate of 6.1 percent, although much of the population is employed in the informal sector (ibid.). The principal types of violence in the capital are related to robberies, delinquency, *mara* activity (gangs involved in many types of violence), drug-related crimes and the proliferation of firearms. According to the register of criminal activity kept by the police, the death rate in Guatemala City was 3.8 times the national average, which was 75 deaths per 100,000 inhabitants. Robberies were also more widespread in the capital, with levels standing at 8.5 times the national average (IEPADES 1998). Chinautla, which is 12 kilometers north of the capital and which has a large Pocomam indigenous population is also included in this category. While the town has lower levels of human development than the city itself, it is more developed than other indigenous areas in the country; for instance, it is one of only three places where literacy levels for indigenous groups are over 50 percent (PNUD 1998: 21).

This area included the research communities of Concepción, Nuevo Horizonte, and La Merced, as well as San Jorge in Chinautla. All communities in or near the capital are vulnerable to environmental change, given their precarious location near rivers, roads, and ravines. Concepción, in zone 6 of the capital, was formed several years after the earthquake of 1976, when families invaded lands owned by an important farming family. Residents are, however, still engaged in the process of trying to secure legal title to the land. Nuevo Horizonte and La Merced, both in zone 13, were formed toward the end of 1983 when residents initiated land invasions. Most residents now own the titles to their land. The populations in all three communities, while predominantly *ladino*, except for San Jorge, in many cases originate from departments affected by the internal armed conflict. Compared with Nuevo Horizonte and La Merced, where problems with drainage and sanitation are particularly pervasive, residents in Concepción enjoy a comparatively high level of public services. These include the supply of potable water, electricity, and drainage systems (100 percent coverage) and public telephone service (70 percent coverage). San Jorge in particular was vulnerable to erosion and increasing levels of pollution that have affected nearby rivers. Also important is that San Jorge is an indigenous Pocomam community founded prior to the colonial epoch. Residents have managed to maintain their cultural traditions, customs and language despite pressures caused by proximity to the capital and high levels of poverty. Access to water and electricity is high (around 90 percent of all homes), although only 18 percent have access to drainage (see AVANCSO 2000, for further descriptions of these communities; also Cabanas Diáz *et al.* 2001).

The second urban category of 'departmental capitals in the Western Highlands' incorporated Huehuetenango, San Pedro Sacatepéquez, San Marcos, and Santa Cruz del Quiché, which are populated predominantly by indigenous groups (comprising 75.9 percent of the total population) (PNUD 2000: 58). This is also one of the areas most affected by the internal armed conflict and in particular by the military's counter-insurgency project, with Huehuetenango and El Quiché (along with Baja and Alta Verapaz which were not included in the research) being the most militarized departments during the conflict. The departments in this region are also the most economically and socially under-developed in the country with all three having some of the lowest levels of human development and the highest levels of social exclusion in the country (PNUD 1998: 199–200). El Quiché is the most deprived department, followed by Huehuetenango and San Marcos. All three have higher proportions of households living in poverty than the national average, as well as higher illiteracy rates. Although the transition to peace has reduced the incidence of political violence, violent deaths have increased throughout the 1990s, with lynching in particular affecting this region. Other types of violence are also on the increase, especially that associated with delinquency, although homicide rates in 1996 were lower in this region than elsewhere in the country (PNUD 1998).

This region includes the communities of Sacuma, Limoncito and Gucumatz. Sacuma, founded in 1969 with a predominantly *ladino* population on the outskirts of Huehuetenango, is reputedly the most dangerous and violent *colonia* (neighborhood) in the town. This is reportedly linked with the proximity of the Mexican border and the transient populations that inhabit the town and *colonia*. It is a relatively well-consolidated settlement, with good access to public services. Limoncito, in San Pedro Sacatepéquez, San Marcos, was founded in 1940. The areas of San Pedro and San Marcos border each other and, while the community of Limoncito was located in San Pedro, its administrative base was in the city of San

Marcos. For this reason, the geographical location of Limoncito is referred to as San Marcos. The predominantly *ladino* residents and minority Mam indigenous population, engage in a variety of economic enterprises. The community is dominated by small-scale, home-based enterprises such as weaving knitted sweaters using knitting machines. These enterprises supply companies in the capital which, in turn, often supply foreign *maquilas* (world market factories). The community has adequate, although somewhat decaying public services. Gucumatz, in Santa Cruz del Quiché, is located in the central urban area of the town dating back to pre-colonial eras. It is a predominantly K'iché indigenous community (around 90 percent), and comprises old and often run-down housing infrastructure.

The third urban category of 'town in the Southern Lowlands' refers to the town of Santa Lucía Cotzumalguapa, located in the department of Escuintla in the Southern lowland area between the highlands and the coastal plains in the Boca Costa area. Economically, the region is characterized by plantation agriculture, especially sugar cultivation, with much of the population in Santa Lucía Cotzumalguapa associated with this sector in some way. As a department, Escuintla has one of the lowest levels of social exclusion and poverty after Guatemala City, with medium levels of human development, the highest proportion of the economically active population working in the formal sector, and relatively high levels of education (PNUD 1998, 1999). Although this area was not severely affected during the armed conflict, the department has witnessed some of the highest increases in violent deaths in the 1990s. Indeed, in 1996, the highest homicide rates in the country were recorded in Escuintla (at 165 per 100,000 inhabitants) (PNUD 1998: 149). This has been part of a general shift in violence towards urban areas and especially secondary cities (Palma 1998).

Included in this category is the community of El Carmen, Santa Lucía Cotzumalguapa. A predominantly *ladino* community, El Carmen was formed around 1820. The population of both the town and community of El Carmen increased dramatically during two historical flash points, first in 1972 and again in 1982, mainly as a result of displacement caused by economic migration and the internal armed conflict. This has led to an increase in indigenous groups, especially from the Department of Quiché, from where most fled. The community is relatively well serviced in terms of infrastructure, given its age.

In the final urban category of 'town in the Eastern Lowlands,' Esquipulas, in the department of Chiquimula, lies close to the borders with both Honduras and El Salvador, with a relatively large transient population from these two countries (usually aiming to go to the United States via Mexico) and a small indigenous population. As a department, Chiquimula has medium to low levels of human development and higher than average levels of social (PNUD 1998: 199–200). Chiquimula has slightly fewer poor families than the national average (Instituto de Investigaciones Económi-cas y Sociales 1994), yet 62.6 percent of the population have received no education (PNUD 1999: annex A.6), and the formal sector workforce is small (PNUD 1999). Although this part of the country was relatively immune from the political violence of the armed conflict, it has tradition-ally been associated with violence, especially in relation to the use of arms (firearms and knives/machetes) and linked with *machismo* (Palma 1998). Indeed, it is this department which has been associated with the recent increases in non-political urban violence in smaller cities and towns.

In Chiquimula, fieldwork was conducted in Villa Real, Esquipulas, which was founded in 1980 close to the center of this frontier town. Located on the banks of a river, the community, although relatively well consolidated, is subject to annual flooding. All homes have electricity and water, with 75 percent having access to a telephone and 50 percent able to use a refuse collection service. Between 15 and 20 percent of the commun-ity are either from El Salvador or Honduras, due to proximity to the border.

APPENDIX 2

Summary of the main PUA tools on violence and recommended number of exercises in each community

Tool	Recommended number of exercises
Matrix of general data	1–2
Matrix of social organization	1–2
Listing of general problems	15–20
Ranking of general problems (scoring, 'onion' diagram, or flow diagram)	5–7
Listing of types of violence	15–20
Ranking of types of violence (scoring, 'onion' diagram, or flow diagram)	5–7
Map of institutional relationships	3–5
Preference matrix on social institutions	7–10
Participatory map of the community	1+
Participatory map of secure and insecure places	5
Matrix on history of the community	1–2
Matrix of trends on general problems	2–3
Matrix of trends on types of violence	5–10
Timeline – daily, weekly, monthly	3–5
Timeline – yearly	3–5
Timeline – long-term (over period of a number of years)	3–5
Causal flow diagram on types of violence and/or other problems	10–15
Problem tree	3
Listing of strategies to cope with violence	10–15
Diagram of strategies to cope with violence	5–7
Listing of solutions to reduce violence	10–15
Diagram of solutions to reduce violence	5–7
Drawings	10–15

Note
The recommended number of exercises was intended as a broad and flexible guide within the current research context, and does not represent strict numerical recommendations for the use of PUA either in this case or in general.

APPENDIX 3

Summary of the principal social actors involved in political violence in Colombia, 1948–98

Social actors in violent armed conflict	1948–58	1959–70	1971–80	1981–90	1991–4	1995–8
Traditional political establishment: Liberals–Conservatives	Urban insurrection of 'El Bogotazo,' followed by 'La Violencia;' Liberal–Conservative rural civil war	Political peace established with two party power sharing in a 'Frente Nacional'	1970 Presidential elections widely perceived as fraudulent resulting in M-19 guerrillas. Turbay's National Security Statute	1982 President Betancour's Amnesty; Peace Process attempts at political reform, direct election of mayors	President Gaviria's constitutional reform intended to decentralize and give local level political representation	State weakened by allegations of President Samper's electoral financial support from drug cartels
Peasant movement	Conflict for land	Peasant land invasions under ANUC	Failed land reform: joined guerrillas to fight and/or grow coca		Peasant leaders targeted by paramilitary	
First-generation guerrilla movements	Communist self-defense groups active in coffee-growing areas and remote mountains	National level guerrilla activities in conflict; pro-Soviet FARC formed in 1950s; Maoist EPL in 1960s; pro-Cuban ELN in early 1960s		FARC founding UP; fighting with armed forces/ protection to coca farmers; taxation of drug cartels; kidnapping; extortion	Cold War collapse increases economic reliance on criminally derived domestic resources from drugs (FARC) and oil (ELN)	Intensification of armed forces conflict with forces participating in coca zones; expanding social base of guerrilla forces; conflict with paramilitary

Actor			
Second-generation guerrilla movements			Main guerrilla groups M-19 – pursue armed struggle for political representation; Movimiento Armado Quintín Lame fought for indigenous rights. 1989 Peace Accords made with various groups
Paramilitary forces	Decree 3398 of 1968 giving military the right to arm civilians	Privatization of security forces through self-defense groups	Establishment of CONVIVIR self-defense groups; terrorization of population in guerrilla held areas to control coca trade routes; untouched by military
Marijuana/coca producers		Conflicts associated with coca production with both armed forces, drug cartels, protected by guerrilla forces	Protection of labs and drugs operations by guerrilla forces; sympathizers increasingly attacked by paramilitary and armed forces
Drug intermediaries and cartels		Violent conflict relating to control and organization of drug crime	Establishment of MAS and other ACUs to kill guerrilla forces; early collaboration with armed forces	Violent penetration of agricultural areas to acquire (i) land for cattle ranching and commercial coca production, and (ii) trade routes for coca; increasing collaboration with paramilitary

Source: Adapted from Moser *et al.* (2000).

APPENDIX 4

Types of problems by violence and types of capital asset by community, Colombia (%)

Type of problem	Embudo, Bogotá	14 de Febrero, Bogotá	Jericó, Bogotá	Amanecer, Bucaramanga	Rosario, Girón	El Arca, Cali	Pórtico, Medellín	Cachicamo, Yopal	Colombia Chiquita, Aguazul	Total (average)
Violence-related										
Drugs	16	18	6	10	12	9	5	3	—	9
Insecurity	11	12	21	10	3	8	3	7	4	9
Intra-family violence	5	4	10	3	4	3	2	2	4	4
Robbery	5	11	3	14	5	13	—	6	1	6
Fights	5	6	2	2	—	1	—	2	1	2
Gangs	—	2	6	1	—	3	6	1	1	2
Loitering (vagancia)	—	4	—	6	9	1	3	1	1	3
Killing	11	2	—	1	—	—	2	2	3	2
Rape	5	1	—	1	1	—	—	—	2	1
Alcoholism	—	4	—	2	—	3	—	1	1	1
Prostitution	—	—	2	1	1	—	1	2	—	1
Guerrilla forces	—	—	—	—	—	—	—	1	—	—
Paramilitary forces	—	—	—	—	—	—	—	1	5	1
Threats	—	—	—	—	—	—	—	5	—	1
Subtotal	58	64	50	51	35	41	22	34	23	42
Physical capital-related										
Unemployment	5	11	6	6	7	9	13	11	11	9
Lack of public services	—	2	13	9	9	7	7	8	11	7
Housing problems	5	1	2	1	2	3	9	7	5	4
Transport problems	—	1	3	4	8	4	3	3	3	3
Subtotal	10	15	24	20	26	23	32	29	30	23

Social capital-related										
Lack of unity	—	2	6	10	5	3	13	12	—	5
Absence of the state	—	—	3	1	2	2	2	2	11	3
Discrimination/stigma	5	2	—	3	1	4	—	3	—	2
Corruption	11	3	—	1	—	—	—	—	3	2
Distrust of police	—	2	—	3	1	9	—	1	—	2
Subtotal	16	9	9	18	9	18	15	18	14	14
Human capital-related										
Lack of education	5	—	6	4	10	7	13	6	7	6
Lack of recreation	—	4	2	2	2	—	8	1	4	2
Lack of health services	5	—	—	—	4	3	6	4	6	3
Hunger	—	2	—	—	—	2	1	1	—	1
Subtotal	10	6	8	6	16	12	28	12	17	12
Natural capital-related										
River (flooding)	—	—	—	1	13	1	—	1	7	2
Environmental hazards	—	—	—	—	—	1	1	1	1	1
Erosion	—	—	1	1	—	—	—	1	1	—
Natural disasters	—	—	—	—	—	—	—	—	1	—
Subtotal	—	—	1	2	13	2	1	3	10	3
Financial capital-related										
Poverty	5	8	10	1	2	5	6	5	6	5
Subtotal	5	8	10	1	2	5	6	5	6	5
Total ≈	**100**	**100**	**100**	**100**	**100**	**100**	**100**	**100**	**100**	**100**

Source: 159 listings of problems. Adapted from Moser and McIlwaine (2000).

APPENDIX 5

Types of problems by violence and types of capital asset by community, Guatemala (%)

Type of problem	Concepción, Guatemala City	Nuevo Horizonte, Guatemala City	La Merced, Guatemala City	San Jorge, Chinautla	Sacuma, Huehuetenango	Limoncito, San Marcos	El Carmen, Santa Lucía Cotzumalguapa	Villa Real, Esquipulas	Gucumatz, Santa Cruz del Quiché	Total (average)
Violence-related										
Theft	6	10	13	1	13	9	17	8	8	10
Gangs	11	6	9	13	11	12	6	5	6	9
Intra-family violence	9	7	5	11	4	7	7	1	7	6
Drugs	6	10	6	3	8	6	3	6	6	6
Alcoholism	4	6	5	4	4	8	7	3	7	5
Fights/shooting	2	5	6	—	6	—	—	7	2	3
Rape	4	3	1	1	4	1	2	—	1	2
Killings	7	—	—	—	3	—	—	3	—	2
Kidnapping	3	1	—	—	2	—	4	—	2	1
Loitering	1	1	1	—	1	—	—	—	4	1
Prostitution	—	2	—	—	1	—	1	1	1	1
Danger	—	—	—	—	3	4	—	2	3	1
Human rights abuse	—	—	—	—	—	—	—	—	3	—
Subtotal	53	51	46	33	60	47	47	36	50	47
Physical capital-related										
Lack of public services	8	14	17	6	8	20	12	17	17	13
Lack of transport	—	1	5	2	4	10	2	6	6	4
Unemployment	1	2	2	—	1	4	—	1	4	2
Housing	4	1	1	—	—	1	1	1	—	1
Work conditions	—	—	—	4	—	—	7	1	—	1
Subtotal	13	18	25	12	13	35	22	25	27	21

Social capital-related										
Lack of co-operation	7	5	2	6	3	6	4	8	1	5
Erosion of traditions	—	1	—	6	3	—	4	1	—	2
Discrimination	2	—	1	1	2	1	3	—	—	1
Lack of police	—	3	—	—	3	1	—	—	—	1
Corruption	—	1	—	3	1	—	—	1	3	1
Subtotal	9	10	3	16	12	8	11	10	4	10
Human capital-related										
Lack of education	1	7	4	11	1	—	2	1	7	4
Lack of health services	1	1	4	3	5	4	3	1	1	2
Lack of recreation	1	2	3	1	—	1	—	—	1	1
Lack of family planning	1	2	—	—	—	—	2	1	—	1
Other services	—	2	3	—	—	—	—	2	1	—
Nutrition	—	1	1	1	—	1	1	—	—	1
Subtotal	4	15	15	16	6	6	8	5	10	9
Natural capital-related										
River	2	—	—	11	4	—	—	17	—	4
Environmental hazards	1	4	1	—	—	—	—	4	1	3
Pollution	9	2	2	7	3	—	—	—	—	1
Subtotal	12	6	3	18	7	—	—	21	1	8
Financial capital-related										
Poverty	4	3	7	1	1	6	11	1	4	4
Subtotal	4	3	7	1	1	6	11	1	4	4
Total ≈	**100**	**100**	**100**	**100**	**100**	**100**	**100**	**100**	**100**	**100**

Source: 199 listings of problems. Adapted from Moser and McIlwaine (2001a).

APPENDIX 6

Types of economic, social and political violence by community, Colombia (%)

Type of violence	Embudo, Bogotá	14 de Febrero, Bogotá	Jericó, Bogotá	Amanecer, Bucaramanga	Rosario, Girón	El Arca, Cali	Pórtico, Medellín	Cachicamo, Yopal	Colombia Chiquita, Aguazul	Total (average)
Economic										
Drugs	18	22	12	15	33	12	11	9	—	15
Insecurity	4	13	14	15	9	16	11	18	15	13
Robbery	9	17	15	28	15	25	7	16	8	15
Loitering (*vagancia*)	—	3	3	9	25	—	2	2	3	5
Gangs[a]	—	2	10	3	—	7	18	2	2	5
Prostitution	—	—	—	1	1	—	2	5	—	1
Subtotal	31	57	54	71	83	60	51	52	28	54
Social										
Inside the home	*11*	*10*	*16*	*6*	*11*	*13*	*5*	*7*	*8*	*10*
Intra-family violence	11	10	16	6	11	13	5	7	8	10
Outside the home	*32*	*28*	*22*	*15*	*7*	*10*	*33*	*11*	*10*	*18*
Fights	23	20	10	8	1	4	13	4	5	10
Deaths	8	2	2	3	—	—	20	5	—	4
Alcoholism	—	6	4	3	—	5	—	2	2	2
Encapuchados	—	—	—	—	—	1	—	—	—	1
Other[b]	1	—	6	1	—	—	—	—	3	1
Outside or inside the home	*15*	*2*	*4*	*6*	*4*	*—*	*2*	*—*	*7*	*4*
Rape	15	2	4	6	4	—	2	—	7	4
Subtotal	58	40	42	27	16	23	40	18	25	32

Political										
Police abuses	11	3	2	1	—	8	7	—	2	4
Guerrilla forces	—	—	2	—	—	1	—	2	—	1
War	—	—	—	—	—	1	—	26	22	3
Paramilitary forces	—	—	—	—	—	—	—	2	18	2
Assassinations	—	—	—	—	—	1	—	—	—	2
Private security forces	—	—	—	—	—	7	2	—	—	1
Extortion	—	—	—	1	—	—	—	—	—	—
Threats	—	—	—	—	1	—	—	—	—	1
Displaced people	—	—	—	—	—	—	—	—	5	1
Subtotal	11	3	4	2	1	18	9	30	47	14
Total ≈	**100**	**100**	**100**	**100**	**100**	**100**	**100**	**100**	**100**	**100**

Source: 104 listings of types of violence. Adapted from Moser and McIlwaine (2000).

Notes

a Gangs were classified as an economic form of violence due to their close links with theft.

b This includes *machismo*, discrimination, mistreatment of children in the street.

APPENDIX 7

Types of economic, social and political violence by community, Guatemala (%)

Type of violence	Concepción, Guatemala City	Nuevo Horizonte, Guatemala City	La Merced, Guatemala City	San Jorge, Chinautla	Sacuma, Huehuetenango	Limoncito, San Marcos	El Carmen, Santa Lucía Cotzumalguapa	Villa Real, Esquipulas	Gucumatz, Santa Cruz del Quiché	Total (average)
Economic										
Drugs[a]	12	8	12	6	12	15	10	—	12	10
Insecurity	1	—	—	1	3	3	—	2	1	1
Robbery/assault	11	11	12	4	5	18	22	6	18	12
Delinquency	3	7	3	—	3	5	2	1	5	3
Loitering	—	1	1	—	—	—	2	—	5	1
Maras/Gangs[b]	5	6	19	9	11	18	10	18	6	11
Prostitution	1	2	—	—	—	—	4	—	2	1
Kidnapping	3	2	1	—	11	—	—	2	6	3
Armed attacks	8	2	10	1	3	—	2	11	—	4
Subtotal	44	39	58	21	48	59	52	40	55	46
Social										
Inside the home	16	13	8	29	6	15	15	9	11	14
Intra-family violence	16	13	8	29	6	15	15	9	11	14
Outside the home	23	35	20	35	30	26	15	44	20	28
Fights	15	20	2	23	18	21	2	18	5	14
Deaths	2	5	3	1	4	—	3	13	—	3
Alcoholism	5	6	11	7	7	5	7	11	10	8
Lynchings	—	—	1	—	—	—	1	2	—	1
Other[c]	1	4	3	4	1	—	2	—	5	2

Outside or inside the home	13	7	11	10	9	—	12	7	5	8
Rape	13	7	11	10	9	—	12	7	5	8
Subtotal	52	55	39	74	45	41	42	60	36	50
Political										
Police abuses	1	1	2	1	1	—	1	—	4	1
Assassinations	2	2	—	—	3	—	—	—	3	1
Discrimination	1	—	1	—	1	—	—	—	—	—
Threats/terrorism	—	—	—	—	2	—	1	—	—	—
Human rights violations	—	3	—	1	—	—	3	—	1	1
Subtotal	4	6	3	1	7	—	5	—	8	3
Total ≈	100	100	100	100	100	100	100	100	100	100

Source: 154 listings of types of violence. Adapted from Moser and McIlwaine (2001a).

Notes

a Drugs were classified as an economic form of violence due to their close link with theft and mugging.

b Gangs were classified as an economic form of violence due to their close link with theft.

c Includes *machismo*, presence of satanic cults and accidents.

APPENDIX 8

Composite listing of types of intra-family violence in Guatemala and Colombia

Colombia	Guatemala
Mistreatment of children	Family verbal abuse and quarrels
Physical violence between spouses	Family physical fighting
Verbal violence between spouses	Men verbally abusive to spouses
Husband killing wife and burying her in the yard	Men physically beat/hit their wives
Mothers hitting children hard and making them bleed	Sexual violence against wives
	Parents hit their children (to correct them)
Aggression against children by parents	Fathers hitting their sons
Children hitting parents	Mothers hit their sons
Mistreatment of the elderly	Sexual abuse of children
Parents fighting	Robbery of children
Violence of husbands towards mothers-in-law	Rape of girls and young women
Rape of girls by fathers	Rape and strangulation of young women
Rape of girls by renters	Brothers beat each other
Rape of girls by stepfathers	Sexual abuse between brothers
Rape of girls by fathers when they are under the influence of *bazuco* (crack cocaine)	Killing between brothers
Children having sexual relations with their mothers when they take *bazuco*	Young men hitting their fathers
Mothers raping sons under the influence of drugs	Older children hitting younger ones
Fights between siblings	Violence against the elderly
Abandonment of children	
Physical and emotional trauma	

Source: Listings of general problems and types of violence.

APPENDIX 9

Types of drug-related problems identified in nine communities in Colombia

---

Presence of drug addicts, including female addicts
Presence of *viciosos* (people with vices, usually referring to drugs)
Robbing for drugs
Killing for drugs
Drug use among children
Parents forcing their children to obtain drugs
Fathers under the influence of *bazuco* raping their daughters
Children under the influence of *bazuco* having sexual relations with their mothers
Mothers under the influence of drugs raping their sons
Violence by women anxious to get drugs
Drug addicts making others leave the basketball court
Drug addicts mistreating people in the community
Sex offered in exchange for drugs
Husbands killing wives who don't give them money for drugs
Police belief that everyone is a drug addict and/or *desechable* (disposable)
Young women forced to smoke drugs against their will
Smoking and sale of drugs
Drug trafficking
Youth under the influence of marijuana
Many people using marijuana
Easy access to drugs
Death from drugs

Source: 159 focus group listings of general problems.

217

APPENDIX 10

Household drug expenditure in Pórtico, Medellín, Colombia reported by two adult groups

(a) Household expenditure noted by one mother in a group of four women aged 25–40

Expenditure item	Cost per month (pesos)	Cost per month ($)	% of total
Alcohol, drugs, gambling	540,000	336.7	49.3
Food	400,000	249.3	36.6
Transport	95,800	59.7	8.8
Services	50,000	31.2	4.6
Education	8,500	5.3	0.8
Total	1,094,300	682.2	100.0

(b) Aggregate household expenditure from a mixed group of adults aged 17–40

Expenditure item	Cost per month (pesos)	Cost per month ($)	% of total
Food	200,000	124.7	30.7
Services	100,000	62.3	15.3
Rent and credit	85,000	53.0	13.0
Transport	60,000	37.4	9.2
Education	50,000	31.2	7.7
Bazuco	40,000	24.9	6.1
Parties	40,000	24.9	6.1
Alcohol	30,000	18.7	4.6
Cocaine/perico	20,000	12.5	3.1
Gambling	12,000	7.5	1.8
Marijuana	8,000	5.0	1.2
Pepas	6,000	3.7	0.9
Total	651,000	405.9	100.0

APPENDIX 11

Gang, robbery and delinquency-related violence as a proportion of total violence related problems, Guatemala

Community	Violence-related problems as a proportion of general problems (%)	Gang, robbery, and delinquency-related violence as a proportion of violence-related problems (%)
Concepción, Guatemala City	54	55
Nuevo Horizonte, Guatemala City	51	45
La Merced, Guatemala City	46	63
Sacuma, Huehuetenango	60	60
Limoncito, San Marcos	49	42
El Carmen, Santa Lucía Cotzumalguapa	47	57
Villa Real, Esquipulas	36	63
Gucumatz, Santa Cruz del Quiché	51	43
San Jorge, Chinautla	33	42
Total	48	55

Source: 199 listings of general problems.

APPENDIX 12

Types of violence related to gangs, robbery and delinquency, Guatemala

Maras	Street violence
Pandillas	Violence between men
Maras killing people	Fights
Maras breaking windows	Fights at night
'*Cholos*' who disturb	Danger in the streets
Maras who paint the walls	Dangerous places
Actions between *maras*	Assassinations
Gang fights – to death	Killing
Maras abuse women	Killing fights
Young men who go around upsetting people	Delinquency
Young people who make problems	Robbers
Problems with youth	Thieves
Youth who insult	Assaults
People with guns	Loiterers
	Kidnapping
	Guerrillas

Source: 199 Listings of general problems and types of violence. Adapted from Moser and McIlwaine (2001a).

Note
Cholos – Slang term for *maras*; literally means mixed race.

APPENDIX 13

Prevalence of membership and service delivery social institutions in Colombia

Type of institution	Embudo, Bogotá	14 de Febrero, Bogotá	Jericó, Bogotá	Amanecer, Bucaramanga	Rosario, Girón	El Arca, Cali	Pórtico, Medellín	Cachicamo, Yopal	Colombia Chiquita, Aguazul	Total number and (%)
Membership organizations										
Violence-related groups	4	10	9	—	—	6	1	8	4	42 (24)
Neighborhood committees	2	7	9	2	2	7	3	1	5	38 (21)
Religious groups[a]	4	5	7	3	2	1	3	3	5	33 (19)
Women's and childcare organizations	4	3	7	5	2	3	3	1	4	32 (19)
Youth, sports and recreational organizations	—	4	3	1	2	7	3	1	1	22 (12)
Organizations for elderly people	—	4	1	—	—	3	1	1	—	10 (6)
Subtotal	14	33	36	11	8	27	14	15	19	177 (≈ 100)
Service delivery organizations										
Social service organizations	3	9	3	5	1	12	4	11	6	54 (28)
State/government organizations	1	4	7	5	5	—	2	12	9	45 (23)
NGOs	3	2	6	1	—	9	—	10	3	34 (18)
State security/justice institutions	2	3	—	2	2	2	1	5	5	22 (11)
Private sector organizations	1	—	—	1	1	1	—	5	8	17 (9)
Productive service organizations	1	—	—	1	4	1	1	1	3	12 (6)
Drug rehabilitation centers	3	—	2	1	—	4	—	—	—	10 (5)
Subtotal	14	18	18	16	13	29	8	44	34	194 (≈ 100)
Total	**28**	**51**	**54**	**27**	**21**	**56**	**22**	**59**	**53**	**371**

Source: 92 institutional listings, maps and matrices. Adapted from Moser and McIlwaine (2000).

Note:
a Religious groups refer to churches and prayer groups only. Religious organizations that provide social services are included in the appropriate service delivery category.

APPENDIX 14

Prevalence of membership and service delivery social institutions in Guatemala

Type of institution	Concepción, Guatemala City	Nuevo Horizonte, Guatemala City	La Merced, Guatemala City	San Jorge, Chinautla	Sacuma, Huehuete-nango	Limoncito, San Marcos	Villa Real, Esquipulas	Gucumatz, Santa Cruz del Quiché	El Carmen, Santa Lucía Cotzu-malguapa	Total number and (%)
Membership organizations										
Religious groups[a]	2	5	2	6	2	7	3	2	8	37 (44)
Neighborhood committees	3	3	3	—	1	2	3	1	2	18 (21)
Violence-related groups	—	1	3	2	1	2	2	—	—	11 (13)
Youth, sports and recreational organizations	2	3	3	—	2	—	—	1	—	11 (13)
Women's and childcare organizations	—	2	2	—	—	—	—	2	—	6 (7)
Organizations for elderly people	—	—	—	—	—	—	—	1	—	1 (1)
Subtotal	7	14	13	8	6	11	8	7	10	84 (≈100)

Service delivery organizations

										Total
Social service organizations	2	12	9	7	9	10	1	8	10	68 (29)
NGOs	4	12	7	5	1	2	3	23	5	62 (26)
State/government organizations	2	—	4	5	2	1	1	21	5	41 (17)
Productive service organizations	1	2	—	1	2	9	1	10	5	31 (13)
State security/justice institutions	—	1	2	—	2	1	2	5	5	18 (8)
Drug/alcohol rehabilitation centers	2	1	—	1	1	1	3	1	2	12 (5)
Private sector organizations	—	—	—	1	5	—	—	—	—	6 (3)
Subtotal	11	28	22	20	22	24	11	68	32	238 (≈100)
Total	**18**	**42**	**35**	**28**	**28**	**35**	**19**	**75**	**42**	**322**

Source: 126 institutional listings, maps and matrices. Adapted from Moser and McIlwaine (2001a).

Note

a Religious groups refer to churches and prayer groups only. Religious organizations that provide social services are included in the appropriate service delivery category.

APPENDIX 15

Perceived importance of social institutions by type in Colombia

Type of institution	Embudo, Bogotá	14 de Febrero, Bogotá	Jericó, Bogotá	Amanecer, Bucaramanga	Rosario, Girón	El Arca, Cali	Pórtico, Medellín	Cachicamo, Yopal	Colombia Chiquita, Aguazul	Total number and (%)
Membership organizations										
Neighborhood committees	2	26	10	5	12	21	6	4	12	98 (30)
Violence-related groups	5	11	13	—	—	11	6	15	10	71 (22)
Women's and childcare organizations	7	3	8	7	7	7	5	1	12	57 (17)
Religious groups[a]	4	10	10	3	6	1	3	8	10	55 (17)
Youth, sports and recreational organizations	—	5	3	2	4	11	3	1	3	32 (10)
Organizations for elderly people	—	7	2	—	—	5	1	2	—	17 (5)
Subtotal	18	62	46	17	29	56	24	31	47	330 (≈ 100)

Service delivery organizations

										Total
Social service organizations	8	20	4	7	3	17	13	21	16	109 (29)
State/government organizations	3	4	8	6	7	—	2	33	19	82 (22)
State security/justice institutions	3	7	—	4	2	4	2	22	21	65 (17)
NGOs	4	2	7	1	—	19	—	13	3	49 (13)
Private sector organizations	1	—	—	1	5	3	—	14	17	41 (11)
Drug rehabilitation centers	7	—	2	1	—	5	—	—	—	15 (4)
Productive service organizations	1	—	—	1	4	1	1	1	3	12 (3)
Subtotal	27	33	21	21	21	49	18	104	79	373 (≈ 100)
Total	**45**	**95**	**67**	**38**	**50**	**105**	**42**	**135**	**126**	**703**

Source: 92 institutional listings, maps and matrices. Adapted from Moser and McIlwaine (2000).

Note
a Religious groups refer to churches and prayer groups only. Religious organizations that provide social services are included in the appropriate service delivery category.

APPENDIX 16

Perceived importance of social institutions by type in Guatemala

Type of institution	Concepción, Guatemala City	Nuevo Horizonte, Guatemala City	La Merced, Guatemala City	San Jorge, Chinautla	Sacuma, Huehuete-nango	Limoncito, San Marcos	El Carmen, Santa Lucía Cotzu-malguapa	Villa Real, Esquipulas	Gucumatz, Santa Cruz del Quiché	Total number and (%)
Membership organizations										
Religious groups[a]	7	15	13	20	8	9	15	13	5	105 (49)
Neighborhood committees	8	8	13	—	1	2	3	10	2	47 (22)
Youth, sports and recreational organizations	8	8	5	—	3	—	—	—	1	25 (12)
Women's and child care organizations	—	11	6	—	—	—	—	—	2	19 (9)
Violence-related groups	—	2	3	4	1	2	—	2	—	14 (7)
Organizations for elderly people	—	—	—	—	—	—	—	—	3	3 (1)
Subtotal	23	44	40	24	13	13	18	25	13	213 (≈ 100)
Service delivery organizations										
Social service organizations	7	27	30	14	18	18	31	1	36	182 (32)
NGOs	7	28	19	8	1	2	7	6	48	126 (22)
State/government organizations	2	—	4	6	5	6	14	7	49	93 (16)
State, security/justice institutions	—	6	11	—	7	3	18	6	20	71 (12)
Productive service organizations	1	2	—	1	3	11	10	4	23	59 (10)
Drug/alcohol rehabilitation centers	2	4	—	5	4	2	9	9	3	38 (7)
Private sector organizations	—	—	—	—	—	—	—	—	—	4 (1)
Subtotal	19	67	64	34	42	42	89	33	179	569 (≈ 100)
Total	**42**	**111**	**104**	**58**	**55**	**55**	**107**	**58**	**192**	**782**

Source: 126 institutional listings, maps and matrices. Adapted from Moser and McIlwaine (2001a).

Note

a Religious groups refer to churches and prayer groups only. Religious organizations that provide social services are included in the appropriate service delivery category.

APPENDIX 17

Evaluation of trust of social institutions in Colombia (%)

Category of social institution	Positive evaluation (high level of trust) (%)	Negative evaluation (low level of trust) (%)
Membership organizations		
Women's and childcare groups	88	12
Youth, sports and recreation organizations	86	14
Religious groups	79	21
Neighborhood committees	75	25
Elderly groups	67	33
Violence-related groups	18	82
Subtotal	69	31
Service delivery organizations		
Drug/alcohol rehabilitation centers	100	0
NGOs	91	9
Social service organizations	87	13
Private sector organizations	72	28
State/government organizations	70	30
Productive service organizations	67	33
State security/justice institutions	49	51
Subtotal	77	23
Total	**73**	**27**

Source: 92 institutional listings, maps and matrices.

APPENDIX 18

Evaluation of trust of social institutions in Guatemala (%)

Category of social institution	Positive evaluation (high level of trust) (%)	Negative evaluation (low level of trust) (%)
Membership organizations		
Elderly groups	100	0
Youth, sports and recreational organizations	82	18
Religious groups	79	21
Women's and childcare groups	76	23
Neighborhood committees	68	32
Violence-related groups	0	100
Subtotal	68	32
Service delivery organizations		
Drug/alcohol rehabilitation centers	81	19
Social service organizations	76	24
NGOs	66	34
State/government organizations	60	40
Productive service organizations	49	51
State security/justice institutions	39	61
Subtotal	62	38
Total	**65**	**35**

Source: 126 institutional listings, maps and matrices.

APPENDIX 19

Strategies for coping with violence[a] in Colombian and Guatemalan communities, by percentage of total

Type of coping strategy	Colombia (%)	Guatemala (%)
Avoidance strategies		
Avoid 'bad company/friends'	4	4
Avoid those involved in violence-related activities	7	2
Remain silent/ignore situation	21	9
Avoid dangerous areas	11	—
Change spatial mobility patterns	—	11
Change temporal mobility patterns – don't go out at night	10	10
Scream	—	2
Leave your husband	—	1
Flee from attacker	11	4
Don't carry valuables	3	1
Change habit of dress (rape) and be a good wife (intra-family violence)	—	1
Avoid gossip	2	—
Leave *barrio*	2	3
Lock houses/put bars on windows	4	4
Subtotal	75	52
Confrontation strategies		
Confrontation	2	2
Carry weapons	2	2
Use violence	2	3
Subtotal	6	7
Conciliation strategies		
Develop relations with those involved in violence	2	1
Turn to religion/pray for those involved	2	4
Subtotal	4	5
Others		
Report to family members or teachers	5	11
Report to human rights institution	—	1
Report to judge or other institution	—	5
Report to police or army	2	15
Submit, cry, abortion (in the case of rape)	5	4
Subtotal	12	36
Total	**100**	**100**

Source: 133 focus group listings in Colombia, 176 listings in Guatemala. Adapted from Moser and McIlwaine (2000, 2001a).

Note

a The types of violence-related activities include drugs, insecurity, intra-family violence, perverse social institutions (gangs, militias etc), rape, robbery, murder and fights in the street.

APPENDIX 20

Solutions for reducing violence by type of capital asset, Colombia (%)

Type of capital	Embudo, Bogotá	14 de Febrero, Bogotá	Jericó, Bogotá	Amanecer, Bucara-manga	Rosario, Girón	El Arca, Cali	Pórtico, Medellín	Cachicamo, Yopal	Colombia Chiquita, Aguazul	Total (average)
Physical capital solutions										
Job creation	5	6	4	9	8	9	11	6	24	9
Housing provision	3	—	2	2	—	5	—	—	3	2
Infrastructure provision (building community centers)	—	1	11	8	—	5	—	2	—	3
Build more prisons	—	6	—	2	—	—	—	2	—	1
Household security (locks, bars)	—	2	—	2	8	2	—	—	—	2
Land reform in rural areas	2	1	—	—	4	—	—	6	12	3
Urban planning	6	—	—	—	—	—	—	—	—	1
Other[a]	—	1	—	—	8	—	—	4	6	2
Subtotal	16	17	17	23	28	21	11	20	45	23
Human capital solutions										
Academic and vocational education	13	9	15	5	12	22	17	24	9	14
Drug and alcohol rehabilitation	10	10	—	2	4	5	3	2	3	4
Drugs and sex education for youth	2	4	4	—	—	2	10	—	7	2
Self esteem training	5	2	2	2	—	2	—	4	3	2
Sports and recreation	—	3	—	5	4	2	—	2	9	3

Health care	—	2	2	—	—	10	—	4	—	2
Conflict-resolution education	—	5	2	—	—	—	5	—	—	1
Family counseling	—	—	—	—	—	2	—	2	3	1
Subtotal	30	35	23	14	20	45	35	38	34	29
Social capital solutions										
Productive social capital										
Promotion of dialog and family values	20	11	21	12	4	17	32	7	3	14
Effective peace process	—	—	2	9	20	—	—	2	6	1
Assistance for/formation of community organizations	10	7	—	—	—	—	—	6	—	6
Programs to integrate youth to society	—	1	11	7	—	2	7	—	—	3
Construction of trust	5	2	13	9	12	2	7	12	12	8
Police reform (positive)	—	7	4	9	8	2	—	—	—	3
Perverse social capital										
Police reform (negative)	3	8	4	5	4	2	—	—	—	3
Social cleansing	11	6	4	7	4	5	7	—	—	5
Military protection/ stronger state presence	4	6	—	5	—	2	—	12	—	3
Provision of arms	—	—	—	—	—	—	—	2	—	1
Subtotal	53	48	59	63	52	32	53	41	21	47
Total	**100**	**100**	**100**	**100**	**100**	**100**	**100**	**100**	**100**	**100**

Source: 133 focus group listings.

Note

a This includes solutions such as reporting violent incidents to authorities (Girón), leaving the country (Cachicamo), disarming offenders (Cachicamo) or prohibiting the sale of alcohol (Colombia Chiquita).

APPENDIX 21

Solutions for reducing violence by type of capital asset, Guatemala (%)

Type of capital	Concepción, Guatemala City	Nuevo Horizonte, Guatemala City	La Merced, Guatemala City	Sacuma, Huehuetenango	Limoncito, San Marcos	El Carmen, Santa Lucía, Cotzumalguapa	Villa Real, Esquipulas	Gucumatz, Santa Cruz del Quiché	San Jorge, Chinautla	Total (average)
Physical capital solutions										
Job creation	2.5	5	9	9	5	5	2	12	3	5
Infrastructure provision	—	—	—	1	7	3	2	2	3	1
Build more prisons	—	1	—	—	—	—	—	—	—	1
Household security (locks, bars)	—	—	—	—	—	—	—	—	2	1
Urban planning	—	—	—	1	—	—	—	—	—	1
Disarming offenders/ control of firearms	2.5	1	—	—	—	—	7	—	—	1
Poverty reduction	—	—	—	2	—	—	—	—	—	1
Prohibition of the sale of alcohol	—	1	2	2	—	—	5	2	—	1
Subtotal	5	8	11	15	12	8	16	16	8	12
Human capital solutions										
Academic and vocational education and scholarships	10	5	9	1	5	6	5	6	11	7
Drug and alcohol rehabilitation	8	13	5	9	10	2	12	2	4	8
Drugs, sex and violence education for youth	8	10	5	10	4	6	2	6	2	7

Training, orientation and therapy	—	2	—	4	2	5	3	6	—	3
Sports and recreation	3	2	2	2	10	—	—	—	2	2
Conflict resolution education	3	1	—	—	4	—	—	—	—	1
Family counseling	5	1	16	5	7	5	2	2	7	3
Subtotal	37	34	37	31	42	24	24	22	26	31
Social capital solutions										
Productive social capital										
Promotion of family values	8	7.5	15	3	6	19	6	13	2	7
More governmental institutions	3	—	—	—	—	—	—	4	—	1
Construction of trust	3	13	9	5	8	9	5	5	19	8
Formation of community organizations	5	15	2	4	6	2	5	3	3	5
Use of religious organizations	—	—	4	—	4	3	2	13	9	3
More human rights institutions	—	3	—	2	—	3	—	—	—	2
Greater police presence	5	7.5	9	6	12	8	13	2	9	7
Perverse social capital										
More discipline in families	3	1	—	2	—	—	—	—	7	3
Deport foreign gang leaders	—	—	—	2	—	—	4	3	—	2
Social cleansing	8	1	—	6	—	8	2	—	2	5
Military protection/stronger state presence	8	2	11	12	5	6	8	8	9	7
Catch criminals and longer prison sentences	15	8	2	12	5	10	15	11	7	8
Subtotal	58	58	52	54	46	68	60	62	67	58
Total	**100**	**100**	**100**	**100**	**100**	**100**	**100**	**100**	**100**	**100**

Source: 176 focus group listings.

NOTES

1 URBAN VIOLENCE AS A CONTESTED DOMAIN

1 Social cleansing refers to the systematic murder of people belonging to certain social groups, usually those assumed to be linked with the perpetration of violence.

2 The term 'cultures of fear' or 'terror,' although still widely used (Corradi *et al.* 1992), has been criticized. This relates to what Margold (1998: 64) has termed: 'totalizing conditions that orchestrate all the rhythms of daily life' such that those experiencing violence are assumed to have no or limited agency in resisting this violence. Thus, 'societies of fear,' as suggested by Kruijt and Koonings (1999), is a preferable notion.

3 Garretón (1992: 17–22) referring to the military regimes of Argentina, Brazil, Chile and Uruguay, calls the first phase of fear 'the reign of terror' when the previous socio-political regime is dismantled; the second, 'impotence and sublimation' involving the reconstitution of a new social order; the third, 'hope and uncertainty' when the regime begins to crumble and civil society starts to mobilize; and the terminal phase of 'regressions, residues and exorcisms' which involves devising ways in which the armed forces can step down. After this, the transition to a democratic state is possible.

4 See Kleinman *et al.* (1997) on the construction of suffering.

5 Memory becomes collective when it moves beyond an individual account and is accepted and shared by a group. It must also have historical and emotional relevance (Chirwa 1998).

6 National security refers to 'safeguarding of the state's sovereignty over the territory and population within its borders, and implies policies to confront any threat to that sovereignty.' Public security refers to the maintenance of civil order, while citizen security relates to the freedom of individuals or groups to enjoy rights and freedoms (Kincaid 2000: 40).

7 The United Nations Interregional Crime and Justice Research Institute (UNICRI) data set on crime in eighteen developing country cities collected through the International Crime Victimization Survey (ICVS) constitutes the most detailed global information on urban violence available. Crime was measured and categorized into five types: (1) vehicle-related crime; (2) break and enter crime; (3) victimization experienced by the respondent personally; (4) consumer fraud; and (5) bribery/corruption. Data were collected in the largest city in each of the selected countries. Although it is not representative of the urban population in each country, it provides a starting point for regional comparisons of urban crime (bearing in mind issues of under-reporting and other

caveats). In Latin America, the countries included were Costa Rica, Brazil, Argentina, Bolivia, Paraguay and Colombia (UNICRI 1998).

8 In Colombia, for instance, violence experts (*violentólogos*) have identified the difference between geographically confined rural mountain violence (*la violencia del monte*) and urban street violence (*la violencia de la calle*) as central in understanding violence in the nation (Deas 1998).

9 As defined by the *Oxford English Dictionary*, for instance, '*violence* is (i) the quality of being violent; violent conduct or treatment, outrage, crying; (ii) by law, violence is the unlawful use of physical force; or intimidation by the use of this.' In contrast, '*conflict* is (i) a state of opposition or hostilities; fight or struggle; the clashing of opposed principles; (ii) the opposition of incompatible wishes or needs in a person; an instance of this or the distress resulting from this' (see also Bowman, 2001, on variations on dictionary definitions of violence).

10 Indeed, it has been argued that many violence analysts are often more preoccupied with measurement issues rather than understanding its causes (Marenin 1997).

11 Under-reporting is particularly prevalent in crimes such as sexual assault. The UNICRI (1998) report, for instance, shows that Bolivia, Brazil, Colombia and Costa Rica had the lowest global average reporting rates for sexual incidents.

12 These distinctions are based on Galtung's (1996: 197) definition of violence as 'avoidable insults to basic human needs, more generally to life, lowering the real level of need satisfaction below what is potentially possible.'

13 For example, a kidnapping does not give rise to costs in macroeconomic terms, since it is a transfer and neither adds nor removes value.

14 For instance while Londoño (1996) estimated that Colombia lost an estimated 4 percent of its GNP annually as part of the human cost of homicides, Trujillo and Badel (1998), writing two years later, estimated a more modest 1 percent of its GNP annually as part of the human cost of homicides.

15 This builds on previous research and analysis undertaken by the authors (see Moser and Holland 1997; Moser and McIlwaine 2000, 2001b; Moser and Winton 2002).

16 The concept of social capital is based mainly on the seminal theoretical work of Bourdieu (1993), Coleman (1990) and Putnam (1993). See Portes and Landolt (2000) for a review in the development context.

2 TOWARD A POLICY-RELEVANT POSITIONING OF VIOLENCE

1 For a policy-focused description of the differences between 'emic' and 'etic' research methods, see Moser *et al.* (1996).

2 At its most simplistic, this concerns two 'polarized' alternative approaches to poverty (Baulch 1996). First, is the 'conventional,' 'objective,' approach that identifies income/consumption as the best proxy for poverty (Ravaillon 1992). This is usually measured through large-scale, random sample household surveys, with a preference for consumption expenditure over income as more stable over time (Lipton and Ravaillon 1995). Second is the subjective, 'participatory' approach, that rejects the income/consumption approach as a narrow reductionist view, serving the technocratic needs of development professionals, while failing to understand the complex, diverse, local realities in which the poor live (Chambers 1992, 1995). The 'participatory' approach uses multiple, subjective indicators of poverty status that emerge out of the realities of the poor, collected through participatory techniques.

3 An important instrument to achieve this has been the integration of participatory poverty assessments (PPAs) into the World Bank's country poverty assessments that are implemented in all their borrower countries (Brock 2002; Norton *et al.* 2001; Robb 1999).

4 Chambers (2002) and Rademacher and Patel (2002) both provide illuminating reflexive 'auto-critiques' of their experiences as academic researchers participating in the production of the 'voices of the poor' components of the *World Development Report* (2000/2001).

5 Of particular importance were the capture, and later assassination of Pablo Escobar of the Medellín cartel in 1993, and the capture of the Rodríguez Orejuela brothers and other 'bosses' of the main Cali cartel in 1995 (Harding 1996).

6 The full name of the area where the community was located was San Pedro Sacatepéquez in the Department of San Marcos. However, hereafter, this will be shortened to San Marcos.

7 Pocomam is one of the largest Mayan indigenous cultures in Guatemala, along with K'iché, Kakchikel and Mam. *Ladino* is the term used to refer to the Spanish-speaking population of European ancestry, often called *mestizo* in other Latin American countries.

8 One of the anthropologists, María Eugenia Vásquez Perdomo, is a former member of the M-19 (see Vásquez Perdomo 2000, for an account of her experiences).

9 See Moser and Holland (1998) for a description of a similar approach to violence PUA in Jamaica.

10 The Office of Human Rights of the Archdiocese of Guatemala conducted the Recuperation of Historical Memory (*Recuperación de la Memoria Histórica*, REMHI) project. Based on oral testimonies, the report documented 55,021 cases of brutal atrocities, of which 79.2 percent were attributed to the Guatemalan military. Unfortunately, it is perhaps best known because of the assassination of the director of the project, Monsignor Juan Gerardi Conadera, in April 1998, 48 hours after the findings were made public.

11 At the same time, those who provided oral testimony material collected via the REMHI project (ODHAG 1999) also noted the cathartic role of sharing their experiences.

12 The issue as to whether qualitative data can be robust or representative is further explored in Moser (2001b).

3 THE MULTIPLE COMPLEXITY OF DAILY VIOLENCE IN URBAN COLOMBIAN AND GUATEMALAN COMMUNITIES

1 Colombia's annual per capita income is U.S.$2,500 (World Bank 2000: 274), whereas in Guatemala it is only U.S.$1,660 (ibid.: 300).

2 The FARC, the oldest of the guerrilla groups which began as a pro-Soviet group, was formed in the 1950s, while the ELN, which is pro-Cuban, was established in the 1960s (Vargas Meza 1998).

3 'A survey of Colombia: drugs, war and democracy,' *The Economist*, 21–27 April 2001. Although Plan Colombia was implemented after the fieldwork for this book was undertaken, it is mentioned here because of its importance in the national context.

4 Colombia also has small populations of indigenous peoples residing mainly in the Amazonian region, with some in the highland areas of Cauca and Nariño to the south of Cali, and in the Sierra Nevada de Santa Marta and Guarija

peninsula (Harding 1996). Also significant is the Afro-Colombian population concentrated in the Chocó region (Wade 1993). Both indigenous groups and Afro-Colombians have complained of systematic discrimination on the part of the dominant white/*mestizo* population.

5 The state was effectively acting as a 'facilitator of low-cost labour for the agro-export landowners' (Palencia Prado 1996: 3).

6 See Gleijeses (1991) for a detailed analysis of this period.

7 Civil patrols were assigned the task of policing their own communities and defending them from the guerrillas. By 1982–3 they consisted approximately 900,000 male *campesinos* (almost 10 percent of the entire population), and about 375,000 members remained in 1995 (ODHAG 1999: 14). The PACs were controlled by the army and, although membership was, in theory, voluntary, it became obligatory. As a critical element of the military's counter-insurgency project, linking the military and rural indigenous communities, they were responsible for carrying out many of the massacres that took place in rural Guatemala during the conflict (ODHAG 1999; see also Popkin 1999).

8 De León *et al.* (1999: 25) point out that 39 percent of all cover stories in the two main newspapers – the *Prensa Libre* and the *Siglo Veintiuno* – relate to violence.

9 Unofficial figures from the *Guardianes del Vecindarios* suggest that a total of 1,452 kidnappings occurred in 1997 (IEPADES 1998: 33).

10 Community Homes (*Hogares Comunitarios*) are run by *Madres Comunitarias*. The Homes comprise a range of different types, although there are two main forms; first, the HOBIS (*Hogares de Bienestar Social* – Social Welfare Homes), that provide childcare for children up to 5 years of age; second, FAMI (*Programa Familia, Mujer e Infancia del Instituto Colombiano de Bienestar Familiar* – Programme of Family, Women and Infants of the Colombian Institute of Family Welfare), that provide care for pregnant and lactating women.

4 COMMUNITY PERCEPTIONS OF THE STRUCTURAL FACTORS UNDERLYING POLITICAL AND ECONOMIC VIOLENCE

1 'Violentologists' are commentators from within a uniquely Colombian academic discipline concerned with the study of violence who, for the past thirty years, have analyzed changing patterns of political violence in the country (Moser *et al.* 2000).

2 Pecaut (2001) suggests that in the case of Colombia it is not useful to look for specific causes of violence because its nature is constantly changing.

3 The 'ecological model' has been used by violence researchers to elucidate the complex causes of, for example, child abuse (Belsky 1980), youth violence (Garbarino 1995), sexual coercion (Brown 1995), and 'intimate partner' domestic violence (Heise 1998).

4 Castells (1998) also provides a useful distinction between identities and roles. While roles are defined by norms structured by the institutions and organizations of society, identities are sources of meaning for social actors themselves and by themselves, constructed through a process of individuation. Identities therefore organize meaning (the symbolic identification by a social actor of the purpose of his/her action), while roles organize functions.

5 The creation, in 1968 of the National Association of Rural Farmers (*Asociación Nacional de Usuarios Campesinos*, ANUC), played an important role in the peasant movement for land. With an agenda to provide land for landless

peasants, they used invasions of large *haciendas* and land-holdings to pressure for their appropriation and distribution by INCORA, the National Institute for Agrarian Reform (*Instituto del Estado para la Reforma Agraria*).

6 In this context, the army's presence, as part of the official eradication programs, has provided the paramilitary with protection to fight for control of land with the guerrillas.
7 Landlessness varies according to area, although is concentrated in northern Guatemala, in the highland departments of Baja and Alta Verapaz, San Marcos, El Quiché, Quetzaltenango, Huehuetenango and on the southern coast (PNUD 1998).
8 Under Article 119 of the Constitution, for instance, the Guatemalan state is also obligated to strengthen co-operative land ownership through aid and rural support programs. Many of these provisions were reinforced, in theory at least, through the Accord on Socio-Economic Issues and the Agrarian Situation, signed in 1996. However, it has also been noted that there is still a long way to go in terms of the full implementation of these accords (Kay 2001).
9 The term *pájaro* dates back to the Liberal/Conservative conflict that resulted in *La Violencia* (1948–58). It purportedly refers to the way the Liberals threw the Conservatives out of airplanes, making them 'fly.'
10 However, the so-called 'narcoterrorism' prevalent throughout the 1980s turned into 'narcodemocracy' in the 1990s as the entire state system was permeated by corruption linked with illegal drug money (Gutiérrez Sanín 2001).
11 Focusing primarily on social violence, the *Casa de Justicia* program in Colombia works within the criminal justice system to promote conciliation, to facilitate access to the justice system in low-income communities with high levels of violence and also to educate low-income groups on human rights issues. Since it focuses on low-income areas, it also indirectly addresses economic violence. Overall, the *Casas* aim to play a key role in providing alternative forms of conflict resolution (Klevens 1998; Moser *et al.* 2000).
12 Between August 1995 and October 1998, 176 lynchings were reported to MINUGUA, making an average of 4.5 per month. Sixty-seven percent of those lynched had committed crimes against property. In most cases, they occur when formal investigation into the offense or crime is not conducted, and people feel moved to punish the accused themselves. In turn, lynchings themselves are rarely investigated (MINUGUA 1998: 33).
13 More specifically, this included 'The Agreement on the Strengthening of Civilian Power and the Role of the Armed Forces in a Democratic Society' through which the government agreed to form a new civilian police force.
14 The importance of poverty in particular as underlying violence is reported at the national level (Camacho and Guzmán 1997, on Colombia; PNUD 1998, on Guatemala).
15 As such, a lack of viable legal employment opportunities channels entrepreneurial spirit into better-remunerated, illegal activities. For example, estimated per capita income for guerrillas in 1995 amounted to U.S.$70,000 compared to the national per capita income of U.S.$1,800 and per capita military expenditure of U.S.$900 (Granada and Rojas 1995).
16 After Sudan, Colombia is the country with the greatest number of people displaced by violence, accounting for an estimated 20 percent of the global total of internally displaced persons (Social Watch 2000).
17 The UN definition of extreme poverty is the inability to afford even the products that make up the *canasta básica* (basic food basket) (PNUD 1998, 1999).

5 THE FAMILY AS A VIOLENT INSTITUTION AND THE PRIMARY SITE OF SOCIAL VIOLENCE

1 It needs to be stressed that social violence occurs both inside and outside the home, but that intra-family violence is usually the most prevalent manifestation of it. More specifically, sexual violence – while often discussed as being confined to the home – also takes place in the public domain.

2 As is common in the literature, the terms 'family' and 'household' are used interchangeably. At the same time it is recognized that the term 'household' refers specifically to the residential unit, while family as a concept is more broadly conceived, and may include relatives not living within a particular household unit. The term 'family' also incorporates more intangible value systems (Chant 1997; Moser 1993). The same distinction applies to intra-family and intra-household violence. However, since people in the community themselves referred to it as 'intra-family violence,' this term is used throughout the book.

3 Although this primarily refers to 'wife-beating' usually in the form of punching, choking, stabbing and so on, it can also denote a wide range of other types of abuse involving other actors in the home, with particular countries and cultures having specific forms of intra-family violence (Davies 1994; Pickup et al. 2001).

4 The methodology was also an important factor in the under-reporting in listings. Focus group discussions often used these as 'ice-breakers' at the beginning of the discussion, where people were asked to list and rank problems in the community and types of violence affecting them. At this point, they often had limited confidence. However, as this grew, especially when discussions were held more than once with the same group, people began to open up about violence within the home.

5 This concurs with feminist research on the family as a major source of societal conflict and gender-based violence (Castells 1998; Walby 1997).

6 Household structure is defined as a combination of headship (male or female) and composition (the members of a household). The main structures identified are male-headed nuclear households comprising a couple with children, male or female-headed extended households, where additional kin resided with a core nuclear unit, and a female-headed single-parent unit of a woman head living alone with her children (see Brydon and Chant 1989, for a typology). There is little research on the nature of households in Guatemala in particular, related to the concentration of research on the dynamics of the armed conflict and Mayan culture. In turn, the few studies on families and households tend to focus on rural areas only and rarely mention household structures explicitly (see Katz 1995). For a discussion of household structure in Colombia see Umaña Luna (1994).

7 The survey was conducted with a total of 180 people involved in the focus group discussions in Guatemala, and with 271 people in Colombia.

8 A further 3.4 percent of Guatemalan households and 8.9 percent of Colombian households comprised brother/sister units, grandmother-headed units, and couples living alone with no children.

9 This has been noted as especially problematic in countries undergoing conflict, especially in relation to child soldiers (Bernat 1999; Pridmore 1998).

10 Community members used the word '*machismo*' to refer to patterns of exaggerated masculinity among men, and '*masochismo*' to denote the experiences of women. *Masochismo* is closely associated with the academic construct of '*marianismo*' (Chant with Craske 2003; Ingoldsby 1991).

11 In relation to gender-based violence, it is significant that community members did not identify men's biological urges as a cause of violence, as this is often one of a set of factors discussed in the literature (together with psychological explanations, patriarchal relations and socio-economic conditions see O'Toole and Schiffman, 1997; Pickup *et al.* 2001).

12 Female-maintained households are usually overlooked in estimates of female-headed households because a male spouse is resident, yet not contributing financially.

6 SUBSTANCE ABUSE-LINKED VIOLENCE RELATING TO DRUG AND ALCOHOL CONSUMPTION

1 It is important to note that the nature and level of violence perpetrated while under the influence of drugs depended largely on the type of drug in question and its physiological effects (with cocaine, for example, provoking more extreme violence than marijuana, on the whole). Notwithstanding this distinction, however, many community members in both countries referred to drug users as one group, especially older generations.

2 Central America's location between South and North America makes this region particularly prone to international drug trafficking, especially Guatemala (see for example, Aguilera and Ogaldes 1996).

3 In her analysis of alcohol consumption in Peruvian Andean communities, Harvey (1994: 214) states: 'drinking is ... seen as an act of sharing and collaboration through which the community is created and sustained, community projects for progress realised, and continuing care from the supernatural powers ensured.' However, the importance of 'getting drunk' is also related to the contention that, in many cultures, drinking is associated with the breakdown or redefinition of social convention. Thus, if individuals transgress social norms by drinking alone, without motive and excessively, it becomes unacceptable, and individuals become known as *vicioso* (ibid.: 217). For a more detailed examination of women's drinking in a highland Chiapas community in terms of women's identities, roles and relationships, see Eber (1995). A policy-focused examination of the social significance of drinking patterns is provided by Grant and Litvak (1997).

4 Mondays were referred to as *día de caldo* or *caldo de mano*, which translates roughly as the 'day of the bull.' This was when local *cantinas* prepared a stew from bull meat or shell fish to act as a hangover cure. However, often men went to the *cantina* for the *caldo* then ended up drinking heavily again.

5 The method of payment for this was, for example, to 'buy four, and take one for yourself.' This could apply to joints of marijuana or pills.

6 There are 100 *centavos* in a *quetzal*.

7 In Villa Real, Esquipulas, a bottle of *kuto* cost 2 *quetzales*, whereas a litre of beer cost 10 *quetzales* and a quarter bottle of rum cost 3.75 *quetzales*.

8 Prostitution among young men was also noted in Pórtico, Medellín by a group of four teachers. They noted that when young men wanted to buy something, or find money (which could be for drugs), they sold sexual favors.

9 Leeds (1996) highlights the fact that in Brazil, drug-related activities are an economically viable option for those in poverty.

7 ORGANIZED VIOLENCE AT THE COMMUNITY LEVEL

1 Table 7.1 excludes drug-related organizations as they have different types of internal structures. It also excludes a range of other groups, often associated with youth, especially those linked with music, such *metaleros* (heavy metal groups), and *punkeros* (punk rock groups), because they are not involved in the perpetration of crime or violence. It also excludes state-sponsored groups such as the army, and the police (see Chapter 8).

2 The regional dissemination of gang culture is related particularly to the post-conflict return of many individuals and their families from other Central American countries such as El Salvador and Honduras, as well as deportation from the United States (see Aboutanos 1997; De Cesare 1997, on El Salvador).

3 See Miller (1998) and Laidler and Hunt (1997) on female gangs in the U.S.A.

4 See Rodgers (1999) on a similar pattern in El Salvador.

5 The main focus will be on various types of gangs, such as the *maras* in Guatemala or the *pandillas* or militias in Colombia, as well as delinquency in general. There will be little mention of the causes of joining the highly organized guerrilla or paramilitary groups in Colombia due to lack of primary information (as people were unwilling to discuss these issues in detail).

6 Miller (1998) also suggests that young women involved in gangs in the U.S.A. often turned to them in order to combat violence they faced in other spheres of their lives.

7 See also Curry (1998) on the U.S. and Riaño-Alcalá (1991) on Bogotá. Whether coerced or not, relatively high levels of sexual activity within gangs in El Salvador are suggested by the finding that nearly 56 percent of female gang members surveyed in San Salvador had been pregnant at some time (Cruz 1997).

8 Drug production and distribution organizations, not explicitly included here, ensured the most lucrative earnings of all.

9 It has been suggested that fashion, music and the drug trade are all industries marketed at young people, but markets to which the majority have little or no access. In the case of drugs, this presents a tempting alternative method of income-generation in the face of severe economic exclusion (De Orrellana 1997).

10 Of over 1,000 gang members surveyed in San Salvador, 76 percent were not studying, 74.5 percent did not have a job, and the most commonly reported need was for jobs (Cruz 1997; see also Gonçalves de Assis 1997, on Brazil).

11 See Rodgers (2001) on the protective role of the *maras*.

12 Although leaving the structure of gangs at any time is psychologically and culturally problematic (Rocha 2000).

13 See Dissel (1997), Barbetta (1997) and De Orrellana (1997).

8 VIOLENCE, SOCIAL INSTITUTIONS AND SOCIAL CAPITAL IN COMMUNITIES

1 This section and parts of the chapter draw heavily on McIlwaine and Moser (2001).

2 For further details and critiques of social capital, see Harriss and De Renzio (1997), Dasgupta and Serageldin (2000) and Portes (1998). For an annotated bibliography, see Feldman and Assaf (1999).

3 This is one of three main types of social capital identified by the World Bank (2000) in its recent *World Development Report* on poverty. The others are

'bonding social capital,' denoting strong ties among relatives, neighbors and friends on a horizontal basis, and 'bridging social capital' referring to weak ties among acquaintances also in a horizontal pattern.

4   This program, PROUME (*Proyecto de Urbanización Mesquital*) was funded by the World Bank and implemented through UNICEF (see Cabanas Díaz *et al.* 2001).

5   The total number of institutions identified was used as a proxy for perceptions of the prevalence of social institutions. The number of times an institution was cited was used as a proxy for perceptions of its importance (Groothaert 1998, 1999). Information on individual membership of organizations was not gathered since the participatory methodology does not use questionnaire surveys (see Groothaert 1999). While this has disadvantages, the use of institutional maps and matrices also has advantages. For instance, in highly violent and dangerous settings, people often find it easier to identify criminal or violence-related groups in a context of anonymity, without admitting membership; a gang member may not admit to his/her membership of a gang in a one-to-one questionnaire context, yet may be more willing to discuss the same gang when asked about it in a focus group discussion. The results in this research certainly point to this conclusion.

6   Levels of trust in organizations were assessed through analyzing institutional maps and matrices and identifying whether community members viewed each organization positively (interpreted as indicating a high level of trust) or negatively (interpreted as indicating a low level of trust).

7   Each *taquillero* received 10 percent of what they sold in 24 hours (a 'turn') or a wage of 30,000 *pesos* (U.S.$18.7) per turn.

9 AVOIDING OR CONFRONTING VIOLENCE? COMMUNITY PERCEPTIONS OF STRATEGIES AND SOLUTIONS

1   The distinctions between these four categories to cope with violence are very similar to more general categories identified in studies on coping strategies to deal with poverty (see Moser 1996, 1998).

2   The increasing decision by *ladino* groups to make use of human rights organizations as a means of resolving conflicts and confronting violence has been a significant development. This was notable in several communities, with *ladinos* seeking to resolve rape, *mara* activity and intra-family violence in this way. Indigenous groups used human rights organizations in a similar way, but they also used them for problems of political violence, often related to discrimination. This also indicates that as patterns of violence themselves have changed, so have people's perceptions of what constitutes their human rights.

3   This reflects the rapid spread of evangelical Protestantism throughout Guatemala, such that it is an important institution at the local level (see Winton 2003).

BIBLIOGRAPHY

Aboutanos, M. (1997) 'La violencia juvenil en las Américas,' in *Proceedings of the PAHO Adolescent and Youth Gang Violence Prevention Workshop*, San Salvador, 7–9 May, Washington, DC: PAHO.

ADE/GTZ [Aktionsprogramm Drogen und Entwicklung/Deutsche Gesellschaft für Technische Zusammenarbeit] (2001) *Drugs and Development in Latin America*, Eschborn: ADE/GTZ.

Aguilera, G. and Ogaldes, C. (1996) 'La narcoactividad como amenaza a la seguridad,' in G. Aguilera (ed.) *Buscando la Seguridad: Seguridad Ciudadana y Consolidación Democratica en Guatemala*, Guatemala: FLACSO.

Arce, A. and Long, N. (2000) 'Reconfiguring modernity and development from an anthropological perspective,' in A. Arce and N. Long (eds) *Anthropology, Development and Modernities*, London: Routledge.

Arendt, H. (1969) *On Violence*, New York: Harcourt, Brace and World.

Arriagada, I. (1998) 'Latin American families: convergences and divergences in models and policies,' *CEPAL Review* 65: 85–102.

Arriagada, I. and Godoy, L. (1999) *Seguridad Ciudadana y Violencia en América Latina: Diagnóstico y Políticas en los Años Noventa*, Social Policy Series No. 32, Santiago de Chile: CEPAL.

—— (2000) 'Prevention or repression? The false dilemma of citizen security,' *CEPAL Review* 70: 111–136.

Arthur, J.A. and Marenin, O. (1995) 'Explaining crime in developing countries: the need for a case study approach,' *Crime, Law and Social Change* 23: 191–214.

Auyero, J. (2000) 'The hyper-shantytown: neo-liberal violence(s) in the Argentine slum,' *Ethnography* 1, 1: 93–116.

AVANCSO [Asociación para el Avance de las Ciencias Sociales en Guatemala] (1996) *Por sí mismos: un estudio preliminar de las 'maras' en la Ciudad de Guatemala*, Cuadernos de Investigación No. 4, Guatemala City: AVANCSO.

—— (2000) *'Heridas en la sombra': percepciones sobre la violencia en áreas urbanas y periurbanas de la Ciudad de Guatemala*, Texto para Debate No. 16, Guatemala City: AVANCSO.

Ayres, R.L. (1998) *Crime and Violence as Development Issues in Latin America and the Caribbean*, Washington, DC: World Bank.

Barata, R.B., Sampaio de Almeida Ribeiro, M.C., Lauretti da Sulva Guedes, M.B. and Cássio de Moraes, J. (1998) 'Intra-urban differentials in death rates from homicide in the city of São Paulo, Brazil 1988–1994,' *Social Science and Medicine* 47, 1: 19–23.

Barbetta, A. (1997) 'Situación de la violencia juvenil en São Paulo,' in *Proceedings of the PAHO Adolescent and Youth Gang Violence Prevention Workshop*, San Salvador, 7–9 May, Washington, DC: PAHO.

Bates, R. (2001) *Prosperity and Violence: The Political Economy of Development*, London: W.W. Norton.

Baulch, B. (1996) 'Editorial: the New Poverty Agenda: a disputed consensus,' *Institute of Development Studies Bulletin* 27, 1: 1–10.

Bebbington, A. (1999) 'Capitals and capabilities: a framework for analysing peasant viability, rural livelihoods and poverty,' *World Development* 27, 12: 2021–2044.

Becker, G. (1993) 'Nobel lecture, the economic way of looking at behaviour,' *Journal of Political Economy* 101: 385–409.

Bejarano, J.A., Echandía, C., Escobedo, R. and León, E. (eds) (1997) *Colombia: Inseguridad, Violencia y Desempeño Económico en las Áreas Rurales*, Bogotá: Fondo Financiero de proyectos de Desarrollo-Universidad Externado de Colombia.

Belsky, J. (1980) 'Child maltreatment: an ecological integration,' *American Psychologist* 35, 4: 320–335.

Berdal, M. and Keen, D. (1997) 'Violence and economic agendas in civil wars: some policy implications,' *Millennium: Journal of International Studies* 26, 3: 795–818.

Bernat, J.C. (1999) 'Children and the politics of violence in Haitian context,' *Critique of Anthropology* 19, 2: 121–138.

Bourdieu, P. (1993) *Sociology in Question*, London: Sage Publications.

—— (1998) *Acts of Resistance: Against the Tyranny of the Market*, New York: The New Press.

Bourgois, P. (2001) 'The power of violence in war and peace: post-Cold War lessons from El Salvador,' *Ethnography* 2, 1: 5–34.

Bowman, G. (2001) 'The violence in identity,' in B.E. Schmidt and I.W. Schröder (eds) *Anthropology of Violence and Conflict*, London: Routledge.

Brock, K. (2002) 'Introduction: knowing poverty: critical reflections on participatory research and policy,' in K. Brock and R. McGee (eds) *Knowing Poverty: Critical Reflections on Participatory Research and Policy*, London: Earthscan.

Brock, K. and McGee, R. (eds) (2002) *Knowing Poverty: Critical Reflections on Participatory Research and Policy*, London: Earthscan.

Bronfenbrenner, U. (1977) 'Toward an experimental ecology of human development,' *American Psychologist* 32, 5: 13–31.

Brown, S. (1995) 'Gender stereotypes and sexual coercion,' in L. Heise, K. Moore and N. Toubia (eds) *Sexual Coercion and Reproductive Health*, New York: Population Council.

Brydon, L. and Chant, S. (1989) *Women in the Third World*, London: Edward Elgar.

Buvinić, M., Morrison, A.R. and Shifter, M. (1999) 'Violence in the Americas: a framework for action,' in A.R. Morrison and M.L. Biehl (eds) *Too Close to Home: Domestic Violence in the Americas*, Washington, DC: IDB.

Cabanas Díaz, A., Grant, E., del Cid Vargas, P.I. and Sajbin Velásquez, V. (2001)

244

'The role of external agencies in the development of El Mesquital in Guatemala City,' *Environment and Urbanization* 13, 1: 91–100.

Call, C.T. (2000) *Sustainable Development in Central America: The Challenges of Violence, Injustice and Insecurity*, Central America 2020 Working Paper No. 8, Hamburg: Institut für Iberoamerika-Kunde.

Camacho, A. and Guzmán, A. (1997) 'La violencia urbana en Colombia: teorías, modalidades, perspectivas,' in A. Camacho, A. Guzmán, M.C. Ramírez and F. Gaitán (eds) *Nuevas Visiones sobre la Violencia en Colombia*, Bogotá: FESCOL-IEPRI, Universidad Nacional.

Carney, D. (1998) 'Implementing the sustainable rural livelihood approach,' in D. Carney (ed.) *Sustainable Rural Livelihoods: What Contributions Can We Make?*, London: DFID.

Castells, M. (1998) *The Information Age: Economy, Society and Culture, Vol. III, End of Millennium*, Malden, MA and Oxford: Blackwell.

Ceballos Melguizo, R. (2001) 'The evolution of armed conflict in Medellín: an analysis of the major actors,' *Latin American Perspectives* 116, 28: 110–131.

CEDEC [Centro de Estudos de Cultura Contemporânea] (1996) *Mapa de Risco da Violencia: Cidade de São Paulo*, São Paulo: CEDEC.

CEH [Comisión para el Esclarecimiento Histórico] (1999) *Guatemala, Memory of Silence*, Guatemala City: CEH.

Chambers, R. (1992) *Rural Appraisal: Rapid, Relaxed and Participatory*, Discussion Paper No. 311, Brighton: Institute of Development Studies.

—— (1994a) 'The origins and practice of participatory rural appraisal,' *World Development* 22, 7: 953–969.

—— (1994b) 'Participatory rural appraisal (PRA): analysis of experience,' *World Development* 22, 9: 1253–1268.

—— (1994c) 'Participatory rural appraisal (PRA): challenges, potentials and paradigm,' *World Development* 22, 10: 1437–1454.

—— (1995) 'Poverty and livelihoods: whose reality counts?,' *Environment and Urbanization* 7, 1: 173–204.

—— (2002) 'Power, knowledge and policy influence: reflections on an experience,' in K. Brock and R. McGee (eds) *Knowing Poverty: Critical Reflections on Participatory Research and Policy*, London: Earthscan.

Chambers, R. and Conway, G. (1992) *Sustainable Rural Livelihoods: Practical Concepts for the 21st Century*, IDS Discussion Paper No. 296, Brighton: IDS.

Chant, S. (1997) *Women-Headed Households: Diversity and Dynamics in the Developing World*, Basingstoke: Macmillan.

—— (2000) 'Men in crisis? Reflections on masculinities, work and family in northwest Costa Rica,' *The European Journal of Development Research* 12, 2: 199–218.

Chant, S. and Craske, N. (2003) *Gender in Latin America*, London: Latin America Bureau.

Chant, S. and McIlwaine, C. (1998) *Three Generations, Two Genders, One World, Women and Men in a Changing Century*, London: Zed Books.

Chernick, M. (1997) 'Changing perceptions of violence in Colombia and its implications for policy,' mimeo, Washington, DC: World Bank.

—— (1998) 'The paramilitarization of the war in Colombia,' *NACLA Report on the Americas* 31, 5: 28–33.

Chevigny, P. (1996) 'Law and order? Policing in Mexico City and Kingston, Jamaica,' *NACLA Report on the Americas* 30, 2: 24–30.

Chirwa, W. (1998) 'Collective memory and the process of reconciliation and reconstruction,' in D. Eade (ed.) *From Conflict to Peace in a Changing World*, Oxford: Oxfam.

Choloros, A., Johnston, J., Joseph, K. and Stohl, R. (1997) *Breaking the Cycle of Violence: Light Weapons Destruction in Central America*, BASIC Occasional Papers on International Security Issues No. 24, London: BASIC.

CIEN [Centro de Investigaciones Económicas Nacionales] (1998) 'La violencia en Guatemala: un tema prioritario,' *Carta Económica* 190: 1–8.

—— (n.d.) *Diagnóstico de la Violencia en Guatemala*, internal document. Online. Available HTTP: <http://www.cien.org.gt/espa%C3%B1ol/area%20social/VIOLENCIA/ponencia.htm>, accessed 9 November 2001.

Clark, F. and Laurie, N. (2000) 'Gender, age and exclusion: a challenge to community organisations in Lima, Peru,' *Gender and Development* 8, 2: 80–88.

CODHES [Consultoría para los Derechos Humanos y el Desplazamiento] (1999) *Un País que Huye: Desplazamiento y Violencia en una Nación Fragmentada*, Bogotá: UNICEF.

Coleman, J.S. (1990) *Foundations of Social Theory*, Cambridge, MA: Harvard University Press.

Colletta, N.J. and Cullen, M.L. (2000) *Violent Conflict and Transformation of Social Capital: Lessons from Cambodia, Rwanda, Guatemala, and Somalia*, Washington, DC: World Bank.

Colletta, N. and Nezam, T. (1999) 'From reconstruction to reconciliation,' *Development Outreach* 1, 2: 5–8.

Collier, P. and Hoeffler, A. (2000) *Greed and Grievance in Civil War*, World Bank Policy Research Working Paper No. 2355, Washington, DC: World Bank.

Concha-Eastman, A. (2002) 'Urban violence in Latin America and the Caribbean: dimensions, explanations, actions,' in S. Rotker (ed.) *Citizens of Fear: Urban Violence in Latin America*, New Brunswick, NJ and London: Rutgers University Press.

Cooke, B. and Kothari, U. (eds) (2001) *Participation? The New Tyranny?* London: Zed Books.

Coral, C.I. (2001) 'Social organizations: from victims to actors in peace-building,' in C. Moser and F. Clark (eds) *Victims, Perpetrators or Actors? Gender, Armed Conflict and Political Violence*, London: Zed Books.

Cornwall, A. (1998) 'Gender, participation, and the politics of difference,' in I. Guijt and M.K. Shah (eds) *The Myth of Community: Gender Issues in Participatory Development*, London: IT Publications.

—— (2000a) *Making a Difference? Gender and Participatory Development*, IDS Discussion Paper No. 378, Brighton: IDS.

—— (2000b) 'Missing men? Reflections on men, masculinities and gender in GAD,' *IDS Bulletin* 31, 2: 18–27.

Cornwall, A. and Jewkes, R. (1995) 'What is participatory research?,' *Social Science and Medicine* 41, 12: 1667–1676.

Corradi, J.E., Weiss, P. and Garretón, M.A. (eds) (1992) *Fear at the Edge: State Terror and Resistance in Latin America*, Berkeley and Los Angeles: University of California Press.

Crisis States Programme (2001) *Concepts and Research Agenda*, LSE-DESTIN Development Research Centre, Crisis States Programme Working Paper No. 1, London: DRC.

Cruz, J.M. (1997) 'Problemas y expectivas de los jóvenes pandilleros desde su propia perspectiva,' in *Proceedings of the PAHO Adolescent and Youth Gang Violence Prevention Workshop*, San Salvador, 7–9 May, Washington, DC: PAHO.

Curry, G.D. (1998) 'Female gang involvement,' *Journal of Research in Crime and Delinquency* 35, 1: 100–118.

DANE [Departamento Administrativo Nacional de Estadísticas] (1999) *Colombian Economic Indicators*, Bogotá: DANE.

Dasgupta, P. and Serageldin, I. (eds) (2000) *Social Capital: A Multifaceted Perspective*, Washington, DC: World Bank.

Datta, K. and McIlwaine, C. (2000) '"Empowered leaders"? Perspectives on women heading households in Latin America and Southern Africa,' *Gender and Development* 8, 3: 40–49.

Davies, M. (ed.) (1994) *Women and Violence: Realities and Responses Worldwide*, London: Zed Books.

Deas, M. (1998) *Violence Reduction in Colombia: Lessons from Government Policies over the Last Decade*, Urban Peace Program background paper, Washington, DC: World Bank.

Deas, M. and Gaitán, F. (1995) *Dos Ensayos Especulativos sobre la Violencia en Colombia*. Bogotá: Tercer Mundo Editores.

De Cesare, D. (1997) 'De la guerra civil a la guerra de pandillas: crecimiento de las pandillas de Los Angeles en El Salvador,' in *Proceedings of the PAHO Adolescent and Youth Gang Violence Prevention Workshop*, San Salvador, 7–9 May, Washington, DC: PAHO.

De León, S., Garavito, M.A. and Murillo, N. (1999) *Percepciones de la Violencia en Guatemala*, Guatemala City: Instituto Centroamericano de Estudios Políticos.

De Orrellana, S. (1997) 'Situación de la violencia juvenil en El Salvador,' in *Proceedings of the PAHO Adolescent and Youth Gang Violence Prevention Workshop*, San Salvador, 7–9 May, Washington, DC: PAHO.

DFID [Department for International Development] (2000) *Halving World Poverty by 2015: Economic Growth, Equity and Security*, London: DFID.

DIAL (2001) 'Desplazamiento forzado: tendencias, respuesta estatal y nuevos desafíos,' DIAL Investigaciones No. 4, Bogotá: DIAL. Online. Available HTTP: <http://www.disaster-info.net/desplazados/informes/dial/tendencia.htm#_448>, accessed 19 February 2003.

Dissel, A. (1997) 'Youth, street gangs and violence in South Africa,' in G. Hérault and P. Adesanmi (eds) *Youth, Street Culture, and Urban Violence in Africa*, proceedings of the international symposium, Abidjan, 5–7 May, Ibadan: IFRA.

Dower, N. (1999) 'Development, violence and peace: a conceptual exploration,' *The European Journal of Development Research* 11, 2: 44–64.

Dudley, S. and Murillo, M. (1998) 'Oil in the time of war,' *NACLA Report on the Americas* 31, 5: 42–46.

Dureau, F. and Florez, C.E. (2000) *Aguaitacaminos: Las Transformaciones de las Ciudades de Yopal, Aguazul y Tauramena durante la Explotación Petrolera de Cusiana-Cupiagua*, Bogotá: Tercer Mundo Editores.

Eber, C. (1995) *Women and Alcohol in a Highland Maya Town*, Austin, TX: University of Texas Press.

Ellsberg, E., Peña, R., Herrera, A., Liljestrand, J. and Winkvist, A. (1999) 'Wife abuse among women of childbearing age in Nicaragua,' *American Journal of Public Health* 89, 2: 241–244.

—— (2000) 'Candies in hell: women's experiences of violence in Nicaragua,' *Social Science and Medicine*, 51: 1595–1610.

Fajnzylber, P., Lederman, D. and Loayza, N. (1998) *Determinants of Crime Rates in Latin American the World: An Empirical Assessment*, Washington, DC: World Bank.

—— (2000) 'Crime and victimization: an economic perspective,' *Economia* 1, 1: 219–278.

—— (2002) 'What causes violent crime?,' *European Economic Review* 46, 7: 1323–1357.

Feldman, A. (1991) *Formations of Violence*, Chicago: University of Chicago Press.

Feldman, T.R. and Assaf, S. (1999) *Social Capital: Conceptual Frameworks and Empirical Evidence: An Annotated Bibliography*, Social Capital Initiative Working Paper No. 5, Washington, DC: World Bank.

Ferreyra, A. and Segura, R. (2000) 'Examining the military in the local sphere: Colombia and Mexico,' *Latin American Perspectives* 27, 2: 18–35.

Ferrigno F.V. (1998) 'El estado democrático de derecho frente al conflicto social,' paper presented at Foro-Taller, Linchamminetos: diagnóstico y búsqueda de soluciones, Panajachel, Guatemala, May 1998.

Fine, B. (1999) 'The developmental state is dead: long live social capital?,' *Development and Change* 30: 1–19.

—— (2001) *Social Capital Versus Social Theory: Political Economy and Social Science at the Turn of the Millennium*, London: Routledge.

FLACSO (n.d.) *Programas para la Prevención de la Violencia y Delincuencia Juvenil*, document prepared for the Inter-American Development Bank, IDB: ES-0116.

Foucault, M. (1977) *Discipline and Punish: The Birth of the Prison*, New York: Pantheon.

Fukuyama, F. (1995) *Trust: The Social Virtues and the Creation of Prosperity*, London: Penguin.

Galtung, J. (1985) 'Twenty-five years of peace research: ten challenges and some responses,' *Journal of Peace Research* 22, 2: 145–146.

—— (1991) *Peace by Peaceful Means: Peace and Conflict, Development and Civilization*, Oslo: International Peace Research Institute.

—— (1996) *Peace by Peaceful Means*, 2nd edn, London: Sage Publications.

Garbarino, J. (1995) *Raising Children in a Socially Toxic Environment*, San Francisco: Jossey-Bass Publishers.

Garrard-Burnett, V. (2000) 'Indians are drunks and drunks are Indians: alcohol and *indigenismo* in Guatemala, 1890–1940,' *Bulletin of Latin American Research* 19, 3: 341–356.

Garretón, M.A. (1992) 'Fear in military regimes: an overview,' in J.E. Corradi, P. Weiss and M.A. Garretón (eds) *Fear at the Edge: State Terror and Resistance in Latin America*, Berkeley and Los Angeles: University of California Press.

Gasper, D. (1999) 'Violence, suffering, responsibility and choice: issues in ethics and development,' *The European Journal of Development Research* 11, 2: 1–22.

Gaviria, A. (2000) 'Increasing returns and the evolution of violent crime: the case of Colombia,' *Journal of Development Economics*, 61: 1–25.

Gaviria, A. and Pagés, A. (1999) *Patterns of Crime and Victimization in Latin America*, IDB Working Paper No. 408, Washington, DC: IDB.

Giddens, A. (1991) *Modernity and Self-Identity*, Cambridge: Polity Press.

Giraldo, J. (1999) 'Corrupted justice and the schizophrenic state in Colombia,' *Social Justice* 26, 4: 31–54.

Glaeser, E.L. (1999) *An Overview of Crime and Punishment*, Boston: Harvard University/NBER.

Gleijeses, P. (1991) *Shattered Hope: The Guatemalan Revolution and the United States, 1944–1954*, Princeton, NJ: Princeton University Press.

Gluckman, M. (1958) *Analysis of a Social Situation in Modern Zululand*, Rhodes–Livingston Papers No. 28, Manchester: Manchester University Press.

Gonçalves de Assis, S. (1997) 'Situación de la violencia juvenil en Río de Janeiro,' in *Proceedings of the PAHO Adolescent and Youth Gang Violence Prevention Workshop*, San Salvador, 7–9 May, Washington, DC: PAHO.

González-Cueva, E. (2000) 'Conscription and violence in Peru,' *Latin American Perspectives* 27, 3: 88–102.

Granada, C. and Rojas, L. (1995) 'Los costos del conflicto armado 1990–1994,' *Planeación y Desarrollo* 26, 4: 12–23.

Grant, M. and Litvak, J. (1997) *Drinking Patterns and their Consequences*, Washington, DC: Taylor and Francis.

Green, L. (1995) 'Living in a state of fear,' in C. Nordstrom and A.C.G.M. Robben (eds) *Fieldwork under Fire: Contemporary Studies of Violence and Survival*, Berkeley and Los Angeles: University of California Press.

Greig, A. (2000) 'The spectacle of men fighting,' *IDS Bulletin* 31, 2: 28–32.

Groothaert, C. (1998) *Social Capital: The Missing Link?*, Social Capital Initiative Working Paper No. 3, Washington, DC: World Bank.

—— (1999) *Local Institutions and Service Delivery in Indonesia*, Local Level Institutions Working Paper No. 5, Washington, DC: World Bank.

Guendel, L. and González, M. (1996) 'Integration, human rights and social policy in the context of urban poverty,' in UNICEF/HABITAT (eds) *Adolescence, Child Rights and Urban Poverty in Costa Rica*, San José: UNICEF.

Guererro, R. (1998) *Violencia en las Américas: Una Amenaza a la Integración Social*, Santiago: CEPAL.

Guerrero Barón, J. (2001) 'Is the war ending? Premises and hypotheses with which to view the conflict in Colombia,' *Latin American Perspectives* 28, 1: 12–30.

Guijt, I. and Shah, M.K. (eds) (1998a) *The Myth of Community: Gender Issues in Participatory Development*, London: IT Publications.

—— (1998b) 'Waking up to power, conflict and process,' in I. Guijt and M.K. Shah (eds) *The Myth of Community: Gender Issues in Participatory Development*, London: IT Publications.

Gutiérrez Sanín, F. (2001) 'The courtroom and the bivouac: reflections on law and violence in Colombia,' *Latin American Perspectives* 28, 1: 56–72.

Gutmann, M. (1996) *The Meanings of Being Macho: Being a Man in Mexico City*, Berkeley, CA: University of California Press.

Guzman, G., Fals-Borda, O. and Umaña, L.E. (1963) *La Violencia en Colombia I*, Bogotá: Carlos Valencia Editores.

—— (1964) *La Violencia en Colombia II*, Bogotá: Carlos Valencia Editores.

Halbmayer, E. (2001) 'Socio-cosmological contexts and forms of violence: war, vendetta, duels and suicide among the Yukpa of North-Western Venezuela,' in B.E. Schmidt and I.W. Schröder (eds) *Anthropology of Violence and Conflict*, London: Routledge.

Hamilton, C., Kaudia, A. and Gibbon, D. (1998) 'Participatory basic needs assessment with the internally displaced using well being ranking,' *PLA Notes*, 32: 9–13.

Harding, C. (1996) *Colombia in Focus*, London: Latin America Bureau.

Harriss, J. and De Renzio, P. (1997) 'An introductory bibliographic essay. "Missing link" or analytically missing? The concept of social capital,' *Journal of International Development* 9, 7: 919–937.

Harvey, P. (1994) 'Gender, community and confrontation: power relations and drunkenness in Ocongate (Southern Peru),' in M. McDonald (ed.) *Gender, Drink and Drugs*, Oxford: Berg.

Heise, L. (1998) 'Violence against women: an integrated, ecological model,' *Violence Against Women* 4, 3: 262–290.

Heise, L., Pitanguy, J. and Germain, A. (1994) *Violence against Women: The Hidden Health Burden*, World Bank Discussion Paper No. 255, Washington, DC: World Bank.

Human Rights Watch/Americas (1994) *Generation Under Fire: Children and Violence in Colombia*, New York: Human Rights Watch.

IEPADES [Instituto de Enseñanza para el Desarrollo Sostenible] (1998) *Seguridad Ciudadana en Guatemala: Diagnóstico de la Problemática Post-conflicto*, mimeo, Guatemala City: IEPADES.

Ingoldsby, B.B. (1991) 'The Latin American family: familism vs. machismo,' *Journal of Comparative Family Studies* 22, 1: 57–62.

Jackson, C. (1999) 'Men's work, masculinities and gender divisions of labour,' *The Journal of Development Studies* 36, 1: 89–108.

—— (2002) 'Disciplining gender?,' *World Development* 30, 3: 497–509.

Jacobs, S., Jacobson, R. and Marchbank, J. (eds) (2000) *States of Conflict: Gender, Violence and Resistance*, London: Zed Books.

Jimeno, M. (2001) 'Violence and social life in Colombia,' *Critique of Anthropology* 21, 3: 221–246.

Jimeno, M. and Roldán, I. (1996) *Las Sombras Arbitrarias*, Santa Fé de Bogotá: Editorial Universidad Nacional.

Kaldor, M. and Luckham, R. (2001) 'Global transformations and new conflicts,' *IDS Bulletin* 32, 2: 48–69.

Kaplinsky, R. (2001) 'Globalisation and economic insecurity,' *IDS Bulletin* 32, 2: 13–24.

Katz, E.G. (1995) 'Gender and trade within the household: observations from rural Guatemala,' *World Development* 23, 2: 327–342.

Kawachi, I., Kennedy, B.P. and Wilkinson, R.G. (1999) 'Crime: social disorganization and relative deprivation,' *Social Science and Medicine* 48, 6: 719–731.

Kay, C. (2001) 'Rural violence in Latin America,' *Third World Quarterly* 22, 5: 741–775.

Kaztman, R. (1992) 'Why are men so irresponsible?,' *CEPAL Review* 46: 79–87.

—— (1997) 'Marginality and social integration in Uruguay,' *CEPAL Review*, 62: 93–119.

Keane, J. (1996) *Reflections on Violence*, London: Verso.

Kellett, P. and Tipple, G.A. (2000) 'The home as workplace: a study of income-generating activities within the domestic setting,' *Environment and Urbanization* 12, 1: 203–214.

Kelly, L. (1991) 'Unspeakable acts: women who abuse,' *Trouble and Strife* 21: 13–20.

Killick, T. (1999) *Making Adjustment Work for the Poor*, ODI Poverty Briefing No. 5, London: ODI.

Kincaid, A.D. (2000) 'Demilitarization and security in El Salvador and Guatemala: convergences of success and crisis,' *Journal of Interamerican Studies and World Affairs* 42, 4: 39–58.

Kleinman, A., Das, V. and Lock, M. (eds) (1997) *Social Suffering*, Berkeley, Los Angeles and New York: University of California Press.

Klevens, J. (1998) *Evaluation of Interventions to Prevent or Reduce Violence in Bogotá, Colombia*, mimeo, Washington, DC: World Bank.

Klevens, J., Bayón, M.C. and Sierra, M. (2000) 'Risk factors and context of men who physically abuse in Bogotá, Colombia,' *Child Abuse and Neglect* 24, 3: 323–332.

Koonings, K. (1999) 'Shadows of violence and political transformation in Brazil: from military rule to democratic governance,' in K. Koonings and D. Kruijt (eds) *Societies of Fear: The Legacy of Civil War, Violence and Terror in Latin America*, London: Zed Books.

—— (2001) 'Armed actors, violence and democracy in Latin America in the 1990s: introductory notes,' *Bulletin of Latin American Research* 20, 4: 401–408.

Koskela, H. (1999) ' "Gendered Exclusions": women's fear of violence and changing relations to space,' *Geografiska Annaler* 81B, 2: 111–124.

Kramer, R.C. (2000) 'Poverty, inequality and youth violence,' *Annals of the American Academy of Political and Social Science* 567: 123–139.

Krishna, A. and Uphoff, N. (1999) *Mapping and Measuring Social Capital: A Conceptual and Empirical Study of Collective Action for Conserving and Developing Watersheds in Rajasthan, India*, Social Capital Initiative Working Paper No. 13, Washington, DC: World Bank.

Kruijt, D. (2001) 'Low intensity democracies: Latin America in the post-dictatorial era,' *Bulletin of Latin American Research* 20, 4: 409–430.

Kruijt, D. and Koonings, K. (1999) 'Introduction: violence and fear in Latin America,' in K. Koonings and D. Kruijt (eds) *Societies of Fear: The Legacy of Civil War, Violence and Terror in Latin America*, London: Zed Books.

Kulig, J.C. (1998) 'Family life among El Salvadorans, Guatemalans and Nicaraguans: a comparative study,' *Journal of Comparative Family Studies* 29, 3: 469–479.

Kyle, D. (1999) 'The Otavalo trade diaspora: social capital and transnational entrepreneurship,' *Ethnic and Racial Studies* 22, 2: 422–446.

Laidler, K.A. and Hunt, G. (1997) 'Violence and social organisation in female gangs,' in *Social Justice* 24, 4: 148–169.

Lancaster, R. (1992) *Life is Hard: Machismo, Danger and the Intimacy of Power in Nicaragua*, Berkeley, CA: University of California Press.

Landmann, C., Bastos, F., Viacava, F. and Tavares de Andrade, C. (1999) 'Income inequality and homicide rates in Rio de Janeiro, Brazil,' *American Journal of Public Health* 89, 6: 845–850.

Large, J. (1997) 'Disintegration conflicts and the restructuring of masculinity,' *Gender and Development* 5, 2: 23–30.

Latour, B. (1993) *We Have Never Been Modern*, Cambridge, MA: Harvard University Press.

Laurie, N., Dwyer, C., Holloway, S. and Smith, F. (1999) 'Introduction: geographies and new femininities,' in N. Laurie, C. Dwyer, S. Holloway and F. Smith (eds) *Geographies of New Femininities*, Harlow: Longman.

Leach, M., Mearns, R. and Scoones, I. (1997) *Environmental Entitlements: A Framework for Understanding the Institutional Dynamics of Environmental Change*, IDS Discussion Paper No. 359, Brighton: IDS.

Lechner, N. (1992) 'Some people die of fear: fear as a political problem,' in J.E. Corradi, P. Weiss and M.A. Garretón (eds) *Fear at the Edge: State Terror and Resistance in Latin America*, Berkeley and Los Angeles: University of California Press.

Lederman, D., Loayza, N. and Menéndez, A.M. (1999) *Violent Crime: Does Social Capital Matter?*, Washington, DC: World Bank.

—— (2002) 'Violent crime: does social capital matter?,' *Economic Development and Cultural Change* 50, 3: 509–539.

Leeds, E. (1996) 'Cocaine and parallel politics in the Brazilian urban periphery: constraints on local-level democratization,' *Latin American Research Review* 31, 3: 47–84.

Lennie, J. (1999) 'Deconstructing gendered power relations in participatory planning: towards an empowering feminist framework of participation and action,' *Women's Studies International Forum* 22: 97–112.

Lewis, D. and Gardner, K. (1996) *Anthropology, Development and the Postmodern Challenge*, London: Pluto.

Lewis, O. (1961) *The Children of Sanchez*, New York: Random House.

Lipton, M. and Ravaillon, M. (1995) 'Poverty and policy,' in J. Behrman and T. Srinivasan (eds) *Handbook of Development Economics*, volume 3B, Amsterdam: North-Holland.

Lira, E. (1998) 'Guatemala: uncovering the past, recovering the future,' in D. Eade (ed.) *From Conflict to Peace in a Changing World*, Oxford: Oxfam.

Londoño, J.L. (1996) 'Violence, psyche and social capital,' in S.J. Burki, S. Aiyer and R. Hommes (eds) *Poverty and Inequality: Annual World Bank Conference on Development in Latin America and the Caribbean 1996 Proceedings*, Washington, DC: World Bank.

Long, N. (1992) 'From paradigm lost to paradigm regained? The case for an actor-oriented sociology of development,' in N. Long and A. Long (eds) *Battlefields of Knowledge: The Interlocking Theory and Practice in Social Research and Development*, London: Routledge.

—— (2000) 'Exploring local/global transformations: a view from anthropology,' in A. Arce and N. Long (eds) *Anthropology, Development and Modernities*, London: Routledge.

Lykes, M.B. (1997) 'Activist participatory research among the Maya of Guatemala: constructing meanings from situated knowledge,' *Journal of Social Issues* 53, 4: 725–746.

McDonald, M. (1994) 'Introduction: a social-anthropological view of gender, drink and drugs,' in M. McDonald (ed.) *Gender, Drink and Drugs*, Oxford: Berg.

McGee, R. (2002) 'The self in participatory poverty research,' in K. Brock and R. McGee (eds) *Knowing Poverty: Critical Reflections on Participatory Research and Policy*, London: Earthscan.

McIlwaine, C. (1997) 'Vulnerable or poor? A study of ethnic and gender disadvantage among Afro-Caribbeans in Limón, Costa Rica,' *The European Journal of Development Research* 9, 2: 35–61.

—— (1999) 'Geography and development: violence and crime as development issues,' *Progress in Human Geography* 23, 3: 453–463.

—— (2002a) 'Perspectives on poverty, vulnerability and exclusion,' in C. McIlwaine and K. Willis (eds) *Challenges and Change in Middle America: Perspectives on Development in Mexico, Central America, and the Caribbean,* Harlow: Prentice Hall.

—— (2002b) 'Women, children and violence,' in R. Potter and V. Desai (eds) *The Companion to Development Studies*, London: Arnold.

McIlwaine, C. and Moser, C. (2001) 'Violence and social capital in urban poor communities: perspectives from Colombia and Guatemala,' *Journal of International Development* 13, 7: 965–984.

—— (2003) 'Poverty, violence and livelihood security in urban Colombia and Guatemala,' *Progress in Development Studies* 3, 2: 113–130.

Macmillan, R. (2000) 'Adolescent victimization and income deficits in early adulthood: rethinking the costs of criminal violence from a life course perspective,' *Criminology* 31, 1: 553–587.

Madrigal, E. (1998) 'Latin America,' in M. Grant (ed.) *Alcohol and Emerging Markets: Patterns, Problems, and Responses*, Philadelphia, PA: Brunner/Mazel.

Margold, J.A. (1998) 'From "cultures of fear and terror" to the normalization of violence: an ethnographic case,' *Critique of Anthropology* 19, 1: 63–88.

Marenin, O. (1997) 'Victimization surveys and the accuracy and reliability of official crime data in developing countries,' *Journal of Criminal Justice* 25, 6: 463–475.

Marchand, M.H. and Parpart, J. (eds) (1995) *Feminism/Postmodernism/Development*, London: Routledge.

Márquez, P. (1999) *The Street is My Home: Youth and Violence in Caracas*, Stanford, CA: Stanford University Press.

Meertens, D. (2001) 'Facing destruction, rebuilding life: gender and the internally displaced in Colombia,' *Latin American Perspectives* 28, 1: 132–148.

Mexican Health Foundation (1999) *Trends and Empirical Causes of Violent Crime in Mexico*, mimeo, Washington, DC: World Bank.

Miller, J. (1998) 'Gender and victimisation risk among young women in gangs,' *Journal of Research in Crime and Delinquency* 35, 4: 429–453.

MINUGUA [Misión de Naciones Unidas de Verificación en Guatemala] (1998) *Third Report, Verification of Compliance with the Commitments Made in the Agreement on the Implementation, Compliance and Verification Timetable for the Peace Agreements*, New York: United Nations.

Mitchell, J.C. (1956) *The Kalela Dance: Aspects of Social Relationships among Urban Africans in Northern Rhodesia*, Rhodes–Livingston Papers No. 27, Manchester: Manchester University Press.

Mohan, G. (1999) 'Not so distant, not so strange: the personal and the political in participatory research,' *Ethics, Place and Environment*, 2: 41–54.

Mohan, G. and Mohan, J. (2002) 'Placing social capital,' *Progress in Human Geography*, 26, 2: 191–210.

Mohanty, C.T. (1991) 'Under western eyes: feminist scholarship and colonial discourses,' in C. Mohanty, A. Russo and L. Torres (eds) *Third World Women and the Politics of Feminism*, Bloomington, IN: Indiana University Press.

—— (1997) 'Feminist encounters: locating the politics of experience,' in L. McDowell and J. Sharp (eds) *Space, Gender, Knowledge: Feminist Readings*, London: Arnold.

Molina, R. (1999a) 'The struggle against impunity in Guatemala,' *Social Justice* 26, 4: 55–83.

—— (1999b) 'Guatemala's tenuous peace,' *NACLA Report on the Americas* 33, 1: 4–8.

Momsen, J. and Kinnaird, V. (eds) (1993) *Different Places, Different Voices: Gender and Development in Africa, Asia and Latin America*, London: Routledge.

Moser, C. (1993) *Gender Planning and Development*, London: Routledge.

—— (1996) *Confronting Crisis: A Comparative Study of Household Responses to Poverty and Vulnerability in Four Urban Poor Communities*, Environmentally Sustainable Development Studies and Monograph Series No. 8, Washington, DC: World Bank.

—— (1998) 'The asset vulnerability framework: reassessing urban poverty reduction strategies,' *World Development* 26, 1: 1–19.

—— (2001a) 'The gendered continuum of violence and conflict: an operational framework,' in C. Moser and F. Clark (eds) *Victims, Perpetrators or Actors? Gender, Armed Conflict and Political Violence*, London: Zed Books.

—— (2001b) ' "Apt illustration" or "anecdotal information"? Can qualitative data be representative or robust?,' in R. Kanbur (ed.) *Qual-quant: Qualitative and Quantitative Poverty Appraisal: Complementarities, Tensions and the Way Forward*, Working Paper No. 20001-05, Ithaca, NY: Cornell University.

Moser, C. and Clark, F. (eds) (2001) *Victims, Perpetrators or Actors? Gender, Armed Conflict and Political Violence*, London: Zed Books.

Moser, C., Gatehouse, M. and Garcia, H. (1996) *Urban Poverty Research Sourcebook: Module I: Sub-city Level Household Survey*, Urban Management Paper No. 5, Washington, DC: World Bank.

Moser, C. and Grant, E. (2000) 'Violence and security in urban areas: their implications for governance, health and labour markets,' background paper prepared for National Academy of Sciences Panel on Urban Population Dynamics, Washington, DC, August 2000.

Moser, C. and Holland, J. (1997) *Urban Poverty and Violence in Jamaica*, Washington, DC: World Bank.

—— (1998) 'Can policy-focused research be participatory? Research on violence and poverty in Jamaica using PRA methods,' in J. Holland with J. Blackburn (eds) *Whose Voice? Participatory Research and Policy Change*, London: IT Publications.

Moser, C., Lister, S., McIlwaine, C., Shrader, E. and Tornqvist, A. (2000) *Violence in Colombia: Building Sustainable Peace and Social Capital*, Environmentally and Socially Sustainable Development Sector Management Unit Report No. 18652-CO, Washington, DC: World Bank.

Moser, C. and McIlwaine, C. (1999) 'Participatory urban appraisal and its application for research on violence,' *Environment and Urbanization* 11, 2: 203–226.

—— (2000) *Urban Poor Perceptions of Violence and Exclusion in Colombia*. Washington, DC: World Bank.

—— (2001a) *Violence in a Post-Conflict Context: Urban Poor Perceptions from Guatemala*. Washington, DC: World Bank.

—— (2001b) 'Gender and social capital in contexts of political violence: community perceptions from Colombia and Guatemala,' in C. Moser and F. Clark (eds) *Victims, Perpetrators or Actors? Gender, Armed Conflict and Political Violence*, London: Zed Books.

Moser, C. and Norton, A. (2001) *To Claim Our Rights: Livelihood Security, Human Rights and Sustainable Development*, London: ODI.

Moser, C. and Shrader, E. (1999) *A Conceptual Framework for Violence Reduction*, Urban Peace Program Series, Latin America and Caribbean Region Sustainable Development Working Paper No. 2, Washington, DC: World Bank.

Moser, C. and Winton, A. (2002) *Violence in the Central American Region: Towards an Integrated Framework for Violence Reduction*, ODI Working Paper No. 171, London: ODI.

Muggah, H.C.R. (2001) 'Globalisation and insecurity: the direct and indirect effects of small arms availability,' *IDS Bulletin* 32, 2: 70–78.

Narayan, D. (1997) *Voices of the Poor: Poverty and Social Capital in Tanzania*, Environmentally and Socially Sustainable Development Studies and Monograph Series No. 20, Washington, DC: World Bank.

—— (1999) *Bonds and Bridges: Social Capital and Poverty*, Policy Research Working Paper No. 2167, Poverty Division, Poverty Reduction and Economic Management Network, Washington, DC: World Bank.

Narayan, D., Chambers, R., Shah, M.K. and Petesch, P. (2000) *Voices of the Poor: Crying Out for Change*, New York: World Bank.

Narayan, D., Patel, R., Schafft, K., Rademacher, A. and Koch-Schulte, S. (2000a) *Voices of the Poor: Can Anyone Hear Us?*, New York: World Bank.

Nef, J. (1995) 'Demilitarization and democratic transition in Latin America,' in S. Halebsky and R.L. Harris (eds) *Capital, Power and Inequality in Latin America*, Boulder, CO: Westview Press.

Newman, G. (1998) *Global Report on Crime and Justice*, New York and Oxford: Oxford University Press.

Niño Murcia, C. and Chaparro Valderrama, J. (1998) *Usos, Costumbres e Imaginarios en el Espacio Público: El Sector Jerusalen*, Bogotá: Tercer Mundo.

Nordstrom, C. (1995) 'War on the front lines,' in C. Nordstrom and A. Robben (eds) *Fieldwork under Fire*, Berkeley, CA: University of California Press.

North, D. (1990) *Institutions, Institutional Change, and Economic Performance*, Cambridge and New York: Cambridge University Press.

Norton, A., Bird, B., Brock, K., Kakande, M. and Turk, C. (2001) *A Rough Guide to PPAs: Participatory Poverty Assessments*, London: Overseas Development Institute.

Ocquist, P. (1978) *Violencia, Conflicto y Política en Colombia*, Bogotá: IEC.

ODHAG [Oficina de Derechos Humanos del Arzobispado de Guatemala] (1999) *Guatemala: Never Again! Recovery of Historical Memory Project (REMHI), Official Report of the Human Rights Office, Archdiocese of Guatemala*, London: CIIR/LAB.

O'Toole, L.L. and Schiffman, J.R. (eds) (1997) *Gender Violence: Interdisciplinary Perspectives*, New York and London: New York University Press.

Pain, R. (1991) 'Space, sexual violence and social control: integrating geographical and feminist analyses of women's fear of crime,' *Progress in Human Geography* 15, 4: 415–431.

Pain, R. and Francis. P. (2003) 'Reflections on participatory research,' *Area* 35, 1: 46–54.

Palencia Prado, T. (1996) *Peace in the Making: Civil Groups in Guatemala*, London: CIIR.

Palma, D. (1998) *La Violencia Delincuencial en Guatemala: Un Enfoque Coyuntural*, mimeo, Guatemala City: Universidad Rafael Landívar.

Pansters, W. (1999) 'The transition under fire: rethinking contemporary Mexican politics,' in K. Koonings and D. Kruijt (eds) *Societies of Fear: The Legacy of Civil War, Violence and Terror in Latin America*, London: Zed Books.

Parpart, J.L. and Marchand, M.H. (1995) 'Exploding the canon: an introduction/conclusion,' in M.H. Marchand and J.L. Parpart (eds) *Feminism/Postmodernism/Development*, London: Routledge.

Pearce, J. (1998) 'From civil war to "civil society": has the end of the Cold War brought peace to Central America?,' *International Affairs* 74, 3: 587–615.

Pearson, R. and Jackson, C. (1998) 'Introduction: interrogating development: feminism, gender and policy,' in C. Jackson and R. Pearson (eds) *Feminist Visions of Development: Gender Analysis and Policy*, London: Routledge.

Pecaut, D. (1997) 'Presente, pasado y futuro de la violencia en Colombia,' *Desarrollo y Economia* 36, 144: 891–930.

—— (1999) 'From the banality of violence to real terror: the case of Colombia,' in K. Koonings and D. Kruijt (eds) *Societies of Fear: The Legacy of Civil War, Violence and Terror in Latin America*, London: Zed Books.

—— (2001) *Guerra Contra la Sociedad*, Bogotá: Planeta.

Pérez, D. and Mejía, M.R. (1996) *De Calles, Parches, Galladas y Escuelas: Transformaciones en los Procesos de Socialización de los Jóvenes de Hoy*, Bogotá: CINEP.

Pérez Gómez, A. (1998) 'Drug consumption in Latin America,' in E. Joyce and C. Mahamud (eds) *Latin America and the Multinational Drug Trade*, Basingstoke: Macmillan.

Pickup, F., Williams, S. and Sweetman, C. (2001) *Ending Violence Against Women: A Challenge for Development and Humanitarian Work*, Oxford: Oxfam.

Pinheiro, P.S. (1993) 'Reflections on urban violence,' *Urban Age* 1, 4: 3–4.

—— (1996) 'Democracies without citizenship,' *NACLA Report on the Americas* 30, 2: 1–23.

PNUD [Programa de Naciones Unidadas de Desarrollo] (1998) *Guatemala: Los Contrastes del Desarrollo Humano*, Guatemala City: PNUD.

—— (1999) *El Rostro Rural del Desarrollo Humano*, Guatemala City: PNUD.

—— (2000) *Guatemala: La Fuerza Incluyente del Desarrollo Humano*, Guatemala City: PNUD.

Poitevin, R., Rivera, A. and Moscoso, V. (2000) *Los Jóvenes Guatemaltecos a Finales del Siglo XX*, Guatemala City: FLACSO.

Popkin, E. (1999) 'Guatemalan Mayan migration to Los Angeles: constructing transnational linkages in the context of the settlement process,' *Ethnic and Racial Studies* 22, 2: 267–289.

Poppovic, M. and Pinheiro, P.S. (1995) 'How to consolidate democracy? A human rights approach,' *International Social Science Journal* 143: 75–89.

Portes, A. (1998) 'Social capital: its origins and applications in modern sociology,' *American Review of Sociology* 24, 1: 1–24.

Portes, A. and Landolt, P. (2000) 'Social capital: promise and pitfalls of its role in development,' *Journal of Latin American Studies* 32: 529–547.

Pretty, J. (1995) 'Participatory learning for sustainable agriculture,' *World Development* 23, 8: 1247–1263.

Pridmore, P. (1998) 'Children's participation in situations of crisis: introduction,' in V. Johnson, E. Ivan-Smith, G. Gordon, P. Pridmore and P. Scott (eds) *Stepping Forward: Children and Young People's Participation in the Development Process*, London: IT Publications.

PRODEN (1996) *Entre el Olvido y la Esperanza: La Niñez de Guatemala*, Guatemala City: PRODEN.

Putnam, R. (1993) *Making Democracy Work: Civic Traditions in Modern Italy*, Princeton, NJ: Princeton University Press.

Putzel J. (1997) 'Accounting for the "dark side" of social capital: reading Robert Putnam on democracy,' *Journal of International Development* 9, 7: 939–949.

Rademacher, A. and Patel, R. (2002) 'Retelling worlds of poverty: reflections on transforming participatory research for a global narrative,' in K. Brock and R. McGee (eds) *Knowing Poverty: Critical Reflections on Participatory Research and Policy*, London: Earthscan.

Ravaillon, M. (1992) *Poverty Comparisons: A Guide to Concepts and Methods*, Living Standards Measurement Study Working Paper No. 88, Washington, DC: World Bank.

Reiss, A. and Roth, J. (eds) (1993) *Understanding and Preventing Violence*, Washington, DC: National Academy Press.

Restrepo, O.L. (1997) 'Situación de la violencia juvenil en Cali,' in *Proceedings of the PAHO Adolescent and Youth Gang Violence Prevention Workshop*, San Salvador, 7–9 May, Washington, DC: PAHO.

Reyes Posada, A. (1998) 'Rural violence in Colombia,' in C. Moser and S. Lister (eds) *Violence and Social Capital: Proceedings of the LCSES Seminar Series 1997–1998*, Latin America and Caribbean Region Sustainable Development Working Paper No. 5, Washington, DC: World Bank.

Riaño-Alcalá, P. (1991) '*Las galladas*: street youth and cultural identity in the barrios of Bogotá,' in H.P. Diaz, J.W.A. Rummens and P.D.M. Taylor (eds) *Forging Identities and Patterns of Development in Latin America and the Caribbean*, Toronto: Canadian Scholars' Press Inc.

Richani, N. (1997) 'The political economy of violence: the war system in Colombia,' *Journal of Interamerican Studies and World Affairs* 39, 2: 37–91.

Riches, D. (1991) 'Aggression, war, violence: space/time and paradigms,' *Man* 26, 2: 281–297.

Robb, C. (1999) *Can the Poor Influence Policy? Participatory Poverty Assessments in the Developing World*, Washington, DC: World Bank.

Robben, A. and Nordstrom, C. (1995) 'The anthropology and ethnography of violence and sociopolitical conflict,' in C. Nordstrom and A. Robben (eds) *Fieldwork under Fire*, Berkeley, CA: University of California Press.

Rocha, J.L. (2000) 'Pandillas: una cárcel cultural,' in *Revista Envío*, June 2000. Online. Available HTTP: <http://www.uca.edu.ni/publicaciones/envio/2000/esp/junio/Pandilleros.htm>, accessed 12 November 2002.

Rodgers, D. (1998) *Youth Gangs and Violence in Latin America and the Caribbean: A Literature Survey*, mimeo, Cambridge: Department of Social Anthropology, University of Cambridge.

—— (1999) *Youth Gangs and Violence in Latin America and the Caribbean: A Literature Survey*, Latin America and Caribbean Regional Sustainable Development Working Paper No. 4, Washington, DC: World Bank.

—— (2001) *Making Danger a Calling: Anthropology, Violence, and the Dilemmas of Participant Observation*, LSE-DESTIN Development Research Centre, Crisis States Programme Working Paper No. 6, London: DRC.

—— (forthcoming) 'Youth gangs in Colombia and Nicaragua: new forms of violence, new theoretical directions?' Outlook on Development Series, Collegium for Development Studies, Uppsala University.

Rodríguez, B.A. (1996) *El Problema de la Impunidad en Guatemala*, Serie Autores Invitados, Guatemala City: AVANCSO.

Rojas, C.E. (1996) *La Violencia Llamada Limpieza Social*, Coleción papeles de paz, Bogotá: CINEP.

Romanucci-Ross, L. (1973) *Conflict, Violence and Morality in a Mexican Village*, Sacramento: National Press Books.

Rosenberg, M. (1999) 'Violence as a public health problem,' in C. Moser and S. Lister (eds) *Violence and Social Capital: Proceedings of the LCSES Seminar Series 1997–1998*, Latin America and Caribbean Region Sustainable Development Working Paper No. 5, Washington, DC: World Bank.

Ross, T. (2001) 'Response: notes from South America,' *International Journal of Drug Policy* 12: 27–30.

Rotker, S. (ed.) (2002) *Citizens of Fear: Urban Violence in Latin America*, New Brunswick, NJ and London: Rutgers University Press.

Rubio, M. (1997a) 'Perverse social capital: some evidence from Colombia,' *Journal of Economic Issues* 31, 3: 805–816.

—— (1997b) *Los Costos de la Violencia en Colombia*, mimeo, Bogotá: CEDE, Universidad de Los Andes.

—— (2001) 'Homicide, kidnapping and armed conflict in Colombia,' *Forum on Crime and Society* 1, 1: 55–65.

Salazar, A. (1990) *Born to Die in Medellín*, London: LAB.

—— (1994) 'Young assassins of the drug trade,' *NACLA Report on the Americas* 27, 6: 24–28.

Salles, V. and Tuirán, R. (1997) 'The family in Latin America: a gender approach,' *Current Sociology* 45, 1: 141–152.

Salmi, J. (1993) *Violence and Democratic Society: New Approaches to Human Rights*, London: Zed Books.

Sánchez, G. and Meertens, D. (2001) *Bandits, Peasants and Politics: The Case of 'La Violencia' in Colombia*, Austin, TX: University of Texas Press.

Scheper-Hughes, N. (1992) *Death without Weeping: The Violence of Everyday Life in Brazil*, Berkeley, CA: University of California Press.

—— (1995) 'Everyday violence: bodies, death and silence,' in S. Corbridge (ed.) *Development Studies: A Reader*, London: Arnold.

—— (1996) 'Small wars and invisible genocides,' *Social Science and Medicine* 43, 5: 889–899.

—— (1997) 'Peace-time crimes,' *Social Identities* 3, 3: 471–497.

Schröder, I.W. and Schmidt, B.E. (2001) 'Introduction: violent imaginaries and violent practices,' in B.E. Schmidt and I.W. Schröder (eds) *Anthropology of Violence and Conflict*, London: Routledge.

Schuurman, F.J. (2000) 'Paradigms lost, paradigms regained? Development studies in the twenty-first century,' *Third World Quarterly* 21, 1: 7–20.

Schlemmer, B. (ed.) (2000) *The Exploited Child*, London: Zed Books.

Sen, A. (1981) *Poverty and Famines: An Essay on Entitlement and Deprivation*, Oxford: Clarendon Press.

Sen, P. (1999) 'Enhancing women's choices in responding to domestic violence in Calcutta: a comparison of employment and education,' *The European Journal of Development Research* 11, 2: 65–86.

Short, J.F. (1997) *Poverty, Ethnicity and Violent Crime*, Boulder, CO: Westview Press.

Sichor, D. (1990) 'Crime patterns and socioeconomic development: a cross-national analysis,' *Criminal Justice Review* 15, 1: 68–78.

Simon, D. (1998) 'Rethinking (post)modernism, postcolonialism, and posttradi-tionalism: south-north perspectives,' *Environment and Planning D: Society and Space*, 16: 219–245.

Smutt, M. and Miranda, J.L.E. (1998) *El Fenómeno de las Pandillas en El Salvador*, San Salvador: UNICEF/FLACSO.

Soares, K., Blue, I., Cano, E. and Mari, J. (1998) 'Short report: violent death in young people in the city of São Paulo, 1991–1993,' *Health and Place* 4, 2: 195–198.

Social Watch (2000) *2000 Country Report: Colombia, Five Years of Constant Reversals*. Online. Available HTTP: <http://www.socwatch.org.uy/en/informes Nacionales/61.html>, accessed 19 February 2003.

Soley, M. (1996) 'Teaching about international conflict and peace,' *Social Education* 60, 7: 432–438.

Spivak, G.C. (1988) *In Other Worlds: Essays on Cultural Politics*, London: Rout-ledge.

Suárez, A.R. (2000) 'Parasites and predators: guerrillas and the insurrection economy of Colombia,' *Journal of International Affairs* 53, 2: 577–601.

Sudarsky, J. (1999) *Colombia's Social Capital: The National Measurement with BARCAS*, summary, Bogotá: National Planning Office.

Sumner, C. (ed.) (1982) *Crime, Justice and Underdevelopment*, London: Heine-mann.

Taussig, M. (1984) 'Culture of terror – space of death: Roger Casement's Putu-mayo report and the explanation of torture,' *Comparative Studies in Society and History* 26: 467–497.

—— (1987) *Shamanism, Colonialism and the Wild Man*, Chicago: Chicago Univer-sity Press.

Tedesco, L. (2000) 'La ñata contra el vidrio: urban violence and democratic gov-ernability in Argentina,' *Bulletin of Latin American Research* 19: 527–545.

Torres-Rivas, E. (1999) 'Epilogue: notes on terror, violence, fear and democracy,' in K. Koonings and D. Kruijt (eds) *Societies of Fear: The Legacy of Civil War, Violence and Terror in Latin America*, London: Zed Books.

Trivedy, R. (2001) 'Conflict prevention, resolution and management: improving coordination for more effective action,' *IDS Bulletin* 32, 2: 79–88.

Trujillo Ciro, E. and Badel Pueda, M.E. (1998) *Los Costos Económicos de la Criminalidad y la Violencia en Colombia: 1991–1996*, Archivos de Macroeconomía, Bogotá: Departamento de Planeación.

Turpin, J. and Kurtz, L.R. (1997) 'Introduction: violence – the micro-macro link,' in J. Turpin and L.R. Kurtz (eds) *The Web of Violence: From Interpersonal to Global*, Chicago: University of Illinois Press.

Turshen, M. (2001) 'The political economy of rape: an analysis of systematic rape and sexual abuse of women during armed conflict in Africa,' in C. Moser and F. Clark (eds) *Victims, Perpetrators or Actors? Gender, Armed Conflict and Political Violence*, London: Zed Books.

Umaña Luna, E. (1994) *La Familia Colombiana: Una Estructura en Crisis*, mimeo, Universidad Nacional, Colombia.

UNCHS [United Nations Centre for Human Settlement] (2001) *Cities in a Globalizing World: Global Report on Human Settlements 2001*, Oxford and New York: Oxford University Press.

UNDP [United Nations Development Programme] (1995) *Human Development Report 1995*, Oxford and New York: Oxford University Press.

—— (1999) *Human Development Report 1999*, Oxford and New York: Oxford University Press.

—— (2000) *Human Development Report 2000*, Oxford and New York: Oxford University Press.

—— (2001) *Human Development Report 2001*, Oxford and New York: Oxford University Press.

UNICRI [United Nations Interregional Crime and Justice Research Institute] (1995) *Criminal Victimisation in the Developing World*, Publication No. 55, Rome: United Nations.

—— (1998) *Victims of Crime in the Developing World*, Publication No. 57, Rome: United Nations.

Uphoff, N. (1997) *Giving Theoretical and Operational Content to Social Capital*, mimeo, New York: Cornell University.

—— (2000) 'Understanding social capital: learning from the analysis and experience of participation,' in P. Dasgupta and I. Serageldin (eds) *Social Capital: A Multifaceted Perspective*, Washington, DC: World Bank.

Vanderschueren, F. (1996) 'From violence to justice and security in cities,' *Environment and Urbanization* 8, 1: 93–112.

Vargas Meza, R. (1998) 'The FARC, the war and the crisis of the state,' *NACLA Report on the Americas* 31, 5: 22–27.

Varley, A. and Blasco, M. (2000) 'Intact or in tatters? Family care of older women and men in urban Mexico,' *Gender and Development* 8, 2: 47–55.

Vásquez Perdomo, M.E. (2000) *Escrito Para no Morir: Bitácora de una Militancia*, Bogotá: Ministerio de Cultura.

Wade, P. (1993) *Blackness and Race Mixture: The Dynamics of Racial Identity in Colombia*, Baltimore, MD: The Johns Hopkins University Press.

—— (1994) 'Man the hunter: gender and violence in music and drinking contexts in Colombia,' in P. Harvey and P. Gow (eds) *Sex and Violence: Issues in Representation and Experience*, London: Routledge.

Walby, S. (1997) *Gender Transformations*, London: Routledge.

Watson, C.A. (2000) 'Civil-military relations in Colombia: a workable relationship or a case for fundamental reform?,' *Third World Quarterly* 21, 3: 529–548.

WHO (2002) *The World Health Report 2002: Reducing Risks, Promoting Healthy Life*, Geneva: World Health Organization.

Willett, S. (2001) 'Insecurity, conflict and the new global disorder,' *IDS Bulletin* 32, 2: 35–47.

Wilson, R. (ed.) (1997) *Human Rights, Culture and Context: Anthropological Perspectives*, London: Pluto Press.

Wilson, R.A. (1997) *The People's Conscience? Civil Groups, Peace and Justice in the South African and Guatemalan Transitions*, London: CIIR.

Winton, A. (2003) 'Youth, social capital and social exclusion in Guatemala: examining the well-being of the young urban poor in Guatemala City,' unpublished PhD Thesis, Department of Geography, Queen Mary, University of London.

WGSG (Women and Geography Study Group) (1997) *Feminist Geographies: Explorations in Diversity and Difference*, Harlow: Longman.

Woolcock, M. (1998) 'Social capital and economic development: toward a theoretical synthesis and policy framework,' *Theory and Society* 27, 2: 151–208.

World Bank (2000) *World Development Report 2000/2001: Attacking Poverty*, Oxford and New York: Oxford University Press.

Zaman, H. (1999) 'Violence against women in Bangladesh: issues and responses,' *Women's Studies International Forum* 22, 1: 37–48.

INDEX

Page references for figures and tables are in *italics*; those for notes are followed by n

262

271